BIG – BLOCK MOPAR PERFORMANCE

High Performance and Racing Modifications for B and RB Series Engines

D1567310

Chuck Senatore

HPBooks

HPBooks
are published by
The Berkley Publishing Group
A division of Penguin Putnam Inc.
375 Hudson Street
New York, New York 10014

First edition: August 1999

The Penguin Putnam Inc. World Wide Web site address is
www.penguinputnam.com

CONTENTS

Acknowledgments   *iv*

Introduction   *v*

Chapter 1: The Stock Big Block   *1*

Chapter 2: Getting Started   *11*

Chapter 3: Cylinder Blocks   *17*

Chapter 4: Crankshafts   *32*

Chapter 5: Connecting Rods   *41*

Chapter 6: Pistons   *48*

Chapter 7: Bearings   *55*

Chapter 8: Oil System   *60*

Chapter 9: Cylinder Heads   *70*

Chapter 10: Camshafts   *88*

Chapter 11: Valvetrain   *99*

Chapter 12: Induction   *109*

Chapter 13: Ignition System   *123*

Chapter 14: Exhaust System   *132*

Chapter 15: Assembly Tips   *135*

Chapter 16: Engine Combinations   *141*

Chapter 17: General Racing Tips   *146*

Formulas   *150*

Index   *151*

ACKNOWLEDGMENTS

First, I would like to mention the main guys at my shop, Muscle Motors. They are: Mike Ware, Phil Berryhill, Eric Neumann, Eric Budden, Chris Hillyard and Mike Brown. These guys are some of the best machinists in the racing engine business and generally make my life easier and our engines run fast and long. Much of the credit that goes to our shop is due to them and their appreciation for a quality product. They can always be counted on to go the extra mile for anything. Special thanks go to Mike Ware for shooting all the pictures in this book as well as the pictures for all of my columns and feature articles. Mike is also active on our racing team and his efforts there have been over and above the call of duty. Without these guys on my side, the success that we have enjoyed would have been impossible.

I would also like to mention one of my former college professors, Gerry Park, from the Michigan Stage University's College of Engineering. Dr. Park taught me many years ago to be a practical engineer as well as a theoretical one. Without a strong sense of practicality, as well as a strong knowledge of theory, many ideas would go unused. He also drilled into me a phrase that I think about every day: "When the results and the theory disagree, make up a new theory." This means to always believe the results whatever they are. This has proven to be an invaluable thought process for tuning and troubleshooting a racing engine.

My first big break in publishing came from Richard Ehrenberg, the tech editor of *Mopar Action* magazine. With his help, Muscle Motors was launched into the national market and was given the opportunity to grow into larger markets. He also provided the opportunity to write columns and articles in the magazine. Many people have benefited from these articles and it lets me know that we are on the right track with our development of this engine.

The members of our various racing teams have been great, not only providing research and development time, but giving us feedback on how to make engines that are faster and stronger. A thank-you goes to these guys for this aspect and for winning all of the national events and a world championship. Our main race team consists of Roy Holcomb, Todd Avery, Jeff Rudisill and Joe Mayhew; some of the best racers in the country.

I would also like to thank all of our customers over the years, and the friends we've made through our racing and in the business. Without all of you, there would be no "us."

A big thank-you must also go to the editor of this book, Michael Lutfy, for not only giving me the chance to write it but to fine-tune it into something that is readable. He had great patience during the process and is responsible for making it look as good as it does.

Much of the credit for my success has to go to my parents who gave me the opportunity to start this company. Without their help and support through the years, you would not be reading this book or have ever heard of Muscle Motors. My significant other, Denese, has put up with all the long and crazy hours at the shop and all the time spent at the racetrack over the summers. To them I owe a large debt of gratitude.

INTRODUCTION

This book was written to provide the most up-to-date information on building the B series big-block Chrysler engine. Over the last decade, this engine has established itself as a popular choice for bracket racing, street performance and even professional racing. Thousands of these engines are raced all over the country every weekend. Unfortunately, the current information on how to build a good B series engine is extremely outdated, and frankly, not very technically accurate or informative.

As the owner of Muscle Motors, a high performance and race engine facility, I have built hundreds of these engines and have tried just about every modification and employed every trick imaginable. Unlike most other material that is written by people who have limited engine building experience, I am in the trenches every day, building and racing this engine for myself and my customers. I have tried to answer the most common questions I am asked by racers at the track, and by readers of my column in *Mopar Action* magazine.

Racing is a very popular and expensive hobby. Many modifications can consume a lot of money without delivering much in return. Since our race teams compete nearly every weekend, I have tried to develop the least expensive, most durable engine combination that will still deliver enough performance to win races. I am aware that many racers, particularly amateurs, only have the budget to build an engine once a season, so it has to last. Therefore I won't be recommending any rare or exotic parts. The B engine is fairly simple and very strong when properly built. It generally doesn't need any expensive or complex modifications to make it a real screamer. Remember the old axiom KISS: Keep It Simple Stupid. Don't fall into the classic amateur engine builder's mistake of buying a lot of parts that you don't really need.

As with any book of this type, things are subject to interpretation. Some people will disagree with some of the things I recommend, which is fine, because there is more than one way to build an engine. No one has an absolute lock on how an engine is built, myself included. What follows is the culmination of the many years of experience I've gained with this engine. The methods in this book have worked for me, so they should work for you too.

However, every possible engine combination can't be contained in a book of this size. I tried to include the most popular methods and parts, as well as some general tips and tricks. Use this book as a guide to help you understand why certain procedures are done, as well as how. There is always a factual basis behind every procedure, a fact lost on many engine builders. If you can get a few tips to make your engine live longer, run faster and better, then I will have done my job.

The best engine builders are those who "listen" to their engine. An engine speaks its own language, and if you listen hard enough, it will tell you what it wants. Good luck!

If you're a big-bucks racer, you might be able to afford a trick aftermarket block. But if you're like most of us, you'll have to settle for reworking a stock block, like this one shown above. Photo by Don Taylor.

1

THE STOCK BIG BLOCK

If you have the budget and are building an all-out racing engine, the ideal situation would be to buy an aftermarket cylinder block and aftermarket heads, and put on all of the latest high performance parts you can find. But that is not the reality for a lot of amateur racers and street enthusiasts. Most of the readers of this book will be working with what they already have, or can find in a junkyard or swap meet.

But regardless of what your intent is, you can't go wrong with a bit of background on the stock big block Mopar engine, and how to identify the various components. If you go wading through a field of junked blocks how do you know what started life as a 383 or 400? Is that crankshaft in the back of the junkyard the one you're looking for? Is that the kind of thing you'd like to know? Read on, then. These and many other mysteries will be unraveled!

BACKGROUND

The story of Chrysler's big-block engines is the story of their entry into the world of brute horsepower and high performance. It is the story of one horsepower for every cubic inch of displacement; a milestone in the auto industry similar to exceeding the speed of sound in a piston-engined aircraft. The glory days of Chrysler racing are also a part of this story. So are passenger cars equipped with engines powerful enough to drive off the showroom floor and onto the drag strip. Names like Keith Black, Dick Landy and Tony Nancy help write part of the story on the nation's race track.

The history of the big-block Chrysler engine begins in 1958. This is the year the B series engines were introduced in the 350 and 351 cubic-inch versions. It took until 1963 for these engines to mature, but when they did they became some of the highest performing engines available. The basic B block grew from its modest beginnings as a 361 into a 383 and 400. All three displacements had a stroke of 3.38" and respective bores of 4.12, 4.25 and 4.34".

In 1962, the most powerful 383 to hit the street came equipped with dual 4-barrel inline carburetors, special "300" series cylinder heads and a hot camshaft. The factory rating for this smallest of the big blocks was a whopping 345 horsepower.

Meanwhile, Chrysler engineers were looking for more torque—and that meant a longer stroke. Thus, in 1959 a long stroke version of the B block was introduced. This was called the raised block or RB engine. The block casting was modified (or raised) to increase the cylinder bore length by 0.745". This allowed the engineers to increase the stroke from 3.38" to 3.75". The result was the 413 cid. The 413 powered Chrysler's first high-performance B car, the Chrysler 300E.

This engine was the RB 413 with dual 4-barrels on a long-ram manifold. Compression was 10:1 with a factory horsepower rating of 380 at 5000 rpm with 450 lbs-ft. of torque at 3600 rpm. However, the biggest changes were yet to come in the form of the Max Wedge. This was the most radical departure from standard engineering design that Chrysler had offered to date.

The Max Wedge was brute horsepower. This 413 produced 420 horsepower. At 60 mph, you could step down into passing gear and the rear tires would still "burn rubber," at least until Officer Brown caught you doing it—twice. The 426 was introduced in the Chrysler that same year.

A new block casting was made to incorporate larger oil feed passages and to accommodate the big 1-7/8-in. exhaust valves. To do this, notches were fitted into the cylinder bores. The block was also stress-relieved. Forged TRW pistons were attached to beefier connecting rods. The compression ratio was 13.5:1.

Special cylinder heads were developed that breathed more freely and accommodated the larger valves. With two Carter carburetors and in race tune, this engine developed 425 horsepower at 5600 rpm. In 1964, Chrysler reached its zenith with the introduction of the Stage III Max Wedge. This very high performance engine was, and still is, one of the most powerful high performance engines ever to be offered to the public at large. In 1963 and 1964, the 426 Max Wedge could be bought for less than a thousand dollars more than a small-block "A" engine. But time, tide and fast cars roll on and Chrysler rolled with them.

At the end of 1964, the Hemispherical Chambered 426 cid (Hemi) engine burst onto the muscle car scene. Although the Hemi had 426 inches of displacement like its Wedge counterpart, the similarity ended here. This engine reintroduced the hemispherical-shaped combustion chamber and increased intake valves to 2.25" and the exhaust to 1.94". The block was recast to accommodate the changes in the head and was beefed up to absorb the increased horsepower. With a single carburetor, Chrysler gave the engine a horsepower rating of 400. With dual-quads, they quoted 415 horsepower and the 12.5:1 compression version was rated at 425 horsepower.

Chrysler's love of brute force would bring one more engine into the horsepower wars—the RB 440. It incorporated a carryover head from the Chrysler 300 series. This utilized huge valves with excellent breathing capabilities. In 1967, it powered the Plymouth GTX and Dodge Coronet R/T. The 440 heads proved to be real champs and were used to give one last hurrah for the 383.

In 1968, the 383 was equipped with 440 heads, a high-rise 4-barrel intake manifold and the 440 high performance camshaft. These were available in both the Road Runner and Super Bee.

Chrysler would make one final lunge at the gold ring before pollution controls and gas shortages ended the era of the muscle car. In 1969, the factory introduced the 440 "Six-Pack"—three 2-barrel carburetors drawing in 1200 cubic feet of air per minute! These beauties were produced through 1971 and ended Chrysler's 20-year streak of producing some of the best high performance street cars the world has ever known.

IDENTIFICATION NUMBERS

There are three basic pieces of information you need to identify your engine: displacement, year of manufacture and engine number. The engine number is all the information that's needed for positive engine identification.

Assuming the engine you removed from the car was original equipment, this information can be found on the Vehicle Identification Plate (VIP).

Until 1967, the VIP was located on the driver's door post. In 1968 it was moved to the left top of the instrument

VEHICLE ID PLATE INTERPRETATION*

Car line

B	Barracuda
C	Chrysler
	Newport/New Yorker, 77—80
D	Dodge, 73—74 Monaco
E	St. Regis
F	Lebaron
G	Diplomat
H	Volare
J	Challenger
L	Dart
M	Horizon
N	Aspen
P	Plymouth Fury, 77—80 Grand Fury
R	Satellite, 75—80 Plymouth Fury
S	Cordoba
T	Newport/New Yorker
V	Valiant
W	Coronet/Charger, 70—80 Monaco
X	Charger SE—Magnum SE
Y	Imperial
Z	Omni

Price Class

E	Economy
G	Dodge Taxi
G	Grand, 72 and later
H	High
K	Police
L	Low
M	Medium
N	New York Taxi
O	Super stock
P	Premium
S	Special
T	Taxi
X	Fastback

Body Type

21	2-door sedan
22	2-door special coupe
23	2-door hardtop
27	Convertible
29	2-door sports hardtop
41	4-door sedan
43	4-door hardtop
45	6-passenger wagon
46	9-passenger wagon

Sequence Number

1   00001
per day, starting with 1 00001,
1 00002, -3 and so on

Engine Displacement

A	170 CID (60—69)
	1.7 liter (78—80)
B	225 (64—69)
	198 CID (70—80)
C	Special order 6 (60—69)
	225 (70—80)
D	273-2Bbl* (64—67)
	225-2Bbl (77—80)
E	273-4Bbl (64—67)
	Special order 6 (70—80)
F	318 Polysphere (60—66)
G	383 (64—66)
	318-2Bbl (67—80)
H	383 Hiperf (64—67)
	340-4Bbl (68—73)
	318-4Bbl (78—80)
J	426 Hemi (64—68)
	340-6Bbl (71)
	360-4Bbl (73—80)
K	440 (64—67)
	360 (70—80)
L	440 Hiperf (64—67)
	383-2Bbl (67—71)
	360-4Bbl Hiperf (74 & 78—80)
M	400 (72—77)
N	383-4Bbl (68—71)
	400-4Bbl (73—80)
P	400-4Bbl Hiperf (68—78)
R	426 Hemi (68—71)
	360 (78—80)
T	440 (68—78)
U	440-4Bbl Hiperf (68—78)
V	440-6Bbl (69—72)
Z	Special order 8

*Bbl is abbreviation for carburetor barrel.

Model year code

6	1966
7	1967
8	1968
9	1969
0	1970
1	1971
2	1972
3	1973
4	1974
5	1975
6	1976
7	1977
8	1978
9	1979
0	1980
1	1981

Assembly Plant

1 or A	Lynch Road
2 or B	Hamtramck
3 or C	Jefferson
4 or D	Belvidere
5 or E	Los Angeles
6 or F	Newark
7 or G	St. Louis
8	Export
H	New Stanton
P	Wyoming (Export)
9 or R	Windsor

*Pre-'66 models used a ten digit VIN that did not include engine displacement or price class.

3

BLOCK CASTING NUMBERS

CASTING #	CID	YEAR	TYPE	REMARKS
1852029	413	1962	RB	Max Perf. & Truck
2120529	413	1959-65	RB	
2205697	413	1959-65	RB	Passenger Car
2205697	426	1964	RB	Passenger Car
2406730	426	1963-65	RB	Wedge & Max Perf.
2468030	413		RB	
2568130	383	1959-71	B	
2468330	426	1964-71	RB	Hemi Head
2432230	426	1964-66	RB	Wedge & Max Perf.
2536430	440	1966-72	RB	
2658836	426		RB	Industrial
3614230	400	1971-72	B	
3698630	400	1973-78	RB	
3698830-440	440	1973-78	RB	
4006530-400	400	1976-78	B	
4006630-440	440	1978	RB	

panel, at the base of and visible through the windshield. This tag is stamped with 13 digits that give car line, price class, body type, engine displacement, model year, assembly plant and sequence number—the car's position on the assembly line the day it was built. This information becomes the car's serial number. The chart on page 2 gives all the information needed to "read" your Vehicle Identification Number.

Engine Block Stamping Number

Another number you'll need is the engine block stamping. This number is stamped into the engine block and gives the code for engine displacement, year and month of production, performance level and special equipment. The B block or 383 and 400 cid stamping is found on the right side of the block adjacent to the distributor. The 413, 426 and 440 cid, or RB series, can be identified by the stamping on a pad at the left front of the engine in front of the valley cover. The chart on page 5 tells you how to interpret this number.

Casting Number

When a part is cast, be it a head, block or crank, the casting number is incorporated into the casting. It can help identify a part, but it is not necessarily adequate for complete identification. For complete identification you'll also need the engine size, year of production and stamping number.

Particularly important are the casting numbers for the heads. These numbers distinguish between years of production and, consequently, different configurations.

Armed with engine size, year, casting and engine stamping numbers, you can identify various engine components. This information, and a physical description, will help you find out if one part is interchangeable with another. The various tables nearby will help you decipher these numbers.

ENGINE BLOCK IDENTIFICATION

The term cubic inch displacement (cid) will be used quite frequently throughout this book. Therefore, a clear understanding of what cid means will be useful. An engine's size is determined by its displacement, the volume displaced by all of the pistons of an engine as they travel once from the top of their bores to the bottom. For example, on a 400 cid engine it would take 400 cubic inches of liquid to fill all eight cylinders from the top of each piston at the bottom of its travel—bottom dead center or BDC—so the liquid would be level with the top of the piston at the top of its travel—top dead center or TDC. The liquid in our 400 example would be 4.34" wide by 3.38" deep (bore x stroke). Let's use these two figures in a formula to discover how 400 cubic inches was determined. The formula for displacement is:

Displacement = pi/4 x bore² x stroke x number of cylinders

The mathematical constant pi equals 3.1415927, and divided by 4 the value is 0.7854. If we plug in the above numbers of our 400 cid engine, we get:

Displacement = 0.7854 x 18.835 x 3.38 x 8

BLOCK SERIAL STAMPING NUMBERS

There are two locations to look for block serial numbers on the B and RB engines: on a pad at the left front of the engine on top as noted in the body copy on page 47, and also on the very bottom of the engine next to the oil pan flange. The stampings on the top of the block will look something like this: CH 426 B 8-3-32. The "C" designates the series or year the engine was built; the "H" denotes that this engine is hemispherical; the "426" is the cubic inch displacement; and the "B" is the body type. In the date, the "8" is the month, the "3" is the day, and the "32" is the number engine that was built that day. You may also find at this location other stampings such as a Maltese Cross, WT, or an X. These markings are noted below.

The stamping on the bottom of the block will be the formal serial number for that block and read similar to the following:

9-10-68 PT38326010001. These numbers are decoded as follows:
A.   The first numbers are the date of stamping (9-10-68).
B.   The next letters indicate the engine assembly plant—in the case of our example, Trenton.
C.   The next three digits indicate cubic inch displacement: 383 cid.
D.   The next four digits (2601) are the 10,000 day calender numbers: 2601 = Sept 10, 1968.
E.   The final four numbers (0001) show that this was the first engine assembled that day.

SERIES:

S = 1962	A = 1965	D = 1968	G = 1971	4T = 1974
T = 1963	B = 1966	E = 1969	H = 1972	5T = 1975
V = 1964	C = 1967	F = 1970	J = 1973	6T = 1976
				7T = 1977
				8T = 1978

OTHER STAMPINGS:
Diamond = 0.008-in. oversize tappets
Maltese Cross = 0.001-in. undersized crankshaft
Maltese Cross and an X = 0.010-in. undersized crankshaft
A = 0.020-in. oversized cylinder bore
B = 0.010-in. undersized main and rod bearings
E = cast crankshaft
H = standard 4bbl
HP = high performance
LC = low compression
O.S. = 0.005 oversized valve stems
P = premium fuel recommended
R = regular grade fuel may be used
S = special engine
WT or TW = water test
X = oversized valve guides

ASSEMBLY PLANTS
K = Toluca   M = Mound Road   MV or MN = Marysville
PT = Trenton   T = Trenton (400 and 440 only)

	Bore		Stroke	CID
Low Block	4.125"	x	3.375"	361
	4.25"	x	3.375"	383
	4.342"	x	3.375"	400
Raised Block	4.18"	x	3.75"	413
	4.25"	x	3.75"	426
	4.32"	x	3.75"	440

This chart will help you understand the difference between the "B" (Low Block) and "RB" (Raised Block) series of big-block Mopar engines.

Displacement = 400 cubic inches.

The Chrysler big-block family consists of five basic block sizes identified by their cid: 383, 400, 413, 426 and 440. This grouping is called the B series and is further refined into the B and RB series. Refer to the chart above to recall what these designations mean.

As a family, the B series has the following in common: They all weigh about 225 lb and they each have a common cylinder-to-cylinder bore spacing of 4.80". As stock, the low blocks share a stroke of 3.375" and the raised block incorporates a 3.75" stroke. Let's look at them a bit more closely.

B Series 383 and 400 cid

If you go back a zillion years, actually to 1956, Chrysler introduced its "A" series of engines—now referred to as "LA" engines—and composed the series we call the small-block. In 1958 Chrysler introduced its big-block engines, the 350 and 361. If they already had an "A" engine what would be the logical nomenclature for the next? You got it, the B engine! I'm not sure if this is true or not, but it

certainly sounds logical to me.

The original B series engines were the 361, 383 and 400. The 361 sort of slipped into oblivion as a big-block but that displacement appeared as a small-block 360 in 1971. For our discussion we'll only consider the 383 and 400 cid engines.

These are the same block castings but with bores cored differently for the two different sizes. The 383 has a bore of 4.25" and the 400 cid, 4.342". Both have a stroke of 3.375".

Chrysler indicates that both of these blocks may be overbored to 0.040". Mopar Performance, Chrysler's high performance parts division, indicates that these blocks may be bored to 0.060" without danger of making the cylinder walls too thin. However, if the engine is to be used for racing purposes the cylinder walls should be checked very carefully. See Chapter 2 for more details.

The 1976–78 400 cid (and 440 cid) was a thin-wall casting and as such should be bored no greater than 0.030" over unless block filler is used.

Mounts—The engine mounting bosses are the same on all B/RB engines. Therefore, the engines are interchangeable within a car designed

to accommodate either one. In other words, you could install a 400 into a car from which you removed a 383. Because all the mounting bosses are the same, the above holds true for putting a 440 where a 413 came out.

RB Series 413, 426 & 440 cid

RB stands for raised block and refers to a modification of the block casting to allow for additional stroke length. The stroke was increased from 3.375" to 3.75" by increasing the cylinder bore length almost 3/4"— actually 0.745". This also increased the crankshaft centerline to the top of the block dimension from 9.98" to 10.725".

Chrysler wanted a strong block. To that end there are extensive support webs in the mid- and low-portion of the case. Sidewalls supporting the main bore extend below the crank centerline. Additional truss material joins the main webs to these sidewalls. By doing this it extends the block casting more than 2" below the crank centerline, allowing for a completely flat pan-rail surface.

It is important to say something here about the term "wedge." Wedge refers to the shape of the combustion chamber within the head of the engines we've been discussing. This helps us differentiate from that more famous combustion chamber, the hemispherical or "Hemi."

413 cid Max Wedge—As noted above, the 413 was the first of the RB series. The bore was increased to 4.175" and the longer stroke of 3.75" was achieved by extending the height of the bore. It was introduced in 1960 in the Chrysler 300E. This was a dual four-barrel, long-ram inducted, 10:1 compression engine, factory rated at

CONDENSED HISTORY

383:	1-2bbl (RB)		1959-1960
383:	1-2bbl (B)		1961-1971
383:	1-4bbl		1959-1971
383:	2-4bbl	was a dealer installed option	
400:	1-2bbl		1971-1978
400:	1-4bbl		1972-1978
413:	1-4bbl		1959-1965
413:	2-4bbl		1959-1965
426:	1-4bbl		1963-1966
426:	2-4bbl		1963-1971
440:	1-4bbl		1966-1978
440:	3-2bbl		1969-1972
413:	2-4bbl	Max Wedge Stage I	1962

380 horsepower (at 5000 rpm) with 450 lbs-ft. of torque.

Two years later, 1962, marked the introduction of the 413 Max Wedge. This was a dual four-barrel, cross-ram engine with 420 horsepower. The 1963–1964 Max Wedge block had valve clearance notches machined in the block at the top of the cylinder bores. In that same year the 426 Wedge was introduced.

426 cid Wedge—By increasing the bore of the 413 Max Wedge from 4.18" to 4.25", 413 became the 426. Further modifications were introduced to make this a total performance package. A new casting was made incorporating larger oil feeds and notched bores to accommodate the 1 7/8-in. exhaust valves. Additionally, this engine incorporated further refinements of special rods, crankshaft, pistons, heads, valves, valve gear, intake manifolds, carburetors and exhaust manifolds.

440 cid—The biggest of the "brute force" blocks was introduced as the 440 in 1966. To do this the new block was bored to 4.32-in. and retained the RB stroke of 3.75". In 1969 Chrysler added three, 2-barrel carburetors, special rods, crankshaft, timing chain, camshaft, valve springs and intake system. This engine has been affectionately termed the "440 Six-Pack."

Like the 400, the 440 was a thin-wall casting design and the same prohibition of boring the engine no more than 0.030-in. over holds here.

CRANKSHAFTS

Before entering into a discussion of the individual crankshafts, we should discuss the various types of crankshafts and how they differ from one another.

Essentially, there are four types of crankshafts: forged, cast, cast/shot-peened and billet. Each type has specific load capabilities.

The forged crank is a single bar of steel that is heated to about 2000° F.,

then forged under pressure into the crank shape.

The second method of crank manufacture is casting. Here, a sand mold is made in the basic crank shape and molten iron is poured in. This is then machined to crank shape and specifications.

To create the third style, added strength is given to the casting by shot peening. In this process, the casting is submitted to a treatment much like sand blasting or glass beading, only steel shot is used with considerably more force.

The billet crank is the strongest and most expensive of the four. It is a single bar or billet of steel that has been roughly forged, and is CNC machined down to the final shape.

The cast crank is the least strong of the three. It doesn't have a grain structure that flows with the shape of the crank as with the forged steel crankshaft. Rather, its crystalline structure is random. But shot peening compresses the surface, prestressing the casting so it is more resistant to cracking.

Crankshaft Interchange

The "B/RB" series of engines provides a veritable potpourri of displacement combinations because most of the cranks are completely interchangeable. At least 18 different engine displacements can be created through the use of various stroke lengths and block sizes. With only stock parts, displacement variations of more than 100 cubic inches may be obtained. Stroke lengths may be varied from 3.218" to 3.750". If you're into the performance end of engine building, your options are virtually unlimited.

However, the B and RB engines

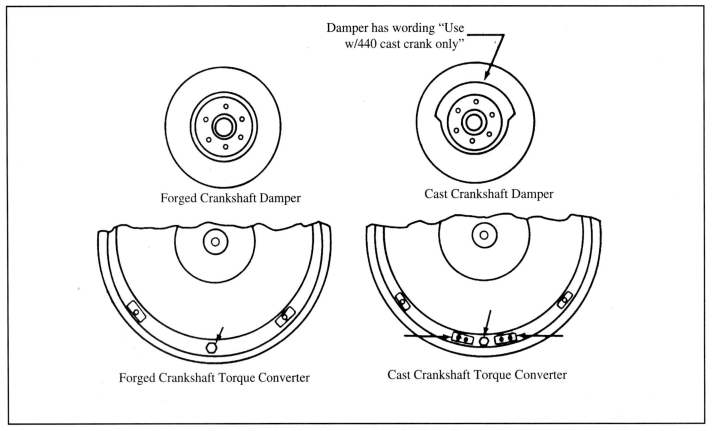

Damper has wording "Use w/440 cast crank only"

Forged Crankshaft Damper

Cast Crankshaft Damper

Forged Crankshaft Torque Converter

Cast Crankshaft Torque Converter

You can determine whether or not you have a cast or forged crank by checking the above diagram. Note the cast crank is externally balanced with weights on the torque converter.

have different main bearing journals and are therefore not interchangeable. The B engine has the smaller main bearing journal at 2.625" as compared to the RB at 2.750". Both cranks incorporate the same rod journal diameter of 2.375". Now let's examine some features of each crankshaft type.

383 cid—The 383 engine started life with a forged crank, but didn't end that way. Late in 1971, the 383 2-barrel was given a cast crank. Cast crankshafts use a specially balanced vibration damper and a specially balanced torque converter or flywheel. This is called external balancing. All cast crankshafts were externally balanced. Refer to the drawing above to see how this is identified.

400 cid—Cast cranks were used in all 400 cid engines except some 1972–74 4-barrels with four-speed

transmissions. These engines used steel cranks.

413 & 426 cid Max Wedge—The Max Wedge crank was a forged steel, flame-hardened unit and was the "weapon of choice" in all high performance buildups.

440 cid—The widest variations in crankshafts are in the 440 series. The 440 4-barrel (1967–1973) used a forged crank of which there are several versions. The first, 1967–70, was a standard forged crank. A stronger unit was developed for the 1972–73, 4-barrel high performance models, although there was also a standard crank in '72-'73 that was balanced for lighter pistons.

The 1970-72 440 Six-Pack used a forged steel crank that utilized external balancing to compensate for the heavier pistons and rods. This was not a modified earlier forging but a

brand-new unit made of premium quality steel.

The cast crank was introduced in 1974. This crank also requires external balancing.

CYLINDER HEADS

All B and RB heads are interchangeable. The only problem arises in trying to use 413–426 Max Wedge heads on a B (383-400) because there is no intake manifold available for this combination.

The history of the B head goes back to 1958. Up to 1961, the B engine used a head with 1.95-in. intake valves and 1.60-in. exhaust valves. The heads (up to 1963) can be identified by their aluminum rocker-shaft attaching brackets and valve covers retained with only four bolts.

In 1962, the intake valves were

CRANKSHAFT VIBRATION DAMPER

P/Cast #	Years	CID	F/C	Remarks
2275897	1962-65	383 413	F	
2275897	1964-66	426	F	Wedge
2532105	1964	426	F	Hemi
2532795	1965	426	F	Hemi
2658457	1966	383 440	F	
2658457	1967-69	383 440	F	
2658457	1970-71	383-4bbl.	F	
2658457	1970-71	440	F	W/Low Performance
2658871	1966-71	426	F	Hemi NC#
3512017	1970-71	440	F	W/Hi Performance
3577180	1970-71	383-2bbl.	C	W/Auto Transmission
3577785	1973-74	440	C	W/Auto Trans/Low Perf
3614371	1972	400 440	F	
3614371	1972-74	400-4bbl.	F	W/Man Trans/Hi Perf
3614371	1974	400-2bbl.	F	
3614371	1973-74	440	F	W/Auto Trans
3614372	1972	440	F	W/Hi Performance
3614374	1972	400-2bbl.	C	W/Auto Trans
3614374	1973	400	C	W/Auto Trans
3830183	1975	440	C	W/Hi Performance
3830184	1975	400	C	
3830482	1975	440	C	W/Lo Performance

F = Forged
C = Cast
NC# = No casting number found on part

You can determine whether or not you have a cast or forged crank by checking the casting numbers on your damper (located on the front or rear) and referencing it to the above chart. Note the cast crank is externally balanced with weights on the torque converter. See drawing on previous page.

increased to 2.08-in. on the intake but the smaller 1.60-in. exhaust valves were retained. With the introduction of the now-famous 300J head, the exhaust valves were increased in size to 1.74-in. and the 6-bolt valve cover became the standard.

The "modern" B engine head that was produced from 1964 to 1966 retained the 2.08" intake valve but reduced the exhaust valve back to 1.60". This head was quite similar to the 1962 design, but continued the 6-bolt valve cover.

With the introduction of the Max Wedge series in 1962 (413), a much larger exhaust valve (1.88") was incorporated. Additionally, these heads had very large ports and no heat cross-over passage. Many of the Max Wedge heads now incorporated adjustable rocker arms, where previously, only non-adjustable rockers were used.

In 1967, the 440 High Performance head was introduced, returning to the 1.74-in. exhaust valve. This head superseded the old 300J. In 1968, a larger combustion chambered version of the 440 High Performance head was brought to market, and was manufactured until 1971.

In 1972, to meet new emission standards, a flatter intake port was introduced on all B series engines. This can be identified by casting number 3462345. In mid-1973, this head was further refined by adding extra cooling passages, making it a bit more durable. These heads remained the same through 1978, with only a few changes such as the addition of hardened valve seats to overcome the effects of unleaded gas.

Today, an active aftermarket exists in highly refined heads. There are high performance heads with revised port shape, improved combustion chambers and oversized valves. Consider these only if you're into high performance or racing.

Design Fundamentals

To further understand the effects of head swapping, let's look at some design fundamentals. Three terms should be defined. These are top dead center (TDC), bottom dead center (BDC) and swept volume (SV).

TDC is the highest position the piston reaches in its upward travel.

B Engine Cylinder Head Casting Numbers

Year	Engine	Casting Number
1960-62	361/383/413	2206324
1962	413 Max Wedge	2402286
1964-67	361-383	2406516
1964	426 Max Wedge	2406518
1963	361/383/413	2463200
1963	426 Max Wedge	2463209
1967	440 High Perf.	2780915
1968-70	383-440	2843906
1971-72	383/400/440	3462346
1973	400-440	3462346
1973	400-440 Motorhome	3751213
1974	400-440	3769902
1975	400-440	3769975
1976-78	400-440	4006452
Stage IV		3614476
Stage V		4286526V

BDC is the opposite, or lowest position reached.

As a piston travels from BDC to TDC, it sweeps through, or displaces, a volume called *swept volume*. Swept volume is a cylinder's displacement.

A cylinder's compression ratio (CR) is directly proportional to its swept volume or displacement, and is inversely proportional to its clearance volume. Therefore, we can make a formula that states:

$$CR = Volume\ BDC/Volume\ TDC$$

This compression ratio formula says that as an engine's displacement is increased, clearance volume must also be increased to maintain the same compression ratio. That's why oversized pistons are manufactured to increase clearance volume by a smaller-than-original dome or larger-than-original dish. Otherwise

compression ratio would be increased.

This is an important consideration when interchanging heads. With today's fuel, compression ratios over 8:1 can cause detonation. If detonation is severe, engine damage will occur. With stock high-compression engines (10.25:1), this is already a problem. At the same time, changing to a head with a combustion chamber volume that is too large will result in a low-compression, poor-performing engine.

Valve & Port Size—Other head design factors affecting performance are valve and port sizes. If these are too small, the engine won't breathe properly and will lose power. In other words, the engine cannot draw an adequate air/fuel mixture through the smaller valve and port openings. On the exhaust stroke it will be unable to expel the exhaust efficiently.

If the valves and ports are too large—particularly on the intake side—the air/fuel mixture will not have enough velocity to keep the fuel mixed with air at low rpm. This creates poor driveability and low-speed sluggishness.

There is a good rule-of-thumb: with an otherwise-stock engine, keep the valve sizes within +/- 10% of engine specifications.

Before you dive into an engine project, you must first develop a plan. Decide how you are going to use the engine, what power level, and how much you can spend before gathering parts. You can save yourself a lot of headache and money with a little foresight. Photo by Michael Lutfy.

From its humble beginning in the 1958 model year, the Chrysler big-block engine has developed into one of the most popular racing engines in use today. Originally offered in 350 and 361 cubic-inch versions, these "B" block engines were built by Chrysler with the intention of replacing the Hemi engines released in the early part of the decade. Chrysler's powerful engines took up where the early Hemis of the 1950s left off. Chrysler wanted to maintain the performance and reliability level that the early Hemis had while having a lighter and simpler engine package. These "B" engines had plenty of performance for their day, but Chrysler wanted even more. So in 1959, Chrysler engineers unveiled their new "raised block" or "RB" version of the big block—the 413. This engine not only produced more power, but unwittingly gave birth to the musclecar movement and the legendary 426 Hemi engine. Chrysler's commitment to performance was shifting into high gear.

BASIC DESIGN FEATURES

The initial design of these engines incorporated several features that gave them certain advantages over the competition. The block was a Y-skirt design, giving it more strength than the traditional non-skirted design. The distributor was located in the front of the engine, allowing easy maintenance of the ignition system. Shaft-mounted rocker arms gave the valvetrain excellent strength and performance. Tall block heights allowed for long, connecting rods. Bearing sizes were selected to give excellent service life and strength, but they were not too large to prevent high rpm usage. Forged steel connecting rods and crankshafts were used that would hold up to high performance abuse. In short, these engines had the foundation necessary to be modified into real screamers with a minimum amount of fuss. Not only were they be able to produce high power outputs, they were able to hold together at these higher

This is a junkyard 440 waiting to be built into a screamer. Most engines you will encounter will probably be in this shape.

horsepower levels.

It's truly amazing that even today, more than 40 years after its introduction, the Mopar big-block design is still the basis for almost every Top Fuel drag racing engine in the world. From 300 horsepower to 6000 horsepower, it still works. Every important dimension like bearing sizes, block height, and bore spacing is exactly the same as it was in 1959. The Top Fuel engine block that you see at the drag races would literally bolt into your late '60s, early '70s Road Runner.

Although the history of the B engine is far more detailed and interesting than this brief overview, I am not going to elaborate on the historical facts, simply because this is not why you bought this book. Most Mopar fans are already familiar with

the great success of the big block anyway, and the reason you purchased this book is to learn how to make them go faster. While it's neat to know the Max Wedge came out in 1962 and the 440 in 1966 and such, these facts will not make you a better engine builder or win any races. You do not need to know what year the long ram intake manifold was produced to be able to build a B-1 engine!

This book is a guide on how to build these engines into competitive and successful race winners. It will go into great detail about the various systems that make up an engine and their effects on each other. Since this is the most up to date modification guide available for this engine, I will not recommend that you use parts that haven't been available for 20 years. It's time that the "B" engine enters the

new millennium. A lot of engine build-up guides are written with the premise that every reader has $20,000 to spend on their project, but I know from experience that this is not the case. For this reason, I will not recommend unnecessary parts or components, nor will I recommend the most expensive choice if there is a cheaper one that will do.

So instead of rehashing history, let's run down the specifications of the big-block Mopar engines—information that will help you with your high performance engine project.

Big Block Specs

Though there were seven different displacements of the B engines available from the factory, they all can be grouped into two separate, general categories—the "low block" B engine

GENERAL SPECIFICATIONS

	Low Block "B"	Raised Block "RB"
Deck Height:	9.980"	10.725"
Rod Length:	6.358	6.768
Stroke:	3.375	3.75
Crank Main Bearing Dia.	2.625	2.750
Crank Rod Bearing Dia.	2.375	2.375

Low Block B Engine Bores

Engine cid	Bore Size Dia.
350	4.06"
361	4.120"
383	4.25"
400	4.342"

Raised Block Engine Bores

Engine cid	Bore Size Dia.
383	4.03"
413	4.1875"
426	4.25"
440	4.32"

and the "raised block" RB engine. These terms are derived from the two separate styles of blocks produced.

Deck Height—The main difference is in the block or deck height of the respective engine families. The block height dimension is more correctly called the "crank centerline to deck surface" dimension. The low block was the first block to be produced at the factory in 1958. When the engineers wanted more displacement, they did it by increasing the stroke of the crankshaft. This required a taller cylinder to keep the piston from banging the cylinder head, so they raised the block height by .745" to provide enough clearance.

Interchangeability—All bolt-on parts interchange between the two engine families except for the intake manifold, pushrods and distributors. All other components—heads, cam timing systems, rocker arm systems, oil pumps, chrome accessories and such—can be interchanged between the two families. This is a great plus because you won't need to buy new parts if you build a larger engine in the future. You can get a good set of heads or rocker arms now for your 383 and if you upgrade later to a 440, you can simply bolt them on.

All B/RB engines share the same 4.800" cylinder bore spacing. This means that each cylinder is spaced 4.800" from each other measured from center to center.

Because the low-block engines are physically shorter by approximately 3/4" on each side, they may fit better into a tighter engine compartment than the taller, raised block. As we will see in later chapters, both block families can accommodate virtually the same displacements.

PLANNING YOUR BUILD-UP

I have spent many years building and racing literally hundreds of big-block Mopar wedge engines. As the owner of one of the largest Mopar specialty engine shops in the U.S., I have had the opportunity to try just about every modification possible. Some modifications are trick, some are unnecessary, and some just don't work. My shop has built everything from 361 cid truck motors for daily use to nitrous engines that have won world drag racing championships. But no matter how diverse the project, all of them have one common thread: planning. There are many different ways to build an excellent engine, even though some people would have you think otherwise. But engines are not particularly intelligent nor are they emotional. They are just a machine that performs a function. Your job as an engine builder is to get it to perform the function that you want over and over again as consistently as possible.

So the first step to building a racing engine is to develop a plan. Get out some paper, take some notes. Use a calculator and figure some things out. Talk to various engine builders. Spend some time at the track checking out other race cars and engines. But most of all develop a plan and stick with it. It is very expensive to change plans in midstream.

A 440 Six-Pack engine from 1969–1971 was the height of big-block street engines. Rated at 390 hp, these cars could hold their own against any street competition of their era.

What Are Your Goals?

Generally an engine is built with three main criteria in mind:

1. Performance
2. Longevity
3. Cost

Depending on your personal goals and budget, these three things will have different levels of importance. For example, if you are on a tight budget, your "importance rankings" would go 3, 2, 1—it's more important that the engine costs under $3000 than that it makes 1000 horsepower. If you want absolute maximum performance, with cost as no object, your order might be 1, 2, 3. Once you determine your priorities, you can develop your plan of attack. Since performance is the reason you picked up this book, performance should be a priority. Set a realistic goal, and stick to it. Hopefully you have spent some time at the track (doing some thinking and planning, of course) and gotten a feel for how fast you would like to go. Once you determine this, you can get an idea of how much it will cost. Don't expect to run the quarter mile in the 7s for only a few thousand dollars. If you can, you should be writing this because I've been at it for years and still haven't been able to do it for that kind of money. Compare and contrast your goals with the reality of your budget and hopefully you'll come up with a good compromise between mortgaging the house and having a slow car. By setting your goals realistically, you will be able to attain them much more easily.

Cost/Benefit—It's my experience that for most people priority ranking is 3,3,3! For many, cost is the only thing that matters, and honestly, it is usually the difference between winning and losing. I mean everybody wants a 6000 horsepower engine, right? They just can't afford it. So you have to perform a cost and benefit analysis of your options. What this means is to determine what things give you the most performance for your dollar. Is it the roller cam or the 1050 cfm Holley dominator carb? The

On the other hand, this 596 cubic inch B1 wedge can easily hold its own on the drag strip in this modern era!

lightweight pistons or the Fluidampr?

Short Block Priority—If you are on a limited budget or a novice building your first engine, try to build the best short block possible in the beginning and skimp on the cam and heads. The short block is the foundation that you build performance on. Granted, a set of aluminum heads or a huge roller cam will make more power than just the mildly reworked short block, but the short block components are the hardest to change at a later date. Even just a piston swap means re-balancing, new rings, bearings, machine work, etc. But if you install good lightweight parts in the short

block in the beginning and spend the extra money for good machining, blueprinting and balancing, then a cam or head swap later on becomes just a quick weekend project. Besides, a killer set of heads on a wimpy short block is a prescription for disaster.

Try to select components that will not limit the growth of your engine project in the future. Select pistons with valve pockets large enough for a big roller cam so you don't have clearance problems later on. If you are buying a new set of heads, choose ones that will allow you to upgrade to new, improved parts as they become available. These little extras usually

have a small initial investment, but will have a major savings down the road. In short, think twice and spend once.

Safety—Always consider the safety aspect of the engine too. Some things like an SFI-approved vibration damper are required by most sanctioning bodies to protect you from a damper explosion. Don't skimp on items like this that may save you money (or your life) in the long run.

Budget-Saving Ideas

To be the most cost effective, you should build the largest possible displacement that you can afford. The

All aluminum 600 cubic inch B1 T/S engine represents about the practical limit of wedge development. Note the dry sump oil pan and the 2 stages of nitrous oxide injection. This is mid-six-second dragstrip wedge power.

reason for this is simple: to make a certain amount of horsepower, the engine needs to burn a certain amount of fuel. This can be accomplished either of two ways: with a small engine turning very high rpm or a larger engine operating at a lower rpm. The larger, lower rpm engine will be cheaper to build and more importantly, to maintain. For a Mopar big block, this means you should start with a 440 cid engine. Since it is the most popular style of big-block

Mopar to build, there are many racing parts readily available and most are sold at a considerable discount over custom components.

Lightweight Components—Try to use lightweight components like pistons and connecting rods because these are examples of the few components that will give you an increase in performance, along with an increase in durability. The increased durability comes from the fact that lighter parts mean less stress.

It doesn't take a genius to figure out that the rods aren't being stressed as much with a 750 gram piston as opposed to the 1100 gram piston. These lightweight components are well worth the additional investment. Keep in mind that at 6000 rpm, the piston goes from TDC to BDC back to TDC (up and down) 100 times per second!

Solid Lifter Cam—Although we address cam selection in Chapter 9, a few words of advice apply here. If you are just starting out, run a solid lifter cam before switching to a roller cam setup. While the roller is a better way to go for an all-out race engine, they are usually three times more expensive than a flat-tappet cam. Several of the newly designed flat-tappet cams can come very close to roller cam performance for less money.

Regardless of what components you choose to use, try to use the parts you already have first. Decide if the intake manifold in your garage will satisfy your performance goals. If it will, then go ahead and run it! Believe me, the easiest thing to do in the racing world is spend money. If you are bracket racing, build a conservative engine with medium compression and camshaft. If your track's fast bracket begins at 11.99 seconds, why spend the extra money for a 9-second engine to race slower cars? However, if your personal goal is to go as fast as possible, by all means go for it! The bottom line to engine building is to think!

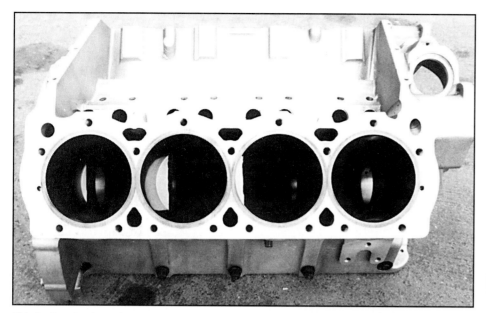

This is the aluminum Indy Maxx aluminum block. Note the thickness of the sleeves. This low-deck block has a bore size of 4.500". These blocks are exceptionally stout and able to withstand the highest horsepower engines this side of Top Fuel.

The first step in any engine build-up should be the cylinder block, because it is the foundation on which everything else is built. An engine is only as strong as its block. It has to hold everything together or disaster will strike. It makes little sense to bolt on a $10,000 set of heads to a used station wagon block.

BASIC DESIGN FEATURES

All Mopar big-block engines are built from the same basic "Y" block design. This design has the crankshaft mounted inside the block above the oil pan rail. This provides more support for the main webbing and lends itself to easy cross-bolting of the main caps. If you study the lower end bracing of these blocks, you will notice that the overall design is similar to that of a triangulated truss. Not only is this very sturdy, but it also allows for a completely flat oil pan rail. Though the Y-block design makes it easy to use the strong cross-bolt method of securing the main caps, it's interesting to note that no

Mopar big block other then the 426 Hemi had cross-bolted mains from the factory. All production wedge engines had two-bolt mains. Unlike some of the other engines from domestic manufacturers, the two-bolt B/RB engine blocks can withstand a lot of abuse. Since it has all of the extended webbing and trusses, the bottom of the block is very resistant to twisting under load. That is why these engines can handle the increased power from racing, even with two-bolt mains.

Head Bolt Pattern—There are seventeen cylinder head bolts on each bank, with a complete ring of five head bolts around each cylinder. This head-bolt pattern provides tremendous clamping force to keep the heads on and the head gaskets intact even under demanding loads.

Measurements—All production blocks have a 4.800" bore spacing. This measurement is the center to center distance between adjacent cylinders and allows for large bores. The relatively tall deck heights for both the low block engines (9.980") and the raised block engines (10.725") allow plenty of room for long connecting rods even with long

Head studs are a good idea if the compression is over 12.5:1 or nitrous oxide is being used. The B-engine has a very strong bolt pattern layout with five head bolts around each cylinder. At the very least, use new head bolts in any performance rebuild.

The factory ID pads on a low deck block (left) and a high deck block (right) are the best way to identify your block. This pad contains a lot of information about the displacement, year, and any factory "goofs" that the block may contain.

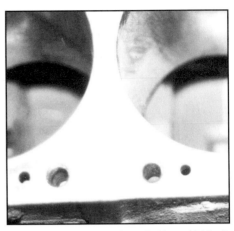

Small coolant holes along bottom of block between head bolts identify block as being from a motor home. These holes circulated coolant around the spark plugs to keep them cool. Special heads with mating holes were also used. These blocks are of no advantage over any other block for racing use.

This additional stiffening rib is standard on all big blocks from 1969 to 1978. Try to choose a block that has it. All Mopar blocks have a casting date cast into them. This one is 12/13/72.

strokes. In short you could do a lot worse than using a production block.

When it comes time to actually design and build your engine, there are three basic block choices that you can make: production cast iron, aftermarket cast iron and aftermarket aluminum.

The block choice that you make will be determined by the power level that you plan on making and how much money you are willing to part with.

All three of these blocks have certain advantages and disadvantages. Since the production block is the most common piece to use, let's start there.

PRODUCTION BLOCK

As stated earlier, the production block is a very stout piece. However, as with any production 30-year-old component, there are ways to make something that's already good even

better. Remember, that most every component is interchangeable from block to block so every modification discussed here can apply to the 383 or 400 as well as a 440.

Initial Selection

After you have decided on which engine family to build (either low block or raised block) you will need to actually find a block to use. There actually are some differences in all of these blocks. As a quick note: all 350, 361, 383, 413, 426 blocks are the same. There is no year-to-year difference, so if you choose to use one of these, they all will work fine. But

This 440 block ID pad shows it's a 1971 model due to the "G440" and that it is a high performance Six-pack model with the "HP2" markings. Normal high performance engines are stamped "HP". The upside W is part of the stamping "WT," which stands for "water test," a factory pressure test.

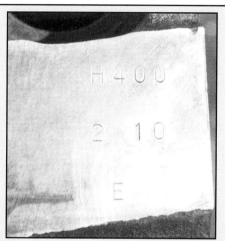

S =	1962
T =	1963
V =	1964
A =	1965
B =	1966
C =	1967
D =	1968
E =	1969
F =	1970
G =	1971
H =	1972
J =	1973
4T =	1974
5T =	1975
6T =	1976
7T =	1977
8T =	1978

This 400-block ID pad shows the displacement as well as the model year of the block. The H means it's a 1972 model block. This system can be found in the key above. The E at the bottom indicates that the engine has a cast crankshaft.

because the vast majority of Mopar racing engines are built from 400 and 440 blocks, we will concentrate on these.

The 440 Block—Though any 400 or 440 block will physically work, there are a few year-to-year variations that are worthy of a closer look. There are three different 440 blocks that you will encounter in your junkyard search. The first type will be found with casting dates from mid-1965 until mid-1968. These first series blocks are a thick-wall design and will make a good starting point for your engine.

The next series goes from mid-1968 up through 1975, and are the same as the earlier blocks, but have additional stiffening along the outside in the form of cast-in ribs. These blocks are also a thick-wall design and would be the best ones to use.

The third series of blocks will be the 1976–1978 blocks which have a thinner cylinder wall design. These thin-wall blocks still have the external stiffening ribs but they don't have as thick a cylinder wall as the earlier blocks. This really isn't a problem, but keep the over-boring on these to .030"

There is a 400 block in circulation that has extra thick webbing as the pointer shows. This is the "cold weather or industrial" 400 block, which was only cast from approximately April 4, 1971 to October 10, 1971. It can be identified by the casting date and the larger than normal "3614230" casting number on the side. This is the best block to use, but they are very scarce.

or less. This does not mean that these later blocks should be avoided. On the contrary, many killer engines have been built with these later blocks as they still have the same bottom end strength.

The 400 Block—The 400 block has a similar situation. There are three choices here as well. First and best choice would be the blocks cast in mid-to late-1971 that have the casting

Extra side webbing on cold weather 440 block was done to resist external cracking. No doubt this will also slightly increase strength of the block. But don't worry about finding one: I have only seen one in over 15 years.

number ending in "230." These blocks have thick cylinder walls and also have a thicker support area for the main bearings. These blocks are fairly hard to find, but if you do find one,

The low-deck block, on the other hand, has more material around the bearing due to its smaller main bearing diameter. This helps to support the load better. As a result, these blocks can withstand considerably more power than the RB engine.

The main bearing support area of the RB block leaves a little to de desired in the support area. These block are prone to cracking in engines putting out 650 horsepower or more.

save it for your wildest engine combination.

The next 400 series would be the 1972 through 1975 blocks. These have the thick cylinder walls and the stiffening rib much like their 440 cousin, and make an excellent starting point.

The final series would be the 1976–1978 blocks. Just like the 440, the same things apply to the thin wall 400. Don't throw it away, but don't overbore too much.

Basic Prep & Inspection

After you get your new (junkyard) block home, it's time to check it out. As you disassemble the engine, pay close attention to the main bearings and caps. If the bearings have lost their ability to fit tightly (called *bearing crush*) into the main caps, the engine was probably overheated and will need line honing. Same deal

applies if the main caps do not fight tightly into their register in the block. Both of these things are signs of abuse and should be noted. If possible, turn the crank by hand once all the pistons are out. If there are any signs of binding or any tight spots, the block will definitely need line honing for correction.

As long as the block doesn't have any glaring problems like a gaping crack or hole somewhere, load it up and take it to your machine shop for a through cleaning. Most machine shops use either a caustic liquid or an oven of some kind to clean. Either way will do a good job.

After all the grease and grime are off, have the block Magnaflux checked to find any hidden or smaller cracks. This process is well worth the small additional cost, especially if you can spot a cracked block before hundreds of dollars are spent on machine work. Since you are spending the money, make sure the shop checks the entire block, because they can crack anywhere. Hopefully

your shiny clean block passed the Magnaflux check and you are ready to spend more money on block machine work!

Clean Threads—But before this is done, carefully run a bottoming tap through all of the threaded holes in the block to make sure they are clean. One of the keys to fastener reliability is to have good, clean threads.

Fasteners—As long as we are talking about block fasteners, it's a good idea to replace the main cap bolts with some stronger fasteners. These new fasteners can be either bolts or studs. The studs are the preferred way to go because they are stronger than the bolts. Since the studs have fine threads on the nut end, they have more holding power than the coarse-threaded bolts. The superior main studs usually cost about the same as the bolts do, so they are effectively a cheap upgrade.

Deburr Casting Flash—If you are feeling ambitious, take a small die grinder and remove any factory casting flash present in the valley and

Line honing the main bearing caps will ensure that all the caps are parallel to each other. This will allow the crank to spin freely and greatly extend bearing life. It is always a good idea to do this even for a mild rebuild. For a serious engine or one that has had the main caps changed, it is a must.

main web area. Do not try to enlarge or remove any more than is necessary. The removal of the flash will not make the block any stronger, but it will ensure that no pieces of cast iron will break off and get stuck in the oil pump. If you are feeling even more ambitious, the lifter valley can be smoothed out to aid in oil drainback.

Torque Main Caps—After all this is done, torque the main caps to specification. This will allow the bottom of the cylinder bores to distort correctly (due to the twisting effect of the main fasteners) prior to boring. This will help to ensure a perfectly round cylinder when the engine is running. Also, take a small ball hone to the lifter bores and very lightly hone them to remove any rust or burrs. This will ensure that the lifters will be free to spin correctly in their bores.

Line Honing

Line honing the block is a machining process that aligns and restores the factory dimension of the main bearing saddles. During normal operation, the block will distort slightly. This is due to the thermal cycling of repeated use and the general stress of running. In time, the main bearing saddles may no longer be in perfect alignment. When this happens, there will be an increase in friction and bearing wear. To correct this, have the block line honed at the machine shop. Since the main caps will also move with use, the caps can be restored to factory specifications by line honing as well. This will ensure uniform and correct main bearing clearance and bearing crush.

If main studs are installed, the caps may shift slightly in their register. Line honing will correct this also. Loose main caps can be welded on the sides to tighten them up before line honing. If you plan on installing a different set of main caps than the block originally came with, the block will have to be line bored before it is line honed. Unless the budget is really

tight, have it line honed even if you suspect everything is okay. Line honing increases performance by reducing friction, which in turn increases durability. If the engine is going to be seriously raced, line honing is a must.

Cylinder Boring & Honing

After all the initial prep work is done, the block is ready to be bored. Boring is critical to ensure that the cylinders are exactly 45 degrees from the crank centerline. This will free up any power that is lost to excess friction generated from mis-located cylinders. There are several methods available for boring a block and all work fine. You basically have to accept the method your shop uses as correct.

Selecting Overbore Size—Make sure the overbore you have selected won't leave the cylinder walls too thin. If you have access to a sonic checker, make sure that the cylinder walls are at least .080" thick after boring. This is considered a minimum and any thicker is better, especially for performance use. All the thick-wall blocks can be safely bored .060" over. Some of the early 400 blocks can actually go .100" over, but sonic check first. The later model thin-wall blocks should be limited to a .030" overbore. If the water jackets have been filled with cement, the overbore can be increased. Even the thin-wall blocks can go .060" over with no problem if the block has been filled. This is a race-only modification. Also remember to check the inside diameter of the head gasket that you plan on using to be sure that it will accommodate your desired bore size. Don't forget to make sure that there are piston rings available too.

All honing should be done with a deck plate regardless of use. This ensures perfectly round cylinder bores when the heads are torqued on. This helps ring seal and ring life in racing engines as well as stock style rebuilds. Make sure your machine shop has one.

Grinding the block for stroker clearance is not an involved process and is easily done with a hand grinder. Only grind enough to give about .060" clearance.

Honing—Have the machine shop bore the block to within .004" of the final size, and then have them hone it to the finished size. Honing is the most critical machining step that is done to a block. It is imperative that the rings seal as tightly as possible in order for the engine to make the most possible power. This means that the cylinders have to be round and stay that way during operation. Unfortunately, it is virtually impossible to hone a block that will be perfectly round during engine operation, but you can come close.

Since the block is subject to a variety of different stresses and thermal loads at the same time, it will never be perfect. The key is to hone the block as close to operating conditions as possible. Some engine builders have actually circulated hot water through the block during honing to simulate operating temperature, but this is a bit extreme.

One important and easy operating condition to simulate is the stress caused by the head bolts when the heads are fully torqued down. The cylinder bores actually distort a

measurable amount when the head is torqued on. There is a device called a "deck plate" that can be torqued on the block during honing that will simulate the stress of the heads. If you use a deck plate to simulate this distortion when the block is being honed, the cylinders will be perfectly round when the heads are on. If the deck plate is not used, the cylinders will be round during the honing process only and will become distorted when the heads are installed. Find a shop with a deck plate and be sure to use the actual type of fasteners that you plan on using for the heads. Most shops charge an additional fee to use a deck plate but it's worth every penny.

The final honed finish will depend on what the engine will be used for, and type of rings that will be installed, but generally a racing engine will use an extremely fine finish. If you or your machine shop is uncertain about this consult the ring manufacturer for their recommendation.

Decking

Machining the block deck surface, called "decking the block," is not always necessary, but if you can afford it, it is a good procedure to have done. Most Chrysler blocks do not have uniform deck heights from side to side. This can be corrected by decking both sides an appropriate amount until they are equal. This process is called "parallel decking" and should be considered a must for a serious racing engine. This will ensure uniform piston deck heights and therefore compression ratios from side to side. To check the block for squareness, simply install the crankshaft and install a piston and rod assembly into the number 1 cylinder.

Partially filling the waterjackets with block filler is a great way to increase cylinder wall strength. By tying the cylinders in with the rest of the block, this cement-based filler will cut down on cylinder wall flex, which equals more power and better consistency. Contrary to belief, the engine will not overheat if properly done since there is still three inches or so of water in the block. This is a drag-race-only modification.

Decking the block will correct for any end to end variation in block height giving more equal compression ratios from cylinder to cylinder. It will also provide a fresh new surface for the gasket to seal on.

Measure the deck clearance, being careful to measure in the exact center of the piston. After this is done, take the same rod and piston combo and check the number two (other side of block) cylinder deck clearance. If it is different, the block should be decked to make the clearances equal. As a side bonus, a decked block will give the head gasket a fresh, new, and perfectly flat sealing surface. This will help prevent gasket failure and is a must for nitrous engines.

Final Prep

Once all the machine work is done, the block should be cleaned thoroughly again to remove any oil and shavings. Water and dish soap can be used, and it should be dried with compressed air. Always scrub the oil galleys completely to be sure that they are clean. Once the block is clean, install the cam bearings, freeze plugs, and the oil galley plugs and it's ready to go. If you are so inclined, the interior of the block can be painted so seal up the pores in the casting. The best thing to use is red insulating varnish. This is easily available in spray cans. Be sure to mask off all of the machined areas. The B engines have good oil drain back, so painting or polishing the valley isn't really necessary.

Increasing Strength

There are a few modifications that can be done to a stock block to make it stronger for racing.

Cement Waterjackets—The first thing to consider is partially filling the waterjackets with cement. I know that it sounds crazy, but it really works well for a race-only engine. When the block is filled in this way, all the cylinders are tied to each other, giving them more strength and rigidity. Remember, the cylinders themselves are only cast-iron tubes suspended in water. They are only tied to the block at the top and bottom. The rest of the cylinder is just hanging in the water. Since the cylinders are fairly long (especially in the RB engines) they are prone to flexing under strain. At best this will mean loss of ring seal and power, less consistency, and more wear. At worst, it will mean a cracked or collapsed cylinder wall. If the block's water passages are filled in with cement, all of these problems are virtually eliminated.

The process is pretty simple. The filler I have had good success with is called "Hard Block." Epoxy can also be used because it is lighter. Set the

End shot of an aluminum main cap. Notice the larger size of the cap. These caps will usually solve cracked and broken main webbing. However, if serious all-out racing is the goal, a cross-bolted main block is the best choice.

A production 440 block fitted with aftermarket aluminum main caps. This modification allows the bottom end to withstand much more power. They are required for applications over 650 horsepower.

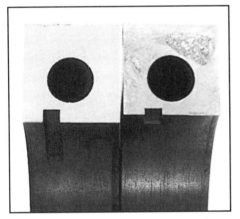

Production main bearing cap on right shows evidence of bouncing in the block. While this doesn't really hurt anything in the short run, it will eventually cause engine failure. Aluminum caps usually will eliminate this problem.

block up so that the deck is level. Make sure that the main caps are torqued to spec and that the freeze plugs are in place. Warning: Carefully study the inside layout of the waterjackets before filling the block. Grab a flashlight and look into all the holes. These blocks have reinforced areas into the waterjacket for the head bolts. The filler has to be below these areas or the water will not be able to

circulate. If this happens, the block is now an even heavier boat anchor. The filler can't be removed, so be careful. It's better to fill the block lower than to turn it into scrap.

Mix up the filler and carefully pour it into the block from the waterjacket holes in the deck. Pour slowly and carefully tap the block with a hammer to settle the filler in the block. After it's filled enough (generally just above the freeze plugs) torque a deck plate on and let it harden overnight.

Aluminum Main Caps—Another good, high horsepower modification is aluminum main caps. These caps will allow the block to flex slightly and therefore not crack and break. Main cap bounce is very common on these engines due to the heavy weight of the internal parts and the two-bolt mains. The bouncing main caps won't be an immediate problem, but in the long run they will definitely cause some type of breakage. With the aluminum caps installed, a two-bolt block can handle a tremendous amount of power. Any block that will be used for over 650 horsepower

should have these caps installed. These caps are generally a race-only modification and are not recommended for the street. They are easily installed by simply line boring them on. This is not to imply that the production caps are fragile. They certainly are not fragile and are capable of handling a substantial amount of power. However the aluminum caps increase long-term durability under high rpm operation. They are a must for heavy nitrous use, and some two-bolt blocks have been used at over 1000 horsepower, which is a testament to the original block design's strength.

Some attempts have been made to install the cross-bolt main caps on the production wedge blocks, but there really isn't enough material in the webbing to really do much good. The factory cross-bolt blocks had the webbing beefed up in these areas for the four-bolt caps. If you want to beef up the bottom end for racing, go with the aluminum caps.

Bushing Lifter Bores—Bushing the lifter bores will not necessarily result

 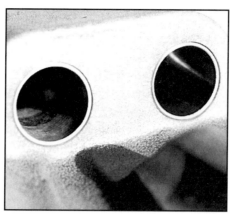

Lifter bores can be bushed to restrict oil flow, correct lifter contact angle, move their position, or change their size. Doing it is not required even for all out racing. Stock, unbushed bores are visible on left.

simple: enlarge the oil galley diameter slightly as deep as the first two lifters. This is easily done from the front of the block with a mill. After the galley is enlarged, tap the front of the block to accept a 1/2" pipe plug instead of the stock 3/8" pipe plug. This additional diameter will allow plenty of oil to flow past the first two bushings and down the rest of the galley.

Bushing for oil restriction on the driver's side galley isn't necessary. This galley is fed from the back of the block via two cross passageways below the oil pressure sender. To restrict oil flow here, simply plug the driver's side galley in the back of the block. This can be done by installing small expansion (freeze) plugs in the galley or by just tapping the galley deeper and installing the galley plug further than normal until it blocks the feed passage. Either way works fine. The passenger side can still be bushed to correct the contact angle if needed.

Remember that the only oil the lifters will get after all this restriction is by "splash." Because of this, this

in increased performance, but it will increase durability. When the lifter bores are bushed, they will not receive any oil, resulting in more oil flow in other, more critical areas such as the bearings. Durability is increased, because the oil system in these engines is designed to feed the main bearings from the passenger side oil galley, which is a potential problem. Since the lifter bores are contained in this oil galley, the lifters themselves act as plugs in the galley. If a lifter were to come out of its bore due to a broken valvetrain component (usually a pushrod or rocker arm) most all of the oil flow from the oil pump would come flooding out of the bore where the lifter used to reside. This will mean that the overall oil pressure to the rest of the engine will immediately drop to about 5 psi and oil volume would be drastically reduced. Needless to say, this is not a good thing. If the lifter bores are bushed, the oil pressure would remain constant regardless of how many lifters may or may not be remaining in their bores.

As an added benefit, the lifter to camshaft contact angle can also be corrected during the bushing process. This may result in a small power gain,

especially if the bores were not drilled properly at the factory.

Some manuals and engine experts say that the first lifter bores on the passenger side (cylinder number 2 intake and exhaust) can't be bushed or bearing failure will result. This is because the larger outside diameter of the bushings will stick farther into the galley than the lifters originally did and the oil flow will be restricted. This is a critical area, because this is where the oil flow changes direction and turns to go down the main galley.

The solution to this dilemma is

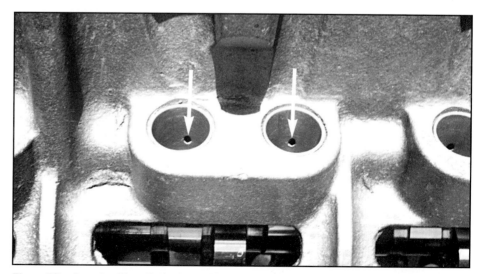

These lifter bore bushings have been drilled for oiling to the lifters. This is required if the engine is going to use through-the-pushrod oiling of the valvetrain instead of the normal through–the-shaft method of oiling. Hole size will depend on the specific application but will generally range from .040" to .060".

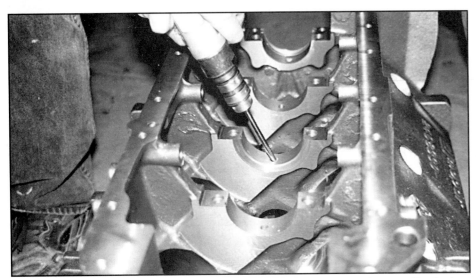

It's a good idea to enlarge the oil galley feeds that supply the bearings as the factory machining can leave steps in the passage. This can be done with a 17/64" reamer chucked into a drill. Only do the passage that goes into the lifter galley, not the one that feeds the cam bearing.

The factory 3/8" oil pickup tube can be easily replaced with the larger "hemi" tube by simply drilling and tapping the block. This is a good idea for a hot street engine and a must for a racing engine that's not going to use some type of external oil system.

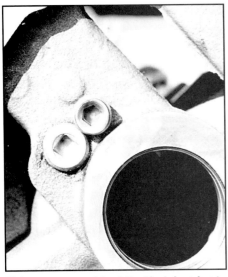

If the passenger side of the block is going to have the lifter bores bushed, it will be necessary to enlarge the oil galley deep enough to go past the bushings for the #2 cylinder. This will allow adequate oil flow to the engine. If this is not done, the oil flow will be restricted in the galley due to the bushing larger diameter intersecting the galley. After the galley is enlarged, a 1/2" pipe plug is used instead of the stock 3/8" which is shown for comparison. Also note the extra material around the cam bearing on this Mopar Mega block. This will allow for a raised cam version of the Mega block to eventually be produced.

modification is not for street use or for hydraulic lifters. It is a track-only thing. I also do not recommend

restricting the oil supply in the block to the heads. If restricted oil supply to the heads is required, it's better to do it in the heads because the amount of restriction is easier to change if it's done in the head.

Other Oil Modifications—On the subject of oiling and galleys, the passageway that feeds the main bearings from the oil galley is usually not a constant diameter and can be restrictive. For additional oil flow these production "steps" in the feed passageway's diameter can be reamed out and the galley can be enlarged. Use a 17/64" reamer chucked into a drill and simply run it down the galley. Since most reamers are 6 inches long and are barely long enough to do the job, make sure that the reamer goes deep enough to connect with the lifter galley. If more length is needed, pull the reamer out of the chuck slightly.

Notice that there are two galleys inside the main bearing feed hole. One goes up to the cam bearing, which should be left as is, and the other goes off at an angle to connect

with the lifter galley. This is the one to enlarge. Be careful when doing this since a broken reamer in the block is very difficult to remove.

AFTERMARKET BLOCKS

No matter what we do to a production block, it will still be just that—a mass-produced passenger car block originally designed to get to the grocery store and back. While the modifications will permit higher levels of performance than the factory ever dreamed of, they are still limited by the inherent constraints of a production block. Face it, nothing lasts forever especially when it's being over stressed.

So if you have the budget and are going racing, consider an aftermarket block. Generally they are a better investment since they will last longer and allow even higher levels of performance with a higher level of reliability. Not to mention that by the time all the tricks are thrown at the

If a gear or belt drive is going to be used on a Mopar Mega-block, some modifications to the casting are required to eliminate interference. The four areas that need machining are shown here.

Aluminum or Iron?—The first decision you have to make is whether or not to go with an aluminum or iron block. Iron blocks are cheaper and heavier, but generally make more power than aluminum because the iron is more thermally efficient than aluminum. Aluminum blocks also tend to shift around more, making ring sealing a little more difficult. While the primary advantage to an aluminum block is its weight, it also offers another important advantage in that its repairable. If there is an internal failure in your engine, such as a broken rod, an aluminum block can be easily welded back into shape while a cast iron block would probably have to be scrapped.

Iron blocks are much more common than aluminum, but both blocks will accept all standard components such as heads, cams, distributors, water pumps, oil pans, etc. Good machine work principles like deck plate honing, oil restriction, square decking, etc. all still apply to these new blocks too. Generally, these new blocks will

production block, you will have put a decent amount of time and money into something that still was designed for a station wagon. Some of the new blocks on the market can be purchased for far less than twice the cost of prepping a production block. When you consider that all aftermarket blocks can accommodate larger bores (allowing for almost "free" cubic inches), have cross-bolt main caps for strength, are available in aluminum for less weight and are brand-new unstressed castings, they appear to have even greater value.

Obviously some engine combinations will require an aftermarket block to be successful. If your combination will make over 850 hp, you had better consider stepping up to a "real" block. The aftermarket has long neglected the Mopar racer when it comes to cylinder blocks. We were forced to build our engines from junkyard parts while the other guys sped by us with their shiny new 600+ cubic-inch engines. But even with our old junkyard parts, we stayed very close to the competition. But now things are different, because we have

the hardware to compete on a level playing field.

Choosing an Aftermarket Block

Okay, you've decided to get a new aftermarket block, but which one? In general, all of the aftermarket blocks currently available are excellent and will withstand significant horsepower and torque output.

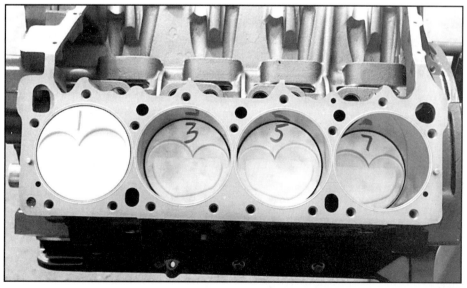

This 4.530" bore Mega-block has had the cylinders O-ringed. This is a must for high compression engines or engines running large amounts of nitrous oxide. When used with a copper head gasket, sealing is maintained even in the most demanding applications.

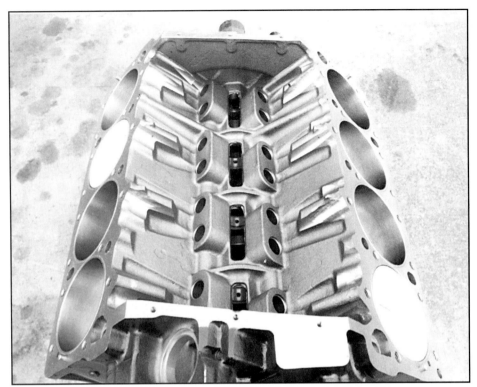

Lifter valley of Mopar Mega block shows where the lifer bores have been beefed up over a production block for strength. Bosses near deck are cast in to allow the same block to be produced in a hemi version.

Bottom end shot of a 600 cubic inch Mopar Mega block. Note the lightweight aluminum rods and the specially lightened crankshaft. Only the center three main caps are cross-bolted. This design has proven itself to be adequate for even top fuel drag racing.

the first available iron block designed strictly for racing. Since Mopar Performance had just reintroduced the 426 Hemi block a few years earlier, it was natural that they would follow with a race version of the 440 block. This block incorporates all of the good features of the original 440 but with the addition of cross-bolt main caps on the center three bearings as the Hemi and the major addition of extra material in the cylinder walls to allow for even larger cylinder bores. This is the first "production" cross-bolt wedge block ever offered by Mopar Performance.

A lot of attention went to strengthening this block, and as a result, it is very stout. The webbed areas around the main bearing saddles and the lifter bores have been beefed up to handle additional power. While the additional strength features are great, the most important new feature is the siamese cylinder bores to allow previously unobtainable cylinder bore sizes. "Siamese" means that there is so much material around each cylinder that the cylinder walls' outside diameter actually touch each other. There is no water circulation between each cylinder.

This additional material allows the cylinders to be bored much larger than normal and allows for a larger engine size. Since the bore spacing is the same as a stock block at 4.800", the maximum bore size is limited to 4.562". Any larger than this and the bore spacing has to be increased. It is possible to increase the bore spacing of this block since it comes from Mopar Performance with 4.200" bores (this allows building every production engine size from a 413 + .030" on up), which requires some type of fixture boring anyway. If the bore spacing is

not require much in the way of modification. Most custom features can be added when the block is ordered. Now let's run down some of

the more common aftermarket blocks currently available.

Mopar Mega Block—The Mopar Mega block with siamese bores was

Close up of the O-ring in the block. Things can get pretty tight in a big bore engine.

The lifter valley of the Indy block has been filled in and strengthened to cut down on lifter deflection.

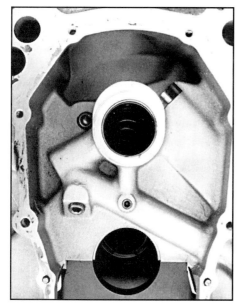

Front view of Indy block shows cross-bolt #1 main cap, oil inlet (plugged) for a dry sump oiling system, and additional material around cam bearing to allow raising the cam to clear longer strokes.

The Indy blocks are the only ones to use cross-bolting on all five main caps. No failures here.

moved, everything else like gaskets, lifters, valve placement, and crankshafts has to be moved to accommodate. This is not a modification recommended for the faint of heart or faint of wallet as it's extremely complicated and expensive. There is no raised cam version of this block yet so maximum stroke capability is the same as stock at around 4.750", depending on the type and size of the connecting rods. At this time, only a raised block style is

available. There is also a two-bolt main version that is legal for stock class drag racing and a version for Hemi heads.

This block is the most affordable of all the aftermarket blocks and can generally be purchased for just a few hundred dollars more than a highly modified stock block.

Indy Maxx Block—Indy Cylinder Heads released their line of aluminum and cast-iron blocks just after Mopar Performance did. The Indy blocks have several unique features designed to benefit racers specifically. The first feature is the cross-bolting of all five main caps rather just the center three main caps, which is more common. Granted, the three cap cross-bolt design has proven adequate for 6000 horsepower Top Fuelers, but Indy wanted even more strength. There is no doubt that the five cross-bolt main caps will contain the highest horsepower engine, one that has yet to be built.

The lifter galley area has also been

The Indy block uses beefy steel main caps which fit right into the block for strength.

The rear main seal on the Indy block is incorporated right into the #5 main cap.

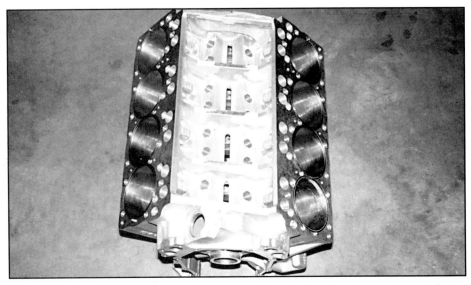

Note the valley reinforcement on the KB block, as shown by the three huge webs right in the valley.

strengthened to the point that it is virtually solid except for the lifter bores. Remember that the block gets its strength from areas like this too. The oil galleys have been modified to allow for more oiling to the bearings and a provision for a dry sump oil system inlet has been added. The oil pan rails can be drilled to accept a wider and more efficient oil pan as well. In short, Indy has thought of just about everything you would ever want to do to a block.

Indy blocks can be ordered with different bore spacings, up to 4.900" for even more bore size, and a raised cam version is available to allow for more stroke, as is a low deck version of the aluminum block.

The iron block is also a siamese bore design while the aluminum block has iron cylinder sleeves. The iron block is extremely heavy due to all of this block's strengthening features, so it would be ideal for uses where weight is not an issue, like a mud bog racing or tractor pulls.

The aluminum block is lighter than its iron twin and is better suited for drag racing. The iron block can accommodate smaller bore sizes, but the aluminum block will have to have different sleeves if a smaller bore is desired. The maximum bore is still limited by the bore spacing. The Indy blocks are priced in the middle of the road: their iron block is more expensive than the Mopar block and the aluminum block is cheaper than a Keith Black.

Keith Black Aluminum—The Keith Black aluminum block really doesn't need much introduction. In production for over 20 years, the "KB" block has powered more professional race cars than all other blocks combined, including virtually

Main web shot of Keith Black aluminum block shows incredible amounts of reinforcement around the main caps. It's no wonder that these blocks have been the standard for Top Fuel drag racing for more than 25 years.

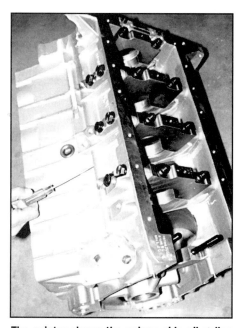

The pointer shows the unique side oil galley in the KB block. By doing this, the bearings get oiled first right out of the oil pump. Note the double cross-bolting on the center three main caps.

all nitromethane and alcohol drag cars. If this block is good enough for the pros, it will probably be fine for you.

The block is a webbed aluminum design, making it relatively light, and it features three cross-bolt mains. The main caps can be either steel or aluminum and the three cross-bolt caps can be double bolted on the sides for even more strength. Since the block is for racing use, the oil system was redesigned to supply the bearings and heads only, via a side-installed main oil galley. Lifter oiling can be ordered for applications that need it.

A variety of bore spacing and head types can be accommodated by the KB block. Low deck and raised cam versions are also available, allowing this block to be built in the largest

displacements. It's interesting to note that for all of its legendary racing accomplishments, the KB block still retains all factory dimensions and most all accessory provisions, which is a true testament to the original factory design. The KB block is truly the ultimate block, and as such is by far the most expensive; a new one currently sells for more than $5000. However, because they have been around for so long, and are so popular, there are many used KB blocks for sale if you know where to look. However, if you are considering a used block, make sure it is a watercooled block instead of a solid block, which makes the hunt even more difficult, because there are far fewer used watercooled blocks around.

4

CRANKSHAFTS

The factory used both a 6-bolt crank flange (right) and an 8-bolt (center) flange. The 8-bolt cranks came only in Hemis while all the wedge engines got a 6-bolt crank. Most aftermarket cranks are 8-bolt units and as such will require the proper flexplate or flywheel and attaching bolts. The crank on the left is a pre-1962 RB 8-bolt crank. Do not mistake these old cranks for Hemi cranks, as their transmission attachment method is completely different. They can be identified by their completely flat (no centering ring) flange. They only fit early transmissions and industrial applications.

If the cylinder block is the foundation of an engine, the crankshaft is the first level. The main function of a crankshaft is to convert the up and down motion of the pistons and connecting rods to a rotational type motion. In addition to this job, the crank must have enough strength to endure tremendous loads yet be light enough so as not to affect performance. Remember that at an engine speed of 6000 rpm, the crank rotates 100 times per second, so rotating weight is a major factor.

BASIC DESIGN FEATURES

All crankshafts, regardless of make, are basically the same, and there is really nothing special about a big-block Mopar crank, but there are some design features that are good for performance.

Bearing Sizes

Fortunately, Mopar engineers designed a crank with bearing sizes large enough to support a tremendous load but not so large as to become a performance disadvantage. Because the crankshaft is supported by a high pressure film of oil (called a hydrodynamic wedge) between itself and the bearings, the journal and bearing sizes become very important. This wedge of oil must be maintained to prevent engine failure. If the crank is allowed to touch the bearing even for an instant, failure can occur. If the sizes are too large, it will become very difficult to maintain this wedge at high rotational speeds, thus limiting the rpm potential of the engine. This is why large bearing engines like Oldsmobiles and Pontiacs are not known for their high rpm durability.

On the other hand, if the journal and bearing sizes are too small, the crank will not be able to maintain the hydrodynamic wedge under high loads and the bearings will most likely fail. This is why small block engines cannot withstand the same tremendous loads as big blocks.

All cast cranks have the engine size cast into them as well as a "casting clock," which is visible above the 440 displacement marking. This is an easy way to identify a cast crank. Though they are not as strong as a steel crank, they will make an excellent crank for high performance street use. Do not be afraid to use them.

Journal Size

All big-block Mopar cranks have a common rod journal size of 2.375". The low-block engines have a main journal size of 2.625" while the raised-block engines have a 2.750" main diameter. Both of these sizes can handle most any load thrown their way given proper oiling. Crankshaft failure is relatively uncommon in a Mopar engine when everything like machine work and oiling systems are done correctly.

CRANKSHAFT SELECTION

A Mopar engine builder has several types of cranks to choose from, so this is where planning becomes critical. Do you use a stock crank or a new stroker crank and if so, from what material? Generally your budget and application will be the deciding factor, but when you start to whittle away the choices and get down to serious modifications, you really only have two basic choices—either a stock modified crank or a new aftermarket

unit. A stock Mopar crank is a very sturdy unit, and unless you need a different stroke, a stock crank will work fine.

Stock Crank

If you are going with a stock crank, there are some things that need to be looked at. All of the early (pre-1971) big-block engines came factory equipped with a forged steel crank instead of a cast iron crank to increase reliability. However, in 1971 as the musclecar era began to taper off and fuel economy became a bigger concern, Mopar engines were detuned and put out less power, so a cast iron crank was installed in some engines. By late 1973 all big-block engines came with a cast crank.

Balancing—All cast cranks are externally balanced. This is because the cast iron did not provide enough weight internally to balance out the rod and piston weight because the density of the cast iron was less than the forged steel previously used. To provide the additional weight required for balancing, weights were added

externally to the vibration damper and the flywheel or torque converter. Because of this fact, balancing these cast crank engines is difficult. Cast crank engines are easy to identify due to the external counterweight on the vibration damper and the letter "E" stamped on the engine identification pad.

A cast crank has adequate strength for a medium horsepower racing engine. In fact, many other popular Detroit engines like some Chevy and Ford only have cast cranks. However, when you add the cost of balancing a cast crank to the purchase, it almost equals the cost of a forged crank.

There are a few disadvantages to external balancing. First, the crank will flex a lot more in an externally balanced setup since a good portion of its weight is very far from its center. The further a weight is placed from a support point, the more deflection it will cause. To give the crank more stability, the weights should be as close to the center as possible. This is why some Top Fuel dragster cranks actually have an additional fourth counterweight installed next to the number three main journal.

The second disadvantage is that most all racing vibration dampers, torque converters, flexplates and flywheels do not have provisions for external balancing. There are a few weighted flexplates and dampers on the market, but most are much more expensive than their internally balanced counterparts. As another balancing option, Mallory metal could be added to the cast crank to convert it to internal balance. This will work fine but like the special flexplates, it is expensive. The point here is that if you are going to spend the extra money to balance the cast crank, why

All production wedge cranks are designed with an undercut fillet. This undercut (pointer) is not as strong as a full radius crank (as used in Hemis) and is where most cracks develop in Mopar cranks. Always check carefully for cracks in this area before using one.

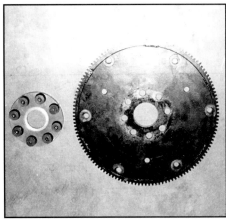

If a non-Mopar transmission such as a Chevy Powerglide is going to be used, a special adapter flexplate is required. This particular example will allow use of a GM converter behind an 8-bolt Mopar engine. It has a starter ring gear on the flexplate, as GM transmission setups don't have it on the converter like Mopars do. The part on the left allows the smaller converter snout to pilot in the back of the larger Mopar crank.

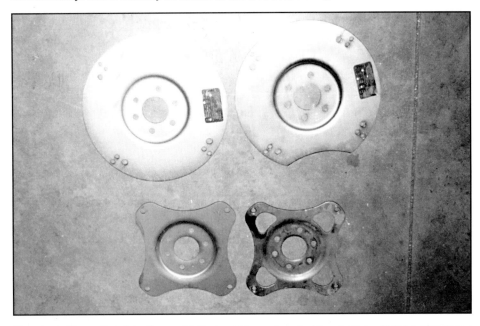

The stock Mopar flexplate (lower right) should be replaced with a better unit for performance use. The Mopar Performance flexplate (lower left) has solid "ears" that can handle more power. The B&M flexplates (top) are stronger yet due to their larger design. They also have all 3 converter bolt patterns and are SFI approved. The cut-out flexplate (top right) is for use with an externally balanced cast 440 crank.

not put that money toward the purchase of a forged steel crank and get the extra strength to boot?

Forged Stock Cranks—The early forged steel cranks make an excellent starting point for all but the highest output engines. Generally they are all the same, so don't worry about trying to find a 440 Magnum crank when a crank from a 413 cid engine will work just as well.

The only stock cranks that were heat-treated were those from a 426 Max Wedge or Hemi engine, but don't bother looking for one of these because they are very hard to find and not really worth the heat treating. Heat treating is really just a surface-hardening procedure, and does not really make the core steel any stronger.

All factory cranks except the 426 Hemi have an undercut in the outer radius of the journals. The Hemi crank by contrast has a full radius journal design. The full radius is a stronger design, but the stock undercut radius will hold up fine.

Modifying Stock Cranks

Any used crank must be Magnaflux inspected by a competent machine shop to check for hidden cracks. Have the machine shop perform a "wet" Magnaflux inspection as opposed to the more standard powder-and-magnet procedure. The wet procedure is much more involved and more accurate, and cracks in the crank are hard to find.

Mopar cranks have a nasty tendency to crack in the undercut areas mentioned above, so make sure the machine shop pays extra attention to these areas.

To install a 440 crank in a low-deck 383 or 400 block, the small counterweights will have to be chamfered as shown to clear the block. A 45-degree bevel about 3/8" wide will usually suffice. Alternately, the block can be ground but that method doesn't add to performance like machining the counterweights.

and bearings will be undersized. This does not appreciably reduce strength. Look at it this way: a .030" undersize journal has only .015" removed from each "side." If you think that this .015" is all that's holding the crank together, you're mistaken. For example, the popular 474 cubic inch modification for the 400 low block requires a 440 crank that is ground .125" on the mains (standard 400 size) and offset ground .165" (standard big-block Chevy size) on the rods. These engines have proven to be absolutely reliable in many different applications.

The 440 Crank/400 Block Combo—Speaking of the 474-style engine, the 440 crank can be easily modified to fit a low-deck block. While it will not give any real cubic inch gain in a stock stroke form, the low deck block with 440 crank is a

Assuming the crank passes the Magnaflux test, it is time to modify it for racing. If you are building a stock displacement engine, simply have the crank ground and micropolished. At this time, tell the crank grinder to chamfer oil holes which will give the oil more room to spread out onto the bearing.

Because most racers don't have access to their own crank grinding machine, there isn't much that you can do to your own crank. If you want, take a grinder and smooth out any flash. Be careful, because one slip can ruin a good crank before you know it.

Resist the temptation to just polish a used crank. By grinding a crank you will wind up with a better piece. If your crank grinding person and machine are competent, the stroke and *throw indexing* (position of the rod throw relative to other rods; a V8 has 90 degree throws) will be corrected. In addition, all the journals will now be perfectly round again, oil clearances will be correct, and any

bend or twist that the crank has will be removed.

Also, don't worry that the journals

"Pendulum counterweighting" of the crank at right is achieved by removing a lot material close to the main bearings. Material located here is mostly dead weight as it does not contribute to balancing as effectively as weight located farther away from the main bearing axis. It is better to remove as much weight as possible from the counterweights and re-locate it where it is needed with the use of Mallory metal as shown on the crank at left. This Mallory metal is made from tungsten and actually adds weight since it's density is greater than the steel it replaced.

Counterweights of full race crank on right have been extensively lightened for improved engine response.

very popular engine combination. The is because the 400 block will produce the same displacement as the 440 block but with a shorter, lighter piston. Remember, the 400 block deck (cylinder), is .745" shorter than the 440. This means that for any given stroke and rod length combo, the piston will be .745" shorter by building the engine in a low-deck block. The 400 is somewhat stiffer and a little smaller physically, but the main reason for this combo is still the piston weight.

This combo can use either the 440 or 400 rod length. To build this combination, simply tell your crank grinder to grind the mains down to 440 block size (2.625") and standard-grind the rods. It's interesting to note that now the crank will use low-deck bearings in standard size but it's actually .125" undersize!

To increase the displacement, the stroke can be increased by offset grinding the journals. This process increases stroke by making the journal smaller in only one direction. Instead

of grinding all the way around the rod journal, the crank grinder is set up to only grind the inside of the rod journal. (To decrease stroke the outside of the journal is ground.) This makes the journal smaller and increases the stroke because the center of the new, smaller journal is further away from the axis of the crank. To gain much stroke change, the journal needs to be ground to a fairly smaller

size because the stroke increase is equal to the amount that is offset ground. This will require rods with a different bearing size, meaning non-Mopar, aftermarket rods. Generally this combination uses rods with a big-block Chevy bearing size, since the rod journals are ground to 2.200", giving a stroke of 3.915" if properly done. Although the Chevy rod is narrower than the Mopar rod, resulting in .060" rod side clearance, this really isn't a problem, but there will be more oil thrown around inside the engine. Because this engine combo is extremely popular, the aftermarket now has rods with Chevy bearing sizes and Mopar widths to maintain correct side clearance.

Other than requiring the correct pistons for your combination, the only other crank modification to fit a 440 crank in a low block is to profile the counterweights for clearance. The low block (and Hemi as well) blocks have slightly different machining under the cylinders. The 440 crank counter-weights will hit the block if installed in one of these other blocks. To gain clearance, the block could be ground

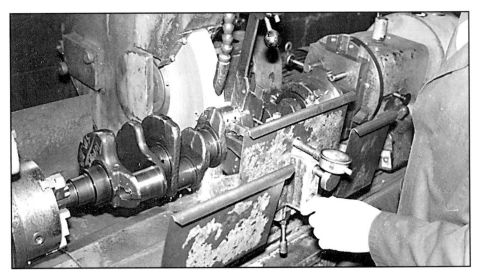

The counterweights can be turned down for block clearance on a lathe. This has the added benefit of also lightening the crank for more performance.

This is about as wild as a crank can get. Machined from a solid billet of steel, it features knife-edged counterweights, a center lightening hole from front to back, and 4 counterweights per half instead of the normal 3. Even with a 4.700" stroke, it actually weighs 3 pounds less than a stock 440 steel crank. You have to get something for $3500!

but the correct way is to simply machine the counterweights for clearance. The inside edges of the two small counterweights need to be machined at a 45-degree angle, 1/4" wide. At the same time, some material can be taken off the overall diameter of all the weights to lighten the crank. The exact amount that can be removed depends on the weight of your rods and pistons, so start with .100" and go from there. Use a lathe to do this. This works out better because not only will the crank fit in the block, it will be lighter too. Since the pistons are so much lighter in this combo, the crank can also be lighter as well and still keep everything in balance. The block grinding method is easier, but turning the counterweights is better.

Aftermarket Cranks

If your engine combination requires a non-stock stroke and your wallet allows, an aftermarket crank is the

way to go. As with everything else, something new is always better than something used. When you consider that an aftermarket crank can accommodate any stroke or bearing size for little or no extra cost, they are really a bargain. However, if you are building a stock stroke engine I would not recommend the extra cost of a new crank. In other words, if you decide to buy a new crank, get one with more stroke and build a larger engine!

Most new cranks are made from either 1053 or 4340 steel. The 4340 cranks are generally stronger and more expensive than the 1053 material. If the engine will make over 1000 horsepower, a 4340 crank is almost a must.

Billet Cranks—There is also the option of a billet crank. These cranks are machined out of a solid chunk or billet of 4340 steel instead of the more common forging process. Since a billet crank is machined from the

ground up, anything can be incorporated into one. For example, all forged cranks are limited by what their raw forging will accommodate. But if you need a crank with a 5" stroke, there is no Mopar forging that I'm aware of that will go this long. No problem for a billet, though. Simply machine it to what you want. As expected they are the most expensive, usually costing about double that of a new forged 4340 crank.

Making Stroker Cranks Fit

If you decide to step up to a shiny new crank and go with more stroke, you now are faced with the problem of making it all fit. Obviously, if you increase the stroke of the crank, the pistons have to change or they will be pushed up too far and hit the heads.

The design of a stroker engine is pretty simple when you know how everything fits into the original parameters of the engine's design. Earlier, I gave the measurement of the deck heights of both styles of big blocks. To refresh your memory, they are 9.980" for the low block family and 10.725" for the raised block family. The secret to stroker engine design are these measurements. Everything related to stroke, rod length, and piston compression height are governed by the block's deck height. All of these factors must fit into the deck height. Imagine that the piston is at top dead center (all the way up) and think about how the block is laid out. Try to get a feel for the fact that the total length of the three main components must be less than the block height or something will collide. The formula for making it all fit is:

Deck Height = Rod Length + Piston

This Mopar stroker crank is of the full radius design. While this design is stronger, it requires special bearings that are chamfered to clear the extra material in the radius.

Compression Height + Deck Clearance + 1/2 Crank Stroke

Only half of the crank stroke is used in the formula, because relative to the centerline of the crank, it "pulls" and "pushes" an amount equal to half of its total stroke. For example, for a stroke increase of 1/2", the rod journal is "moved" 1/4" away from the centerline of the crank. The exception to this is offset grinding to change stroke where the total stroke change is equal to the exact amount of the offset grind. So if we put a crank in the engine that has .500" more stroke, the

piston compression height has to be .250" shorter to compensate if we keep the rod length and deck clearance constant. If you have access to a computer and a spreadsheet program, input the stroker formula so you can easily change a component and immediately see the effects on the other components.

CRANK BALANCING

Any crank that is going to be raced should be balanced even if the racing is of a casual nature. Chrysler quality control in this area was among the worst in the industry. Many engines left the factory with the components poorly weight-matched. Balancing does not create power in itself, but it frees up power that is being lost to vibration. In extreme cases of vibration component failure will be likely. If anything is changed, like rods or pistons, have the crank (and whole assembly) rebalanced. It obviously is a must with a new crank.

Balancing Procedure

There are two parts to balancing an assembly, the static part and the dynamic part.

Static Balancing—The static part consists of weight-matching the pistons and the rods. The pistons are simply weighed and corrected with the seven heavy pistons made to equal the one lightest. The rods are corrected in a similar fashion, but the big ends are all weight-matched separately from the small ends. This is done because the crank bears the weight of the big end of the rod all the time while it only bears the small end part of the time.

Dynamic Balancing—Once all the weights are matched, their actual

Like all production engines, the Mopar big block can benefit from a good balance job. After the weights of the rods and pistons are equalized, special "bobweights" are set up on the crank that equal this weight. When the crank is spun on the machine, it displays where and how much to correct the crank so it will be perfectly balanced. Always have this done during any rebuild.

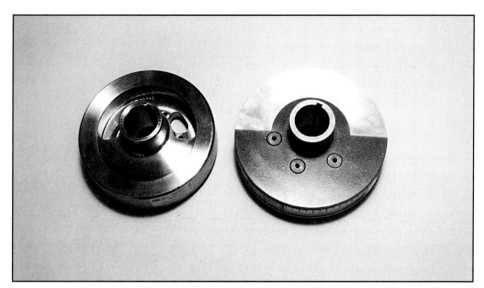

The large eccentric weight on these aftermarket balancers are for use with externally balanced cast cranks.

amounts are entered into a special formula and from them a bobweight is figured out. This bobweight is the weight the crank is actually balanced to during the dynamic part of the procedure. Actual weights are clamped onto the rod throws of the crank. As the crank is spun on a machine, the machine will pick up any vibration that the crank is experiencing and display it to the operator in a way than can be corrected.

As can be found in the bobweight formula, it has both a rotating and a reciprocating component. The rotating component uses the weights of two rod big ends and bearings because they're always attached to the crank. The reciprocating part is another story. Since the engine is a "V" style with one rod and piston assembly from each cylinder bank on each crank throw, there is some weight cancellation of a portion of the small end of the rod and piston due to the relative position of each of the two assemblies per crank throw. This is why the bobweight is not just the total weight of two rod/piston assemblies. As a side note, inline and horizontally

opposed engines do not use bobweights since there is always an equal opposing weight regardless of the position of the crank.

The crank is balanced in two different halves (front and rear) separated by the number three main bearing. One half can be internally balanced and the other externally balanced, the crank really doesn't care from a balance standpoint. From a load standpoint internal balancing is the way to go, since the crank will be more stable if most of its weight is closer to its center. The stroke of the crank has an effect on the crank's balance too. Think of a crank's balance as beam scale (scales of justice style) with the axis of the main bearings being the balance point. If the crank is in balance, any change in one end by, for example, a lighter piston, will require a change (less weight) on the other end to stay balanced. If the weight is kept constant, but one end is moved farther from the balance point (by increasing the stroke of the crank), then more weight needs to be added to the other side to compensate. Alternately, the weight end could be moved to

compensate for the additional stroke but in reality it can't move because it has to fit in the block.

Mallory Metal—This is where Mallory metal comes in to play. Mallory is simply metal (usually tungsten) that is added to the crank to increase its weight. The Mallory is more dense than the steel it replaces in the counterweight of the crank so it effectively adds weight.

Frequency Specific—Though it's very important to balance the crank, remember that balancing is *frequency specific*, which means that the crank will only be in perfect balance within a narrow rpm range. At other speeds it will still vibrate very slightly. Think of it as an unbalanced tire on your car; at some speeds it will vibrate and at others it won't. Add in the poor crank's problem of over 10 pounds of oil flying around everywhere and the constant hammering it gets as each cylinder fires, and you can understand why balancing is not an exact science.

Vibration Damper

Fortunately for the crank there is relief from all of these sources of shake in the form of the vibration damper. This simple device is mounted on the front of the crank and absorbs the vibration. It does its job by counteracting vibrations in the crank. Because it has mass, it can absorb a vibration by "vibrating" in the opposite direction of the crank. If the damper had little mass, as is the case with just a crank hub, it would do a poor job of absorbing vibration, because it can't set up a vibration of equal and opposite intensity to that of the crankshaft. As such, crank breakage is common with these hubs.

On the other hand, a very heavy damper would do a great job of

Common stock vibration dampers for the B engine. They are: stock steel crank, external balance 440 six-barrel (also used on some 440 4 barrel HP engines and some motor home engines), and external balance cast crank engine. Though they both have external counterweights, do not confuse the "six pack" damper with the cast crank damper.

Fluidampr vibration damper is a good choice for a street/strip car as well as for an all out track car. Not only will a damper like this make more power but it will help keep the crank from breaking under heavy load. Newer versions shown here are machined for use with a stock pulley.

Most race sanctioning bodies require an SFI approved damper past a certain performance point. Most drag cars will need one if they run faster than 10.99 in the quarter.

absorbing the crank's vibrations but would slow the acceleration rate of the engine. The factory used a thin damper in two different weights for the production engines. It's interesting to note that the Hemi used a heavier balancer to compensate for its heavier internal parts. So overall it's a trade off between dampening ability and weight. There is no "free lunch" here; the damper needs weight to work. With the advent of higher engine speeds and power, the stock damper was pushed past its limit, making it less effective, and damper failure became common. Sometimes stock dampers can actually explode. For safety reasons, various racing sanctioning bodies have imposed an explosion-proof damper requirement for a certain performance levels.

Fluid Damper—Various methods are used by aftermarket damper manufacturers. One unique design is the fluid damper. These units have a heavy steel ring suspended in fluid inside a sealed housing. These dampers are pretty heavy but their theory is that under quick acceleration the fluid will allow only the outer housing to spin freely while the heavy ring will eventually catch up and start absorbing vibration. In this way, the engine can accelerate quickly and still have a good amount of protection.

Pulley alignment may change with an aftermarket damper so be sure to check it. The Fluidampr® brand damper is one of the most popular for this engine. The older Fluidampr units required special pulleys (available from March Pulleys) but the new dampers are machined for use with stock pulleys.

Another popular damper is made by ATI and uses friction discs to dampen vibration. It seems to work a little better than the Fluidampr in extreme rpm (8000+) situations and is available with a Chevy pulley bolt pattern to allow easier mounting of crank triggers and dry sump pumps.

To sum up, any racing engine should have an aftermarket damper. They increase performance and durability and are well worth the investment. No matter what style you choose, make sure that it's SFI approved.

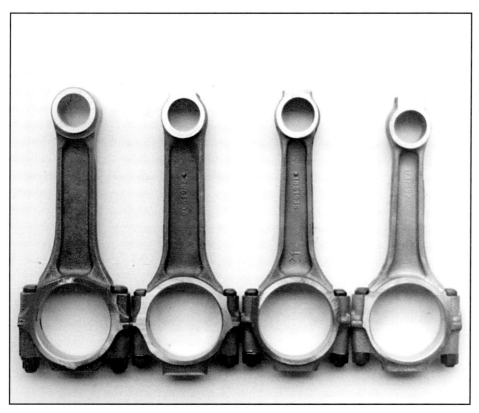

The most common rods for the B engine are (l to r) 426 street Hemi, 440 six-barrel, 440 four-barrel and 383/400 all. Note the extra beam width of the Hemi and 440+6 rod.

5

CONNECTING RODS

O f all the components in the engine, the connecting rod probably has the toughest job. Because it is responsible for converting the reciprocating (up and down) motion of the piston into useful rotational motion of the crankshaft, it is subject to different types of load. Unlike most of the other engine components that experience their load in a constant direction, the connecting rod is constantly being pushed and pulled. Remember, too, that the rod is preventing the piston from twisting and pushing itself out of the block. And consider that at only 6000 rpm, a 440 piston and rod assembly traveling the equivalent of 62.5 feet per second has to come to a complete stop and change direction 100 times per second. Based on these unbelievable facts, it's pretty easy to understand why many engine failures are due to rod failure. Fortunately for us, Mopar engineers realized all of these facts when they designed the connecting rods for the big block.

All of the factory production rods are a typical I-beam design and are forged from steel. No wimpy cast rods here. Because of this, the big-block Mopar rod can withstand a high level of performance. As with any other engine component, the rods can be upgraded with new aftermarket rods if the performance level requires and the budget allows. As with all components, generally anything new is better than anything old. The rods are no exception.

STOCK ROD TYPES

If you decide to go with stock rods, there are three different rods that we need to be concerned with; the low-deck rod #692, which was used in all low-deck engines regardless of displacement or model year; the raised-block rod #535 used in all RB engines from 1958–1978, with the exception of 1970–1974 HP and six-

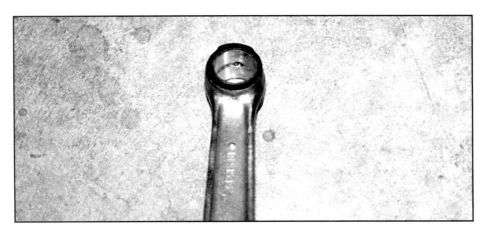

The stock rod can be bushed down to accept a smaller wrist pin if desired. Most of the time the weight saving is not that great since the additional weight of the bushing must be factored in. Lightweight stock-size pins are available that offer considerable weight savings over production pins.

pack engines; and the six-pack rod #908.

Six-Pack Rod

The six-pack rod was used in the 1970–1971 six-pack engines (hence the name) and most 440 HP and motorhome engines until 1974. If you have one of these HP engines and the vibration damper has a small (not the huge weight for a cast crank) eccentric weight on it, there are six-pack rods inside. There were a few other rods for these engines such as the Max Wedge pieces and the old Direct Connection rods, but since the chance of finding any of these is so slim, they really don't warrant any discussion.

Dimensions

The stock rod lengths are 6.358" for the low deck and 6.768" for the raised block. The cross-sectional areas for the low-deck rod and the raised-block rod is the same, except for the six-pack rod, which is much wider. Because of this fact, the low-deck rods can handle more power due to the fact that they are almost 1/2" shorter, but have the same width beam as their longer counterparts.

Load Capability

In the last few years, there has been much discussion about the load capability of a stock rod, most notabilty the #535 rod. With the exception of some mega-power combination, the failure of the stock rod is not as much due to its lack of strength but rather its life cycle in terms of fatigue. Rods, like everything else, have a finite life expectancy. This life expectancy may be perhaps 10 million cycles at a particular load level. The problem is, that unless you have been traveling with the rods since they left the factory, you have no idea how close they are to this 10 million mark. Are they at 50,000 or are they at 19,999,500 cycles? There is no way to tell where your set of rods are in this life cycle time line and as such you may be on the brink of a failure. And to make matters worse, we can't even predict for sure how many cycles they are even good for! No one knows for sure. Obviously the more stress placed on the rod the more critical these numbers become. If you look at most aftermarket rods, their cross sections aren't really much larger than a stock rod, but due to

their better materials and a life cycle clock starting at zero, they would be the way to go if the budget allows. Money spent here will go a long way toward preventing failure because when a rod breaks, it's pretty messy.

Reducing Rod Stress

There are ways to reduce the stress on a rod to make it last longer. The easiest way is to reduce the power level of the engine. Since this is a racing engine manual, reducing the power is definitely out of the question, so we need to find another way to make the rod last.

Reduce Weight—The easiest thing to do is to reduce the weight the rod has to carry. Since these engines were factory-equipped with the heaviest pistons and pins of any engine of the era, the first thing to do would be to get a set of lightweight pistons and pins. Weight reductions of 25 percent or more are not uncommon. It doesn't take a genius to understand that swinging a lighter piston will result in a longer life for the rod it's attached to. Since the crank can be lightened due to the lighter assembly, it will see less stress too as will the block and the main caps. The engine will rev quicker too, which will make it run faster.

Limit Rpm—The second easiest thing to do to increase longevity is to keep the maximum rpm down. Build your combination to yield maximum power at the least amount of rpm. Since the forces inside the engine increase with the square of the rpm, (force = rpm^2), there is almost twice the load at 8000 rpm compared to 6000 rpm. That 2000 rpm increase almost doubled the internal force. There is virtually no reason to rev a big-block Mopar over 7000 rpm,

Connecting rod cap mating surface on the rod is being cut on cap grinder. This material is cut off both the rod and the cap to make them smaller. After this is done, the bearing housing is machined back to its original size. Always have this done during any engine build.

especially with stock connecting rods. There are many combinations that will make excellent power at or below this rpm level.

Beam Polishing—Beam polishing off the stock casting flash will not make the rod stronger. Unless the area or material changes, the rod can't become stronger than it already is. What it will do is prevent any cracks that may occur from points of high stress created from the forging process. As a small side benefit, the rods will be slightly lighter too. If you decide to beam-polish the rods, make sure that you grind in the lengthwise direction of the rod. Do not grind "crosswise." After grinding, polish the beams with a sandpaper roll to get a smooth surface. Don't try to lighten the beams—you are just removing the flash only.

Shot-Peening—If shot-peening is available in your area, consider having it done. It is a method of cold-working the steel (heat-treating for example is a method of hot working) to increase

surface hardness. Again, it doesn't make the rod much stronger, just more resistant to cracking. Many shops think they can shot-peen with some type of air blaster, but in reality it's an industrial process that can only be correctly done by a facility that specializes in it. If you choose to do either or both of the things, do them before the new bolts are installed and any machining is done.

Prepping Stock Rods

If you are still planning on using stock rods they will need some inspection and prep work to make them reliable. The first inspection would be a visual one. Your eyes are the best diagnostic tool ever invented. If something looks strange to your eyes, it probably is a problem. If you see any signs of bluing or blackening around the big end of the rod, scrap it. It means that the rod had experienced some type of oil pressure loss and has gotten extremely hot. Don't take a chance on it for your new engine

because the strength of the core steel may be reduced by this excessive heat. If you find a rod that has evidence of a spun bearing but hasn't turned blue, it can probably be saved by resizing. Check to be sure that the rod cap mating surfaces are clean and free of any signs of galling or pounding. Make sure that the pin end is also free of any gall marks. If you have the old bearings, check them out for signs of unusual wear. If any are present, it's a good bet that the rod is bent.

The last visual inspection would be to make sure that all rods and caps have the same cylinder number stamped on them. This number represents the cylinder the rods and caps were installed in at the factory. It is important to keep the correct caps with the correct rod. If they get mixed up, they are virtually impossible to resize. It's okay for the rod and cap to end up in a different cylinder, but the caps and rods must be a matched set. If they don't, then you shouldn't use them.

Any obvious twist or bend will be cause for discarding the rod. If it's bent enough to see by eye, it's pretty bent. Considering the relative low cost of stock rods versus the high costs of a new cylinder block and rebuilt engine, it's cheap insurance to replace any suspect rods.

Inspection—If they pass the eyeball test, take them to your machine shop and have them checked further. The first step is to have then Magnafluxed. This process will find any hidden cracks in the rod and is the same process used to check heads and blocks for cracks. Do not skip this step even if there is an additional charge for it.

Your machine shop should also have

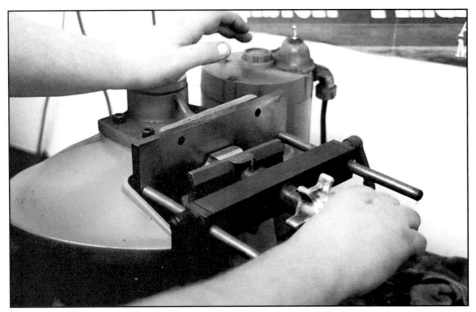

The rod cap is also cut on the cap grinder prior to resizing.

a fixture for checking for twist in a rod. If they do, have them check your set since it will be far more accurate than just using your eyes.

If the rods pass these tests, it's time to have them machined. Machining— With used rods that have been run many cycles, there is a good chance that the big end of the rod has become slightly elliptical or "egg shaped." The rod caps will bounce ever so slightly due to the stretching of the rod bolts. As long as the rod bolt stretch is kept within its *elastic limit*, instead of its *plastic limit,* it will immediately return to its original dimension and everything will be fine. If the bolt is stretched too far, the bearing will probably spin and chances are you won't have the rod in your collection. Inevitably all this stretching will deform the big end into an egg shape, requiring it to be machined to ensure proper bearing crush and oil clearance. Do not even consider using a stock rod without resizing it.

Resizing—The resizing process is unique, in that the rod is honed back to its original size, even though it's already probably larger than stock! How is something honed "smaller"? The rod and cap mating surfaces are cut slightly in a special grinder. This grinder makes sure that all surfaces will be parallel when the cap is installed. When the cap is installed, the housing bore is smaller than stock since material was removed from the mating surfaces. From here, it's a

simple procedure to hone the rod back to its correct dimension. Make sure your shop is competent to prevent big ends that are tapered or barrel shaped. Anything less than perfectly round will result in inconsistent oil clearance and excessive bearing wear.

Rod Bolts—At this time, replace all the rod bolts with some type of aftermarket bolts such as those from ARP. New rod bolts are probably the best durability improvement for the money. Always replace the bolts before resizing the rods because the new bolts can locate the cap slightly different, which can be compensated for during resizing to still end up with a perfectly round bearing bore.

Wrist Pins—If the rods are going to be used with full-floating stock size wrist pins the pin can be floated right to the rod without a bushing. Many people may cringe at this idea but it works fine. To do this the small end can be honed to remove the factory press fit. Give the pins about .0007"–.0009" clearance and drill a 1/8" oil hole through the top of the

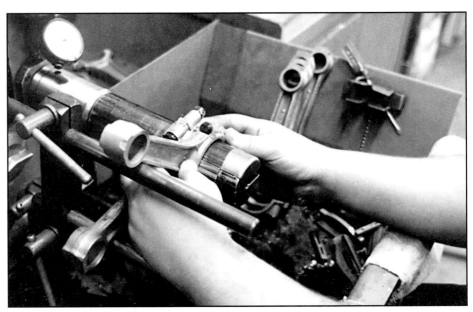

Bearing bores being honed back to their original size. Since this is done by hand, a skilled operator and a high quality machine are a must. This has to be done extremely accurately to ensure that the bearing won't spin under load.

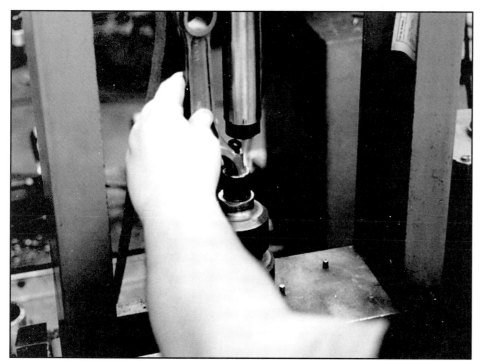

The pin end of the rod can be honed for use with full floating pins if desired. It is not a problem to float the pin right to the steel of the rod. Sounds crazy but it works fine!

Always replace the rod bolts in any rebuild. Install them with a press, not a hammer. After the new bolts are installed, the rods will need to be resized since the new rod bolts may locate the cap in a slightly different position.

rod to give the pin some lubrication. An oil hole in this position does not appreciably weaken the rod. If a smaller than stock pin size like the common .990" big-block Chevy pin is used, the small end will have to be bushed down to accommodate it. This pin swap is a fairly common one, because the Mopar pins are generally so heavy. The Chevy pin is lighter (about 50 grams lighter than the stock Mopar pin) but when the weight of the bushing is added, the actual weight savings becomes less than 25 grams. Given the cost of bushing the rods down, I think that the money could be better spent elsewhere in the engine.

For general race applications, use the stock 1.094" pin size and float it right to the rod. The upsides to full floating pins are ease of assembly and disassembly of the piston and rod assembly, and the fact that if the pin starts to seize in the piston, the rod

can still pivot on the pin.

Some light pistons can crack while they are being pressed off, so always use floaters for this type of piston. However, there is no reason why a pressed pin won't work for a race

engine, and because there is a more rigid connection between the rod and the pin, it is actually a slightly stronger setup. The downsides to pressed pins are that if the pins start to seize in the piston, additional friction will result and unless you have access to a press and a heater, piston removal is very difficult, especially at the race track. When everything is working correctly, there is no operational difference in the two methods.

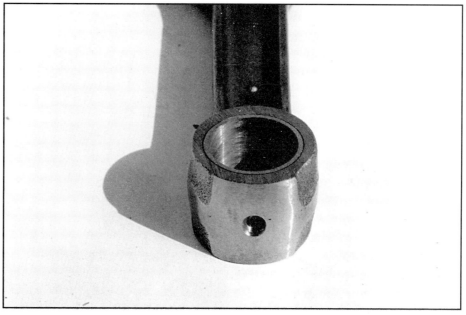

If the rod is set up for floating pins, drill a 1/8" oil hole from the top to provide lubrication for the pin.

AFTERMARKET RODS

If your budget allows, I recommend a set of aftermarket rods. All of the aftermarket rods available for this engine are made from superior materials and are far superior to any production rod. Most all feature larger 7/16" bolts to secure the caps. A rod is still ultimately only a strong as the bolts holding the caps, so if the beams can hold 5000 hp but the bolts can only hold 300 hp, you are in trouble.

New rods have obviously not been subject to any cycling, so fatigue is not a factor like it is with used rods. And because the B/RB engines are so popular to build into racing engines, the cost of new rods is now very reasonable. When you total the cost of fully restoring and prepping used stock rods, you would probably have spent 1/2 the total cost of a new set.

Aluminum or Steel?

Deciding on whether to go with aluminum or steel is dependent on the application. There are also rods made from titanium, but because they are about $3000 per set, they are not very common or practical for the average racer.

Aluminum—For short blasts of power, such as in drag racing, an aluminum rod would be best. Aluminum rods are also used to a small degree in circle track engines, but usually only for qualifying engines.

Because aluminum work hardens at a rate much faster than steel, aluminum rods' life expectancy is considerably shorter. However, because aluminum rods are much lighter than steel, they will be a performance advantage in a drag engine. As mentioned before, lighter internal parts mean less stress and allow the engine to rev quicker. A very lightweight assembly consisting of aluminum rods with lightweight pistons will go a long way toward keeping the block and crank from breaking, not to mention a large improvement in performance.

You may have heard horror stories about people getting only 20 drag race runs on a set of aluminum rods before they broke, but let me set the record straight. If properly installed, aluminum rods will last a long time. I know many people who have made over 600 passes with aluminum rods, and they are still going strong. Most of the aluminum rods on the market for the B engine are designed on blanks originally designed for Top Fuel Hemi engines, but with additional lightening since they won't be used for 5000 horsepower engines. As such they are much stronger than their GM counterparts. A steel rod is very rigid and transmits any shock right into the crank, while an aluminum rods can actually cushion some of the shock that occurs from combustion. This can be beneficial for engines that are prone to detonation, like nitrous engines. Aluminum rods are required for nitro engines, since they generate so much combustion shock.

To have adequate strength, aluminum rods are physically larger than their steel counterparts, so be sure to check for clearance with the block, crank, and camshaft. Generally, aluminum rods need more side clearance (usually .020" minimum), because they expand more than steel. Piston-to head clearance should be at least .050" since the aluminum rods

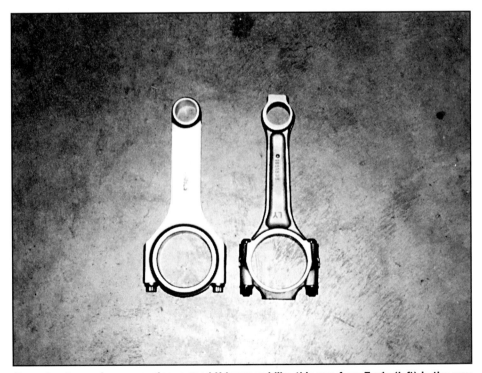

For a street or endurance engine, a good H beam rod like this one from Eagle (left) is the way to go. The H beam design is more resistant to twisting than the production I beam design and their 7/16" bolts are 35% larger than the stock 3/8" bolts. Not only are they much stronger than the stock rods but they are new! This means that their life cycle is starting at zero.

It's a good idea to balance the rods for any rebuild but it's a must for racing purposes. To do this, all the rods are equalized first on the big end (shown here) and finally the small end. This requires a special fixture and a very accurate scale to do properly.

will stretch more under load.

Always make sure that the cap of an aluminum rod has a dowel pin in it. This pin helps prevent spun bearings, because the aluminum rod will flex more and can't always maintain good bearing crush. If the dowel pin is missing, or your set doesn't have it, you are almost certain to spin a bearing. Special bearings that have a hole for the dowel pin are required. Always oil all threads and mating surfaces and torque the rod bolts in several steps.

As with steel rods, always follow the rod manufacturers' recommendations and specifications to ensure a long and trouble-free life.

The easiest way to ensure long life with aluminum rods (and valve springs) is to warm the oil up to operating temperature before your first pass down the track. Don't take it off the trailer and floor it. Warm it up and then get ready to run.

Steel Rods—As a general rule, if the engine is going to be run for long periods, such as on the street, in circle track racing or for boating, you should use a steel rod.

There are two basic types available; the stock I-beam style or the H-beam style. Both types work very well. The H-beam rods are more resistant to twisting but the I beam rods are generally lighter. In this situation, with the rods being so similar, cost will be the deciding factor.

Most all aftermarket steel rods are ready to run right out of the box and usually come in balanced sets. If you want to fine tune the balancing, the rods are usually so close it will only take a few minutes. After checking the big- and small-end sizes, simply bolt them in. Any of the rods on the market will take all the power you can put to them.

All aftermarket rods can be ordered with either the 1.094" or the .990" pin size. If you are getting new pistons at the same time, go with the .990" pin in both the rod and the piston and save some weight for no extra cash. There are many different brands on the market now and all seem to be working well. Always be sure to follow the manufacturers' specifications for their rods.

6

PISTONS

From left to right; a dished piston (for B1 heads), a flat-top piston and a domed piston. These are the three main styles of pistons available for your Mopar engine. All have a specific purpose. Note the machined flame travel area on the domed piston.

On the surface, it looks like the piston has a pretty easy life. All it has to do is go up and down inside the cylinder. While that does indeed sound easy, let's look at the real life of the piston.

PISTON FUNCTION

Obviously, the piston's main function is to push on the connecting rod as the pressure from combustion pushes on it. By doing this, the energy that is released by the burning fuel is converted into useful mechanical motion. Unfortunately for the piston, it has to be exposed to this high temperature (over 3000 degrees) and high pressure (over 1500 psi) all the time that the engine is running. In addition, it must be able to support the rings to allow them to provide a good seal for the combustion pressure on top and a good seal for all the oil that is trying to get into the chamber from below. Also consider the fact that at 6000 rpm the piston moves from top dead center (TDC) to bottom dead center (BDC) back to TDC 100 times in a second. With a stock 440 stroke of 3.75", the piston is traveling at a speed of 62.5 feet/second at this rpm level. In other words, this is about 43 mph!

For an extreme example, consider a 600 cubic inch nitrous wedge Mopar engine. It is not uncommon to twist these engines to 8000 rpm, and with a stroke of 4.625", the piston speed is 103 ft/sec or 70 mph. Add to this speed all the temperature, load and pressure, and it's a wonder the piston doesn't just disintegrate. When you consider that the piston has to do this millions of times without failure, it has to be the most complex "simple" part in the engine.

Piston Weight

Because the piston has mass, it stresses the rod. While the piston has a hard job considering the forces it is subject to, the rod still has to hold it in the block. The Mopar B engines have absolutely the heaviest stock pistons in the industry. Each piston and pin

This is a flat-top piston for the 440 manufactured by Ross Pistons. This piston has valve pockets for big cams and weighs 25% less than a stock piston.

weighs over 1000 grams in a typical 440 engine. Over the entire engine, that's just under 20 lbs of mass swinging around. Part of the reason the Mopar has such heavy pistons is because of the tall block heights (Chapter 2) and the relatively short strokes. Even with longer rods, the piston compression heights of most B engines are over 2 inches. I suppose that the theory was to make a tall piston to make it more stable in the cylinder to increase ring life. That's fine for an engine that will never see over 5000 rpm, but for racing, it causes a loss of performance.

Ideally, the piston should be as short as possible. Any material between the bottom ring and the wrist pin is strictly along for the ride. For racing, the shorter the piston, the better. For this reason, many racers prefer to use low deck cylinder blocks. With a low deck block, you can use a piston that is .745" shorter than a raised block piston, for any given rod and stroke. It has nothing to do with displacement or bore size. It's strictly about piston height and weight.

It is possible to use a piston that is so short that the wrist pin will actually intersect with the oil ring groove. This is an acceptable situation for racing, but is not really the most durable setup for everyday driving, though many engines like this are getting away with it. A piston and pin weight can weigh less than 600 grams, saving nearly 8 pounds of internal engine weight! This increases rpm speed and rod life, and overall performance.

CAST VS. FORGED

There are 2 types of pistons that you will encounter in any engine build up. They are: cast and forged.

Cast

The stock factory pistons are cast from molten aluminum, which is poured into a mold and finish-machined into a piston. This results in a good, inexpensive piston. The factory pistons have steel struts cast inside of them to control thermal expansion. This allows them to be fit tightly into the bores to ensure long life, low oil consumption, and quiet operation.

Hypereutectic Pistons—These are newest pistons to come along in recent years. They are basically classified as a cast piston, but the material is a special aluminum and the process is different. They have almost as much strength as a forged piston

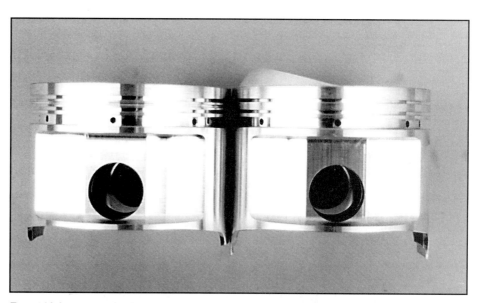

To get high compression in a stock head 440 domed pistons (right) are required. If the dome is properly done flame travel problems will be minimal. Any loss in power due to flame travel will be more than offset by the additional power of the added compression.

Here is an example of a stock cast piston that has actually melted due to detonation. Not only are forged pistons stronger when things are going right inside the engine, they are more resistant to failure when things go wrong.

but with the tight-fit properties of a cast piston. Most Mopar versions of this piston are slightly lighter than a stock cast piston, which is an added bonus. For a street car or a casual racer, this type of cast piston will work very well.

Forged

The other type of piston is a forged piston. These are made by forging (pounding) a piece of aluminum into a mold or die and then finish-machining. Because the aluminum is forced into the mold at tremendous pressure, a forged piston is more dense than a cast one. This increased density makes the piston much stronger. But it's impossible to forge in expansion control struts, and

because the denser aluminum will expand more, the forged piston will expand more than a cast piston when heated by combustion. Because of this, forged pistons must have more clearance in the bores to prevent seizing. This looser fit will make more noise and burn more oil. A tighter fit will stress the rings less (since the piston is not rocking around as much) and the engine may make more power. Most newer forged pistons are designed to fit tighter than some older design. Even the superlight Ross pistons can be fit as tight as .004".

There is usually no "free lunch" with engines and everything is a trade-off. In this case it's strength vs. noise and oil usage. Because almost every race engine has forged pistons, strength is more important.

While we are on the subject of strength, how much do you need? This will have to be answered by the intended use of the engine. The main advantage of forged pistons is strength. But where and how much?

Pin Bosses

The first area to look at would be in the pin bosses. Because it may travel at over 100 feet per second and change direction over 100 times per second, the pin boss needs to be strong enough to prevent the piston from literally flying off the rod. Cast pistons are prone to failure in the pin bosses. It's not uncommon to pull the pin right out of a cast piston. In reality, the pin didn't pull out, the rest of the piston flew off. If your rpm range is anywhere near 7000, forged pistons are a must. I would suggest 6500 as the cut-off point. Below this point the cast pistons should work okay.

Both of these pistons are for 451 cubic inch engines with stock 440 stroke and rods. The shorter piston on the right is for use in a 400 cid block while the taller piston is for a 440 block. Note the difference in compression height which makes the 400 block piston much lighter.

Top & Ringlands

The other strength area would be the top and the ringlands. Because the top of the piston takes most of the force from the combustion pressure, it has to be very strong. The temperature and pressure inside the combustion chamber of a racing engine is extremely high. The piston must be able to handle the stress with virtually no deflection. Any deflection will weaken the piston and create a loss of power. If the piston can't handle the temperature on the top it will melt. While this is not too common with production engines, it can happen in racing engines, especially those running nitrous oxide.

The ringlands of the piston need to be strong, because they too are bearing some of the pressure. Most ringland failures are caused by detonation. Overall the piston's biggest enemy is detonation. When the engine experiences detonation, the forces of combustion aren't smooth like normal, but they are like sledge hammer blows. This hammering can instantly break or melt the piston. Always make sure to run fuel with enough octane to prevent detonation. Don't run excessive ignition timing either, as over-advanced timing will immediately cause detonation.

GENERAL PISTON TIPS

Compression Ratio

Since the piston's job is to convert the heat and pressure of combustion to motion, it stands to reason that if we move the top of the piston closer to the source of the heat, more energy transfer will occur. Because the source of the heat is in the combustion chamber, we can do this by moving the piston closer to the chamber. This

The Keith Black cast pistons feature a unique quench dome that partially fills the dead area of a stock open chamber head. This allows for greater combustion efficiency and lessens the chance of detonation. These pistons are also lighter than stock and great for high performance street use.

is exactly what a high compression piston does. To get higher compression, the piston has to come up higher in the block than normal at TDC. The piston can't come fully out of the block because it would hit the head, but it is possible to use a piston that can actually extend up into the combustion chamber. This is more commonly called a *domed piston*.

The piston dome effectively puts the piston closer to the fire of combustion, allowing for maximum heat transfer. Since the mixture is compressed more, it will burn with more intensity and more completely, resulting in even more heat. More compression always makes more power up to the point of detonation. At this point, further horsepower production stops and engine damage can occur.

High compression engines are very hard on the bottom end and head gaskets. This is because the pressure built up on the compression stroke has nowhere to go, it just keeps building, although on the power stroke, the piston will move and the pressure will lessen. For this reason, high

compression engines should be built with strong (preferably aftermarket) rods and a strong block.

Recommended Ratios—For most street cars, a compression ration of 10:1 or so is pretty much maximum with today's premium unleaded fuel. For general bracket racing, I would go with a max of about 12.5:1 if racing fuel with a minimum of 110 octane is available. Maximum performance drag engines can be built with 14 or 15:1 compression, but generally they have no production components and require 114+ octane fuel.

More radical camshaft timing will allow more compression before detonation sets in, since the larger overlap will reduce lower speed cylinder pressure somewhat.

Alcohol fuel engines should be built at 14:1 or more compression, because this fuel is highly detonation-resistant. Any engine with compression over 13:1 should have the block O-ringed and run soft copper head gaskets for maximum reliability. Avoid aviation fuel, since it has many compounds in it (like de-icing chemicals) to help

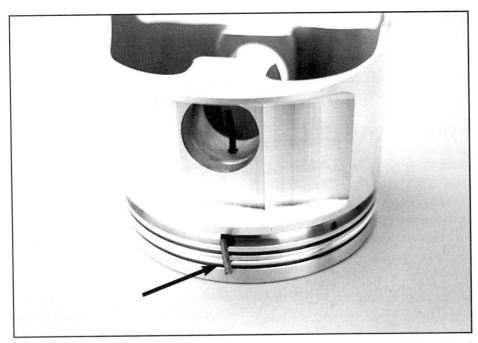

True race-quality pistons feature forced pin oiling. This oil is scraped from the cylinder wall and channeled onto the pin. The wire in the piston shows how the passage is actually routed through the piston.

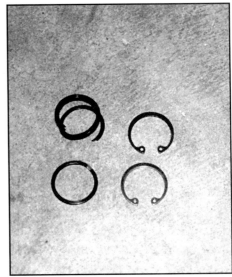

The older Tru-Arc locks (right) have given way to the more reliable spiral-locks (left). To install the spiral locks, simply stretch it out (top left) and coil it into the lock groove in the piston. Not only are the spiral-locks hard to install, they are even harder to remove, which is exactly what you want in a pin lock.

planes, not race cars. It generally has a different specific gravity than racing fuel so the carb jetting may be way off too.

Nitrous Oxide & Pistons

Nitrous oxide injection can provide instant horsepower gains at the touch of a button. It can also melt a set of pistons just as quickly. If you plan on running nitrous, forged pistons are a must. The only way to make more power is to increase the combustion pressure by burning more fuel. Obviously this additional pressure will increase the stress on the pistons, so the absolute strongest pistons are needed. The only way the engine can burn more fuel effectively is if it gets more oxygen at the same time. If more fuel is dumped in without more oxygen, the mixture will not burn completely and the combustion temperature will be low.

Unfortunately our atmosphere is not oxygen rich, with a pure O2 content of only about 30%. Additional oxygen will have to come from a source other than Mother Nature. This is where nitrous oxide comes in.

How Nitrous Works—The way nitrous works is pretty simple. The nitrous kit sprays additional fuel into the engine at the same time as nitrous oxide. Under the heat and pressure in the engine, the oxygen and nitrogen of the nitrous oxide split. This free oxygen gives the engine more oxygen to use so it can burn the additional injected fuel. The nitrogen acts as a soothing buffer and promotes a smooth burn. Unfortunately, if this free oxygen doesn't have enough fuel to burn with it, the cylinder will run excessively lean. Too much oxygen for the amount of fuel is coincidentally the same way a cutting torch works. That's what will happen to your pistons if things go or are setup wrong.

Despite this, do not be afraid of running nitrous. It really works great in Mopar engines. Because they have such strong bottom ends, B engines can take a good dose of "juice" without a problem. If you have a production block, try to keep the dose under 200 hp. More can be added, but ultimately, reliability will suffer. If you have a cross-bolt block equipped with the best aftermarket racing components, then spray away. I know of some Mopar engines that are injected with over 750 hp of nitrous, and they hold up fine. Strong pistons, good head gaskets, a good fuel and ignition system, and strong bottom ends are all required. Always follow the nitrous kit manufacturer's suggested tuning tips for jet size and ignition timing adjustments.

Designing Custom Pistons

With all of the crank and block swaps that are available for Mopar engines, you may find the need for a custom piston. There are so many different displacement and head

When custom pistons are made, anything can be done. This piston is for a Brewer head and has a dish due to the small combustion chamber and the large, 604 cubic inch engine size. Even with the dish compression is still 14:1. Note the extremely high pin placement due to the long stroke and rod length and how the shape of the dish matches the combustion chamber.

combinations possible today that the old reliable TRW pistons may not cut it. Because the Mopar B engines has the heaviest stock piston and tallest block deck heights of any common engine, you can gain a lot of performance with a custom piston. Because these pistons are truly custom, any combination of rod, stroke, block, head, or compression ratio can be designed. Generally, you want the piston to be as short as possible to minimize weight. If a .990" pin is used, the minimum compression height should be limited to about 1.100". The larger 1.094" pin (stock size) is limited to 1.150". These pistons will require the tops of the rods to be rounded to prevent interference. Aftermarket rods will work fine, but stock rods usually won't fit because they are flat on the top and will interfere with the underside of the piston. Any engine of this caliber should be using aftermarket rods anyway. With pistons this short, oil ring support rails are needed since the wrist pin wall is up so high that it cuts into the oil ring groove. This is not a problem and is very common for racing engines.

Domed pistons will be required in some situations to get the necessary compression ratio. A domed piston is not a performance disadvantage if the dome is properly designed. A very tall domed piston should incorporate a spark plug relief to allow for better flame travel across the top of the piston. A slight loss of flame travel may be experienced with a dome, but usually the extra compression (and power) that the dome gives will more than make up for any small loss due to flame travel.

Rings

The best pistons in the world won't do a very good job without an equally good set of rings. These days the only way to go is with moly rings. Most moly rings are made from some type of iron that has a moly-filled edge that contacts the cylinder wall. The moly serves the purpose of holding oil which aids in longer life and less friction. Since the moly is usually sprayed on the ring through a plasma process, it is there to stay. While regular cast rings are a little cheaper, the extra money for the moly rings is a good investment. Do not use chrome rings, as they are very hard to break in. If the cylinder wall finish is correct (extremely smooth), a moly ring will seal almost instantly.

An engine that is going to use a large amount of nitrous oxide (over 450 hp) should consider a top ring made of stainless or tool steel. These rings will hold up better to the pressure and there is no danger of any of the moly flaking off under the detonation that is common in these engines.

The stock ring sizes are 5/64," 5/64" and 3/16", which were common for most engines of the era. Because most of the friction in the engine is caused by the rings, reducing it can recover some of the power that is being lost. In fact, the production engines today are fitted with narrower rings for an increase in performance and fuel economy. Sometimes the auto manufacturers actually learn something from racing!

The first step for performance use is to go with a narrower compression ring setup. This is usually a 1/16", 1/16" and 3/16" stack and this combination works very well for both track and street use.

Dykes Ring—If this still isn't wild enough, a .043 top ring can be fitted

The extremely short compression height required by a 4.15" stroke crank and a 440 length rod in a 400 block actually located the pin inside the oil ring. The spacer rail (left) is a thick ring that fits in the oil ring groove to support the oil ring. The oil rings fit on top of the spacer rail. An alternate, older way to support the oil ring in this situation is to use pin buttons. This piston is still stable in the bore due to its 360 degree skirt design.

or some type of Dykes ring can be used. The Dykes style of ring is unique, in that it is an "L"-shaped ring to reduce radial friction and weight. This type of ring should only be used for racing.

Reducing Friction—The oil ring friction can be reduced by using low tension oil rings. These rings will exert less tension on the cylinder wall, thus reducing friction. Unfortunately, less tension also means a less effective job of controlling the oil, so increased oil consumption may result. Generally the low tension oil rings are for track use only.

The 3/16" oil ring width can be changed to the smaller 1/8" or 3mm rings for even less friction, but be sure that these rings are available for the bore size you plan to use.

Choosing Rings—In general, your ring choice will be determined by your piston choice; changing the ring grooves in the piston is usually not possible. Most street pistons use the 5/64" ring stacks while most of the race pistons use the 1/16" ring stack.

If any other combination is needed, the pistons will have to be custom made. As a general recommendation, for any engine other than one built for all-out racing, use the 1/16", 1/16", 3/16" stack with low tension oil rings. This setup is the best overall way to go, figuring in cost, ease, performance, and durability.

Gapping Rings—File-fit rings will need to be fit to each cylinder and should follow the ring manufacturers guidelines for proper gap. As a starting point, a gap of .004" times bore size for the top and .003" times bore for the second ring will work. This works out to .017" and .013" for a typical B engine. If the engine is being used with nitrous, increase the gap about 25%. If the gap is too tight, the ring ends will butt together and in extreme cases, the rings can seize in the bore, ruining the piston and the block. If the gap is too loose, a small increase in blowby may happen. For this reason, err on the loose side when fitting the rings.

Gapless Rings—Gapless rings can

be used but do not expect large gains. My experience with these rings has shown very little, if any, gain in performance. Consistency may increase slightly, but it is impossible to verify unless you built two identical engines and tested them. Most racers do not have the capability to do this, so they must rely on advertising and hearsay. You can find a number of racers that swear by gapless rings and an equal number that swear at them. Actually there is some thought being given to actually increasing the gap on the second ring to let the pressure out that builds up between the two rings to lessen ring flutter somewhat. This is just another case of two opposite theories that both work. Many things in an engine are this way. Unfortunately engine building is an inexact science and nobody has all the answers.

Crankcase Ventilation

Always run some type of crankcase ventilation system on your engine. There will always be some blowby that will cause pressure to build up in the crankcase. This pressure has to be vented somewhere. On a racing engine, do not run the breathers from the valve covers into the intake manifold like a stock engine does, since this will contaminate the fuel charge with oil. In this situation, run the valve cover breather into the headers as this will create a slight vacuum inside the engine, which will make the rings seal better. All-out racing engines actually use an air pump connected to the valve covers to create a larger vacuum inside the engine to gain even more power. That's the trick setup if you can afford it.

Mopar cam bearings are all of different sizes. If you are installing them yourself, pay attention to their sizes and oil hole alignment. Note that the number 4 bearing has two additional oil holes to provide oil to the heads for valvetrain oiling. If you suddenly experience a loss of oil flow to one or both heads, you probably have spun the #4 cam bearing.

The bearings in a racing engine are definitely unsung heroes. They are one of the only components that do not have a real racing quality replacement. Sure, the factory used cheap aluminum bearings and you may buy tri-metal or babbitt material bearings for your racing engine, but they are still essentially the same thing. Pistons and rods can be made higher-tech to be lighter, valves can be made of exotic materials like titanium, cranks can be machined out of solid billets of steel but for the most part, a bearing is a bearing. Even the best, most expensive set of bearings are relatively cheaply made. These days, with all of the corporate mergers occurring between car companies, there really are only a few brand choices to consider when purchasing bearings for your racing engine. However, there are still different types and styles of bearings to choose from.

CAM BEARINGS

The simplest bearings in your engine are cam bearings. These five bearings are pressed into the block with a special tool and serve to support the camshaft. They are fully round bearings with an oil hole to supply oil for the camshaft. The number four cam bearing has two additional oil holes that feed the cylinder heads to supply pressurized oil to the valvetrain.

Installation

It is very important to align all of the oil holes with the proper oil passages in the block or disaster will result. Check and double check that all of the holes are lined up correctly before the engine is assembled. For some reason, Mopar engineers designed each cam bearing with different outside and inside diameters. Because of this, it is very important to pay attention to how they are

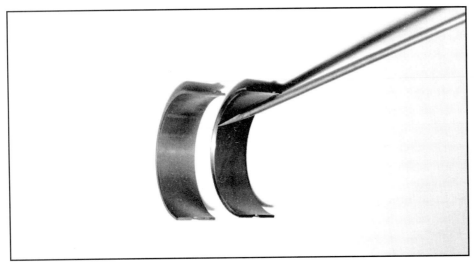

Only one side of the rod bearing comes close to the crank, so these bearings are only chamfered on one side. Make sure to install the chamfer on the correct side. Kellogg, Mopar Performance, and all other aftermarket cranks with full radius fillets require these special bearings.

installed. Most of the cam bearing manufacturers offer a chart with bearing location and individual bearing part numbers in the bearing set to tell you where they need to go.

When installing cam bearings, make sure to always use the proper tools and procedures to prevent the bearing from getting cocked in its bore. Most people have the machine shop install cam bearings, because a special tool is required. If you have a shop install the cam bearings, give them the cam that you plan to use to allow them to test-fit it in the block.

Buffing—Regardless of who installs the cam bearings, make sure to test-fit the cam before any other engine assembly is performed. The cam can fit slightly snug but you should be able to turn the cam by hand. Because of the five different sizes, sometimes the cam will not fit very well with new bearings in a used block. If this is the case, the bearings can be "buffed" slightly with fine emery cloth or a bearing knife to provide the necessary clearance. This is a very common hang-up with Mopar big blocks so don't panic if

your bearings need this treatment. The tight area will show up as a shiny spot on the offending bearing, so clearancing it should only take a few minutes.

Cam Bearing Styles

There are really only two styles of cam bearings for these engines, the solid bearing and the rolled bearing. The solid bearing is just that—a solid cylinder of bearing material.

The rolled type starts out as a flat strip of material, then is rolled into a cylinder and the two ends are interlocked. Both types work fine, but the solid ones are much easier to install without damage. The solid ones are more reliable too since they can't unravel inside the engine. In reality, I haven't seen an interlocked cam bearing for these engines in years, so the chance of running into them is slim.

Any of the bearings will work fine regardless of cam type or application. Just make sure the holes line up, the cam fits nicely, and that oil is fed continuously to the bearings.

As a quick note, if your engine

suddenly has no oil flow to one or both cylinder heads, it may be a sign that the number four cam bearing has spun in its bore and the holes no longer align. If everything else checks out, replace that particular cam bearing.

CONNECTING ROD BEARINGS

Connecting rod bearings take the most beating of all the bearings so they need to be selected carefully. Because the force of combustion is trying to push the rods out of the block, the upper rod bearing is the one that is actually subjected to the most abuse. Coupled with the fact that the rod is flexing and the cap is bouncing, it really isn't too hard to see why spun rod bearings are the second most common cause of engine failure behind broken connecting rods. Face it, all that's holding the rod bearing in the rod is the bearing crush. It's simply a snap fit deal here so the rod bearing has to be able to survive during the moments of reduced crush caused by all the hammering going on around it. Fortunately, the bearing manufacturers' realize these challenges and provide bearings properly designed to withstand this abuse.

Types of Connecting Rod Bearings

The two types that you will likely encounter for your Mopar are *tri-metal* and *babbitt*. The tri-metal bearings are the most common these days and are produced by a few different companies, with AE Clevite's CL-77 or M-77 being the most popular. Tri-metal bearings work great for virtually every application, whether it's street or track.

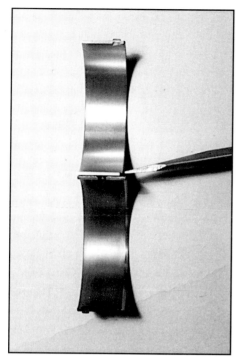

Babbitt bearing on top is not chamfered to clear the radius, instead it is narrowed slightly.

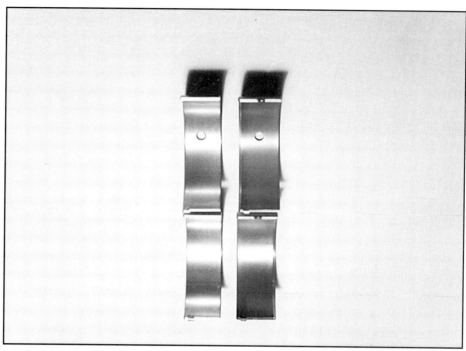

If using aluminum rods, special bearings with dowel pin holes are required to clear the pins in the rod cap. Two types are available: the tri-metal (right) bearing is good for street/strip while the babbitt is preferred for all-out racing use, especially when running with nitrous. These bearings are only available in standard and .010" under. If your crank is .020" or .030", you can make your own dowel holes easily.

The babbitt bearings are much softer than the tri-metal bearings. This is not as good for street use since the babbitt will wear faster. For race use, the softer babbitt bearings have two advantages: They absorb shock better, which is desirable for Top Fuel and nitrous engines, and they allow dirt to embed into them easier, thus preventing the dirt from scratching the expensive racing crank. Figure out what your engine will be used for and select the right bearing.

Prepping Rod Bearings

If you are using aluminum rods in your engine, the lower (cap) rod bearing must have a hole to fit over the dowel pin that's in the rod cap. Most bearings are available with this hole but not in every size. If you can't get the dowel pin bearings in your size, you will have to make them.

Another special rod bearing that you may need is one with a chamfer cut into one side. These chamfers allow the bearing to clear the radius on a full-radius crankshaft. This will only be an issue with aftermarket or welded cranks, because all stock Mopar cranks (except the 426 Hemi) had undercut radii. If you do not use these special bearings on a full radius crank, there will not be enough rod side clearance, since the bearing will

To make your own dowel pin hole rod bearings, you will need to buy one pre-drilled rod bearing and sacrifice an old rod cap. Take the bearing with the hole in it and put it in the rod cap. After this, use the existing hole in the bearing as the location to drill a hole through the rod cap. The rod cap now becomes your fixture to drill other bearings. Simply install a non-drilled bearing into the cap, flip it over, and drill through the bearing.

After the dowel pin hole is drilled into the bearing, flip the rod cap fixture over and chamfer the hole with a chamfering bit.

hit the radius before the rod can hit the cheek of the crank journal. Like the dowel pin bearings, you can install these chamfers if you want. If you do it yourself, be sure that you put in enough chamfer to allow the rod to move over fully to the crank. As a side note, most chamfered bearings also have the dowel pin hole and vice-versa, so if you buy the special "racing" rod bearings, you will get both features. Figure on the race bearings costing about $40 more than the "street" bearing.

MAIN BEARINGS

Your options when it comes to main bearings are similar to those of the rod bearings, with babbitt and tri-metal also being the most common types used. The same rules apply to the mains as do the rods. If the engine is going to be hammered, use the babbitt bearings. Generally, the mains don't get hammered as hard as the rods, so the tri-metal bearing bearings will work well even in the most demanding situations.

Grooved Bearings

The greatest difference between main bearings is the type of oil groove

they have. The grooves in the main bearings are what allows the oil to flow onto the bearing and support the crank. In addition to this, these grooves also provide and control the oil supply to the rod bearings.

Half-Grooved Bearings—Except for some factory race engines, all production engines only had the upper bearing shell grooved. This is why they are called half-grooved bearings. This actually means that the rod bearings do not get a continuous supply of oil, because the oil passage in the crank that feeds the rod bearing

will line up with the groove only during half of a revolution. This works fine in a production engine since the oil holes are strategically placed in the crank to begin the oil flow right before the load is placed on the rod during the power stroke.

Increasing Oil Flow—While this arrangement is fine for low rpm use, it obviously has some limitations. If there isn't enough oil supply to support and cool the bearing, failure will result. What is needed is full-time oiling to supply additional oil to the bearings. This can be accomplished two ways—by cross-drilling the oil holes in the crank or by using bearings that have both halves grooved. If the crank is cross-drilled, there will be two oil holes in the main journal of the crank and as such one will always be in alignment with the oil groove. This takes care of the oil supply problem but having an extra hole through all five main journals will weaken the crank slightly.

The alternative is to simply use a fully grooved set of main bearings. By doing this, the original oil passage in

Extra wide oil groove main bearings are available for RB engines. These will flow enough oil for even the wildest applications. They should be used if rpm is going to exceed 7000 on a normal basis.

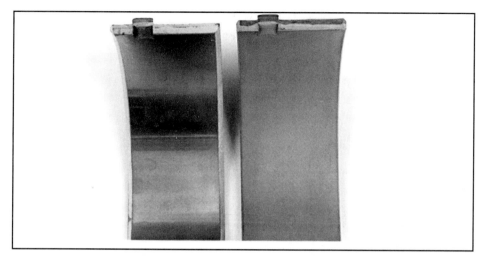

Chamfered main bearing on left is required to clear cranks that have large radius fillets. Most real racing cranks will require their use. Always check during your assembly to be sure that the radius of the crank isn't grinding into the bearings. Stock cranks have undercut radii so this is not a problem.

grooved sets will clear most cranks.

OIL CLEARANCE

On the subject of oil clearance use .002–.003" for rod and main bearings. This is where the clearance should fall if the crank journal and bearing housing are sized in the middle of the factory tolerances. This is adequate for both street and race use. Slightly tighter will be fine for low rpm use and will control the oil slightly better, but should be avoided for high rpm use. Any more than this will cause more oil to flow, but will work the oil system harder, because there is more "leakage" around all the bearings.

the crank is retained and will always be in alignment with the oil groove. This method does not weaken the crank but does slightly lessen the amount of bearing area available for load support. Of the two ways to get full time oiling, the fully grooved bearing way is the easiest, cheapest and the strongest.

Oil System Upgrade—Because the oil flow to the rod bearings has now doubled, full time oiling places more demand on the entire oil system. The oil pump must be able to keep up with the extra demand, so make sure to use a high volume oil pump. Idle oil pressure will probably be a little lower than "normal" too but this will not cause any problems. Also make sure to use a good high capacity oil pan to control the extra oil that will now be flying around inside the engine.

3/4 Grooved Bearings—On the subject of extra oiling, a new trend in bearing design is the use of 3/4 grooved main bearings. As the name implies, these bearings deliver oil to the rods 75% of the time while retaining most all the load-carrying capacity of the bottom bearing. These bearings were made to supply more

oil to the rod bearings while trying to keep the extra flying oil down to a minimum. While these bearings have proven to be a good choice, they are not very common. Because the B engine family has relatively poor oil control because half of the oil pan is actually part of the block, the extra oil inside the engine is not that much of a power loss, so it isn't much cause for concern. A good windage tray will control most of the oil. There are also special main bearings to clear full radius cranks but most of the fully

Never run a clearance over .004" under any circumstance (except Top Fuel where even .008" is common) because the oil system will be too stressed and there will be far too much oil flying around inside the engine. If you plan on using an old crank from a Top Fuel engine, check the journal sizes, because most are undersized to gain the additional clearance. Always check this stuff out before final engine assembly.

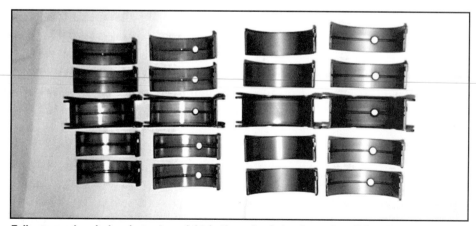

Fully grooved main bearing set on right is the only choice for racing. Using them will provide full time oiling to the rod bearings, allowing them to withstand higher loads and rpm. Coupled with a high volume oil pump, this set-up is bulletproof, even for a stock or restoration rebuild. Never groove or cross-drill the crank to accomplish full-time oiling; use the fully grooved bearings. In the very unlikely event you have a cross-drilled crank, use the 1/2 groove bearings.

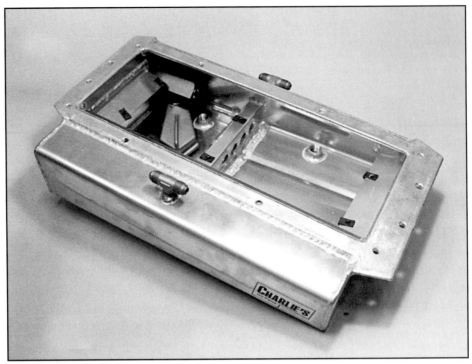

This oil pan made by Charlie's Pans features the state-of-the-art design in a wet sump pan. It features: full kick-outs on both sides; a trap door to keep the oil in the sump during deceleration; a full-length screen-type windage tray (not shown); and a separate mini-sump under the swinging pickup. It just can't be done any better than this. AN "T" fittings are for oil returns from the heads.

Make no mistake, oil is truly the lifeblood of any engine. If the oil supply is interrupted even for a few seconds, serious engine damage will result. The oil in your engine has two main functions—to lubricate the moving parts and keep them cool. As mentioned in the crankshaft section, the film of oil that exists between the crankshaft and the bearings supports the load and keeps the bearings off the crank journals. A Mopar big-block engine has a pretty good oil system that can be easily modified to meet the demands of a racing engine. A race engine has slightly different requirements than a stock passenger car engine. Because most racing engines are capable of turning more rpm than a stock engine, the oil system has to provide additional oil to increase the amount of lubrication and cooling so that parts like bearings and pistons can survive. The additional load placed on the bearings by the higher combustion pressure requires more oil pressure to form a stronger hydrodynamic wedge to keep the bearings off the crank.

OIL SYSTEM DESIGN

Mopar B engines use a fairly standard oil system that's simple and reliable. Unlike most engines that have the oil pump located inside the engine, Mopar B engines have a unique system where the oil pump is located on the outside of the block.

Pressure

This is handy for racers, because an oil pump swap or a pressure adjustment is a snap. The oil pump delivers oil under pressure through a galley that runs across the front of the block behind the upper timing gear. After this, the oil turns into the passenger side lifter galley where additional galleys feed off and supply all five main bearings. At the rear of

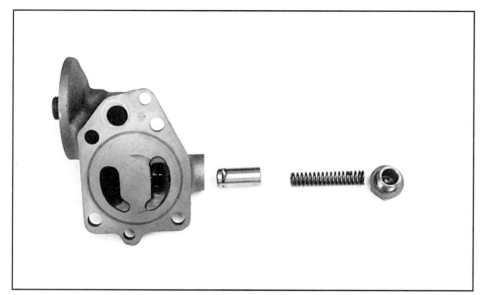

Disassembled oil pressure regulator shows design. The oil pressure of the engine is determined by the pressure of the relief spring. This is easily adjusted from outside the engine. Always check to be sure that the plug is tight before racing. They have been known to loosen up and fly off the oil pump. When this happens, oil pressure drops to zero.

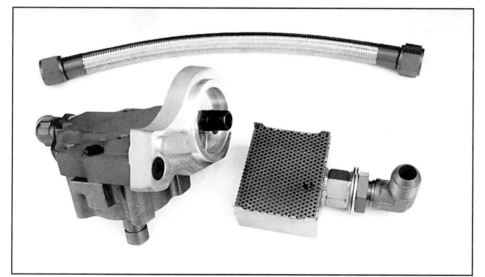

A good medium race oil system is the single-line static pickup system shown here.

the block, the oil crosses the block again and supplies the driver's side lifter galley. The driver's side lifter galley only supplies oil to the lifters, and there are no other things that are supplied off of it. Other than enlarging the galleys that feed the main bearings from the passenger side galley or bushing the lifter bores to restrict the oil to the lifters, there aren't any necessary modifications that are required on the pressure side of the oil

system. The stock layout will be reliable to over 8000 rpm if required.

Suction

The suction side of the oil system is another story. An oil pump is no different than most other pumps in that it is much better at pushing out liquid than it is pulling or sucking it in. Because the pump is located on the outside of the block, but the oil is located on the inside of the engine,

there has to be an oil pickup located in the engine. This 3/8" pipe pickup (1/2" on Hemi and later Max-Wedge engines) is screwed into the block and extends into the pan where it sucks up the oil to supply the pump. The passageway that the pump screws into has to make a severe turn in order to feed the external pump. This turn is a restriction to the oil supply and can stand some modification.

MODIFICATIONS

The first oil system modification you can make for a racing engine is to drill and tap the stock 3/8" pipe inlet to the larger 1/2" inlet size. This is pretty easily done with a hand drill and a 1/2" N.P.T. tap. Be sure to drill the inlet passage in the block the entire length before tapping it. Also, take care to preserve the factory angle on the threads so that the pickup tube will be in the correct position. The intersection point of the two passageways in the pickup tube boss can be radiused with a die grinder to smooth and expedite the flow of oil. Don't go crazy enlarging the passageway with the grinder. Use some common sense and just radius the intersection point.

Upgrade Oil Pump

Other than the larger pickup and radiusing the intersection point, the only thing left to change would be the oil pump itself. Any racing engine should use a high-volume oil pump. These pumps have taller rotors to pump an extra amount of oil. In addition to taller rotors, most high-volume oil pumps also have a higher pressure relief spring to increase the oil pressure at the same time. These pumps can be purchased

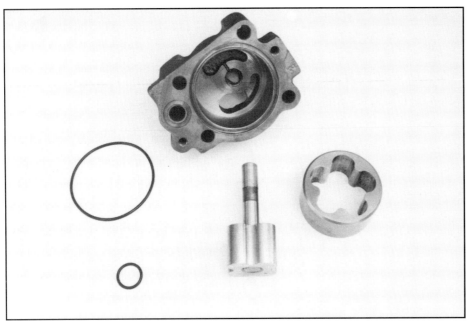

Main components of the stock oil pump body. Regardless of the inlet method, this is what will actually pumps the oil. The gearotor design is far more efficient than the gear design used by other Detroit engines.

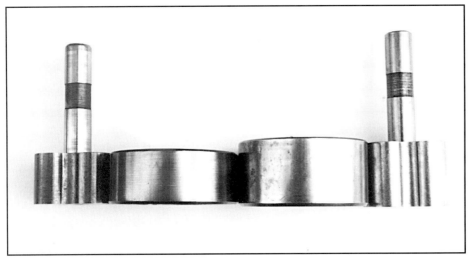

A high-volume oil pump is able to deliver more oil due to its rotor gears being taller. Stock gears on left are shorter.

For all but the most severe use, a good high-volume oil pump can be tricked out with the dual line adapter plates to make a fine oiling system. Use this system under 8000 rpm.

inexpensively and will provide an extra measure of protection for the engine. The Mopar pump is unique in that it uses rotors instead of gears to pump oil. The rotors are more efficient and take less power to turn than a gear pump.

In addition to this feature, the pressure relief system is also unique because the oil that is bypassed to regulate the pressure is kept inside the pump (instead of being dumped into the pan as is common with internal pumps) and eventually pumped into the engine. This reduces the load on the pickup side since the oil has already been sucked into the pump.

High Pressure vs. High Volume

Many people ask if they should use a high-volume pump or just a high-pressure pump. The answer is to use a high-volume oil pump. Higher oil pressure will indeed allow the bearings to support more load but without an additional supply of oil, no additional cooling from oil will occur. If a high-volume oil pump is used it will supply an additional amount of oil and increase oil pressure at the same time. The additional pressure will be the result of pumping more oil through the same restriction (in this case the all the bearing clearances) as with a stock oil pump. While the old rule of 10 psi per 1000 rpm is not scientific, it will actually come close enough for reliable operation. Excessive oil pressure is not required in these engines.

General Tips

With a 1/2" internal system and a good high-volume oil pump, the internal oil system is good for 7000 rpm. Make sure that the bearing oil clearance is between .0025"–.0035" and that the oil pressure is in the 70 psi range. Any more oil pressure than this is unnecessary and will only consume more power. Less than 70 psi will not be enough to support the extra load of a racing engine. If

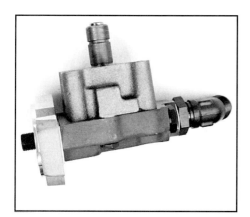

If the rpm demands of the engine are not severe, Milodon also offers a single-line oil system. Available in both fixed and swinging pickup designs, this system is good to 7500 rpm when used with a good high-volume oil pump. The actual kit consists of the pump cover/filter adapter, #12 AN line and the pickup. This system can also be used with a custom oil pan to fit virtually any vehicle possible. By adding the correct spacer plate, this system can be upgraded to a dual inlet setup at any time.

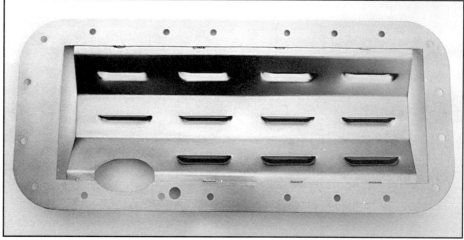

Full-length Milodon windage tray features many louvers for the oil to return back into the oil pan. This design is better than a production tray sine the oil return is much faster. This tray may not work with shallow oil pans.

everything is within specifications, a standard high volume oil pump should deliver this kind of oil pressure.

Compensating for Low Pressure— If the bearing and rod side clearances are a little on the loose side, the pressure may be slightly less. This is easily solved by installing a shim (usually in the form of a washer) on the pressure relief spring. Keep shimming the spring until the oil pressure is where it should be.

Compensating for High Pressure— If the engine has had the lifter bores bushed or any other oil restriction modification, the pressure may actually be too high. In this case, the easiest remedy is to use a stock low pressure spring (usually red in color) in the high-volume pump. This will usually do the job and get the oil pressure down to where it needs to be.

Oil Pan Tips

The oil pan should be one with additional capacity, usually in the seven-quart range. At high rpm, the oil pump can pump the oil to the engine faster than the oil can get back to the sump, so the additional capacity will prevent oil starvation. Additional oil capacity will also dissipate heat faster, which will result in slightly lower oil temperature as well. If the engine is going to be installed in a production car, your oil pan choice will be determined by what will fit in the chassis. There are many pans on the market for these engines and all work fine.

Baffles—Make sure that the pan has both acceleration and deceleration baffles. If you want to check how well the baffles work, take the car to the dragstrip and glance at the oil pressure gauge when you first leave the line. If the oil pressure takes a nose dive and then returns back to normal, your acceleration baffles need some help. The oil pan should have front and rear baffles in the sump area.

At the other end of the track when you start decelerating, the oil pressure should remain constant. If it falls momentarily, the deceleration baffles need help.

Windage Tray—A windage tray can help with the oil slosh situation, but the stock design tray will rarely make more power in a racing engine with a real race oil pan. The reason for this is that the tray can't handle the additional oil flow from high-volume pumps and high rpm engines. The four small slots just can't get the oil through fast enough and the oil that is flying off the crank just bounces back onto the crank. Real windage trays usually have about 10 louvered slots over their entire length. This allows the oil to return to the sump where it belongs, but usually these trays are too deep to use with a stock style oil pan. If you have a production shallow oil pan, the windage tray will be of some benefit, because the oil is so close to the crank with these pans. If you are going to use a tray, take a screwdriver and open the slots up to about three times their original size to allow oil to actually flow through them.

The best way to make power in a B engine oil pan is to get the oil away from the crank. This is hard to do, because the lower skirt of the block actually forms part of the oil pan. In short, go with the deepest pan that

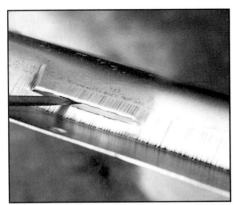

If you are using a production-style windage tray, open up the oil return slots with a screwdriver to allow quicker oil flow back down into the pan. Sometimes these slots aren't even punched all the way through. Looser bearing clearances and high-volume oil pumps require the oil to return back to the pan, not just to bounce around on top of the tray.

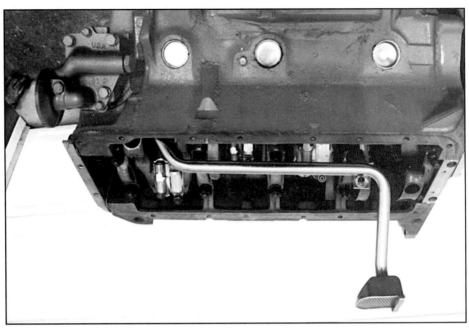

A B engine in a stock truck chassis requires a rear sump oil pan. This obviously requires a special rear oil pickup, shown here.

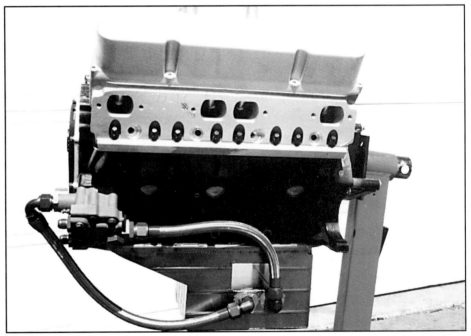

The Milodon external dual-line oil system with high capacity "Super Stock" oil pan has been the standard for many years. This particular system has the aluminum oil pump which will provide adequate oil delivery for engine speeds over 8000 rpm. The rear sump design of the pan is much better for drag racing and the square hole in the oil pan is for the center link of the steering to pass through.

will fit in the chassis and still have some ground clearance. I have seen extreme modifications attempted by actually cutting some of the lower skirting out of the block and making the pan actually wrap up the side of the block. But because this severely weakens the block, I would not recommend it.

Types of Oil Pans

The most common styles of racing pans for the B engine are the "super stock" pan for production chassis cars and the "dragster" pan for tube chassis cars.

Super Stock Pan—The Super Stock style pans usually have the oil sump relocated to the rear (the stock Mopar oil pan usually has its sump in the center rendering it less effective as a real drag race pan) to contain the oil during acceleration. Coupled with good baffling and a swinging pickup, these pans work very well. Due to the relocated sump and the location of the steering linkage of the car, these pans usually have a sealed hole through them for the steering linkage to pass through. Needless to say, they require

some labor to install as the steering linkage will have to be dropped every time the pan or engine is removed.

Dragster Style—If your chassis permits, the best type of race pan to run is the "dragster" style. Usually

these pans resemble a large square box that covers the entire bottom of the block. Because of this, the oil can be kept further away from the crank than with any other pan design. Unfortunately, the entire bottom of the

When an external oil system is used, the passage for the original oil pickup must be blocked off to prevent the sump from sucking air. This can be done inside the block or by tapping the passage externally and installing a 3/8" pipe plug. Either method works fine.

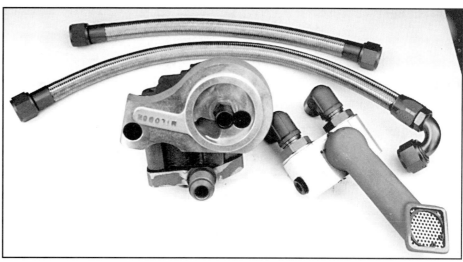

Main components of the external dual-line oil system. With two #12 AN oil lines, oil supply is virtually assured.

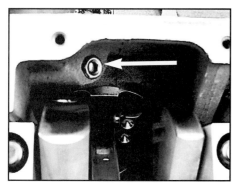

The stock oil passage can also be blocked off inside the block for use with an external oil system.

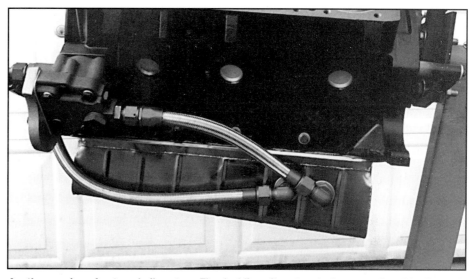

Another version of external oil system. The dual line oil system is the same, but this oil pan is shaped more as a box. This oil pan will only fit in tube chassis cars and dragsters as it will hit the original K-frame in a production chassis. The box-style pan is the best setup because it keeps the oil further away from the crankshaft. This pan also uses a swinging pickup and incorporates a full-length windage tray.

engine has to be open to allow it to fit. Thus the pan won't work in production vehicles with stock K-frames. These box-style pans should always have the swinging pickup, because the oil tends to slosh around more inside because they are so large. They also need to be well-baffled and should feature some sort of trap-door system to keep the oil where it needs to be.

A full-length windage tray can also be used with these pans to keep the oil off the crank, as can things like crank scrapers. A "full kickout" design is popular with box-style pans too. This

kickout is done by making the pan wider than the width of the oil pan mounting surface. Usually, this additional width is added on the passenger side of the block to catch and contain the oil that is flying off the crank. Again, all of this trick stuff is only trying to keep the oil away from the crank.

External Oil System

In cases where rpm will exceed

7000 or the load is very high, say over 650 horsepower, the internal oil system should be upgraded to one with external entry. These external oil systems are extremely popular and are easy to install. Since the pump is conveniently located on the outside of the engine, it provides an easier method for the pump to get oil. Most of these systems have two number 12 AN lines to supply the oil pump. This is more than double the inlet area of

Front view of the Milodon external oil system uses dual lines. Usually this oil filter adapter will hit something in most chassis setups. Check this before final installation of the engine. On a tube chassis car, it will usually interfere with a rack-and-pinion steering system. A kit is available to use an external filter, which can solve some installation problems.

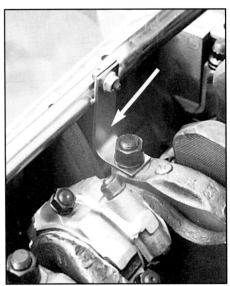

The Milodon rear sump oil pickup is made to withstand rugged use like off-road racing. Note that the pickup is anchored to a #4 main cap stud to prevent breaking or cracking during severe use.

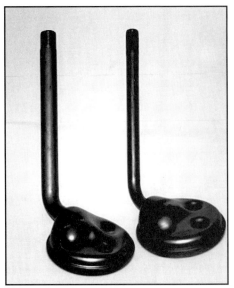

Street Hemi oil pickup tube on left is 1/2" diameter and dwarfs the stock 3/8" pickup on right. The larger pickup is fine to 7000 rpm and is easily installed in a wedge block by drilling and tapping the pickup tube boss in the block. This is a must for racing and a good idea for any performance use. Be sure to match the pickup tube with the oil pan so everything will work.

Internal shot of the swinging oil pickup. This arrangement actually allows the pickup to follow the oil as it sloshes around under rapid acceleration or deceleration. When a large area sump is used, the swinging pickup is a must to prevent oil starvation under extreme acceleration.

an internal system.

These systems can be equipped with larger oil pumps as well. With the larger pumps and the additional inlet area, these systems will support well over 8000 rpm.

Custom Oil Pickups—The external lines also make it easy to install an oil pickup in a custom pan if necessary. Depending on the type of pan, the external pickup can usually be located in a spot where it will be the most effective, depending on the type of racing. For example, circle track

racers would benefit from having the pickup located on the right side of the pan (because they are almost always turning left, oil sloshes to the right).

Drag racers usually use a swinging pickup that, like its name suggests, will actually move inside the oil pan to keep it submerged in oil during acceleration and deceleration. This is very important for drag cars, because both the acceleration and deceleration rates can be very high.

Even if your engine doesn't turn a lot of rpm (remember for under 7000

rpm the internal system will work), an external oil system with swinging pickup can increase power and durability. A good example of this would be a big cubic inch dragster engine. This setup can put these cars into the low 7-second zone running at only 6800 rpm. Even though the rpm range falls within the internal pickup zone, the super-high acceleration rate would immediately uncover the stock oil pickup and damage would result. So it's not always an rpm or oil volume thing that requires the external system.

Most of the pans that are used with external systems are quite a bit larger than a stock oil pan. As mentioned, the key to making horsepower with an oil pan is to keep the oil as far away from the crankshaft as possible. This will help prevent oil from becoming trapped around the crank, which will not only waste power but will also

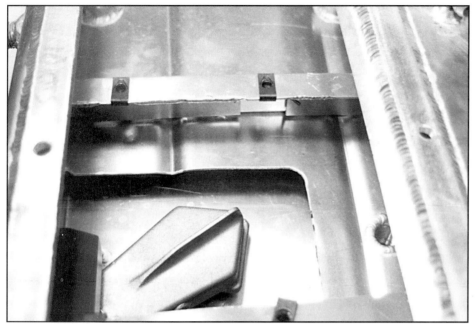

Close up shot of the sump within a sump in a Charlie's Pans oil pan. This ensures adequate oil to the pickup even if a giant slosh occurs.

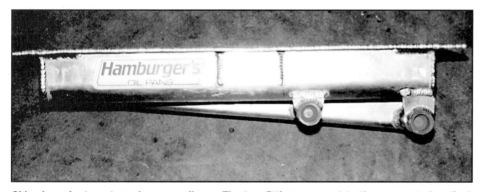

Side view of a two-stage dry sump oil pan. The two fittings connect to the scavenge (suction) side of the oil pump. Notice how shallow the pan is. Since the sump is "dry" (there is very little oil in it), it doesn't need to be very deep.

Interior of dry sump pan shows a full-length unidirectional windage tray and a crank scraper (upper row of "tabs"). All of these things combine to get as much power-robbing oil out of the engine as possible. All the suction from the external oil pump can help to provide a vacuum in the crankcase, which helps ring sealing too.

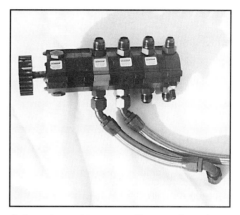

A four-stage dry sump oil pump has three stages of suction from the oil pan and one pressure stage to feed the engine. Usually the pump is belt-driven off the front of the crank. An external tank actually holds all the oil for the engine, giving the system its name.

deprive the oil system of oil.

Dry Sump Systems

Since we are so obsessed with keeping the oil off the crank, the ultimate setup would be one where the oil sump actually has little to no oil in it. This is what a "dry sump" oiling system is. In these systems, the oil is not stored in the oil pan on the engine but rather in an external tank that is mounted somewhere on the car. These systems use a special, external oil pump that has several suction sections and one pressure section all driven off the front of the crank. The suction stages of the pump simply pump the oil out of the engine and into the oil reservoir tank. At the same time, the pressure stage pumps oil from the tank into the engine. Because of this, there is much less problem with oil sloshing around inside the engine because there is so little inside. There's not much worry of oil starvation or uncovering the pickup because there should always be plenty of oil in the tank. Because the dry sump system has several sections of suction or scavenging, as they're called, the oil can be sucked from the

Always replace the oil pump driveshaft with a new HD unit from Mopar Performance or Milodon. Both feature pinned gears and hardened drive hexes to prevent twisting (shown here) or breaking off. The extra demands for a high-volume oil pump and high rpm make them a necessity but they are cheap insurance for any rebuild.

engine in several spots to yield as much power as possible. Most drag cars have two or three scavenge sections, but some all-out engines use up to five sections. With this, the oil can be sucked for every possible area of the engine, thus keeping it as "dry" as possible. If the pan is designed correctly, there will be little to no oil around the crank. This will allow for maximum power. With a typical Mopar engine a power gain of about 30 horsepower can be expected.

While a dry sump system looks and sounds complicated, they really are not. There are many lines and fittings and such but again it's all pretty straightforward. They are however, very expensive. A typical dry sump system usually costs over $2000 by the time it's all set up. If ultimate power is your goal, consider one. However make sure that there is no other modification that could be done on the engine that will offer a larger gain in horsepower for the same money.

Oil Pump Drive

The only other part in the oil system that needs to be considered is the oil pump drive. The B engine uses a unique oil pump drive system that also drives the distributor. What

makes it different from most engines is that the gear that turns it is not part of the distributor but rather is part of the shaft that stays in the block. This shaft rotates in an aluminum bushing that's pressed into the block. Because this bushing gets removed for cleaning, replace it with a heavy-duty bronze bushing instead of an aluminum one.

Distributor Drive—The Mopar design makes distributor installation very easy since its shaft can only go in one of two ways. While it is all a neat design, this distributor drive should be replaced for racing use. The production drive has been known to

fail in two ways. First, the hex end that fits into the oil pump has been known to round off, especially with the higher load of a high-volume oil pump and higher rpm usage. Second, the shaft can actually spin inside the gear, which will result in the shaft no longer being able to turn the pump. Both of these problems can be solved easily by replacing the drive with a heavy-duty one. These heavy-duty shafts feature a heat-treated, hardened hex end to prevent rounding, and are pinned to the gear to prevent the shaft from slipping.

If you are planning on running a roller cam, make sure to use the bronze gear oil pump drive to prevent gear failure. Roller cams are made from a steel billet core that's much harder than a traditional cast iron core. Because of this, the stock iron gear would fail. Hydraulic and flat-tappet cams must use the iron-gear shaft. Don't think the bronze gear is "better" since it is more expensive and use it on your stock cam. If you have one of the dual line external oil systems you will need a oil pump drive that is longer than stock since the pump is

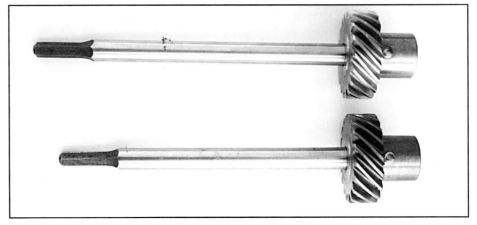

When using an external dual line oil system, the oil pump driveshaft needs to be longer since the pump is spaced away from the block more to allow for the second oil entry. The drive on the top shows the additional length required. The special Milodon aluminum pump system takes its own special driveshaft that's longer than stock but not as long as the "normal" extended-length shaft. Internal pickup oil systems and the single-line systems take a stock length shaft.

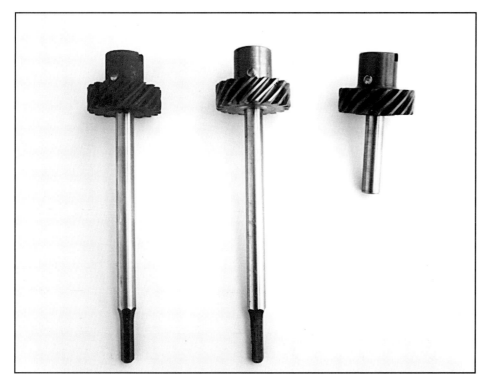

If the engine has a roller cam, it will require a bronze gear oil pump driveshaft, center. This is for metal compatibility with the roller cam's steel billet material. Hydraulic and solid cams do not require this gear. Do not use the bronze gear drive on these cams. It is not better just because it is more expensive! Note the pin through the gear to prevent it from spinning on the shaft. Short gear on right is for use with a dry sump oil system. This gear only has to turn the distributor since the external oil pump is belt-driven off the crankshaft.

also longer than stock.

Installation—Make sure that when the drive is installed, the gear bottoms out on the bushing before the hex bottoms in the pump. There should be about .050" free play in the shaft, and be sure that it rotates easily inside the bushing or it may seize. If you are using a dry sump system, cut the shaft off just below the point that is below the bushing in the block. This will allow the distributor to still be turned by the cam. Also block off the oil pump mounting pad to prevent oil leakage.

OIL

One question I am often asked is, "What type of oil should I run?" By type, they mean what brand and what viscosity. I have tried many different types of oil and had good results with all of them. I would recommend 20w-50w oil for most racing engines. For people that don't like multi-viscosity oils, run straight 30 weight.

As far as what brand to use, I would go with whatever you have been using for the last five years, because it doesn't really matter. All of the major brands on the market are all excellent. Any sub-par oil company would be run out of business in short order these days. If your buddy tells you that they changed to a different brand of oil and immediately blew up the engine, don't believe them. Something else went wrong somewhere.

Synthetic Oils

Over the last 10 years or so the new craze in oil has been synthetic oils. These oils actually do have superior breakdown resistance and will withstand heat and load much better than conventional mineral oil. Since they lubricate so much better than normal oil, you can usually get away with a thinner viscosity, which can increase power slightly. If the oil weight is doubled, it can reduce power by as much as 3-5%. Think about this when you are tempted to pour in some 70-weight oil.

Cautions—If you do use synthetic oil, make sure the engine is broken in with mineral oil first. The synthetic oil is a little too slippery to create the friction necessary for proper break-in. Also consider that synthetic oil is about three times more expensive than conventional oils, so factor this into your decision about using it. For most race cars, the oil is changed too often for synthetic oil to be a cost-effective way to increase performance.

Oil Maintenance

The key to having the oil do its job is to change it often, especially in a race car. The oil itself doesn't wear out but it does get contaminated with all sorts of things like dirt, combustion by-products, and raw fuel. Fuel contamination is the most common problem, especially with high octane racing fuel. Even after a few dragstrip passes, your new oil will smell of fuel. Racing fuel is very harsh and the oil temperature never gets warm enough for a long period of time (especially in a drag car) to burn out the fuel. So the bottom line is to change the oil often. Usually once a month or so should be enough—any more than this is a waste of money.

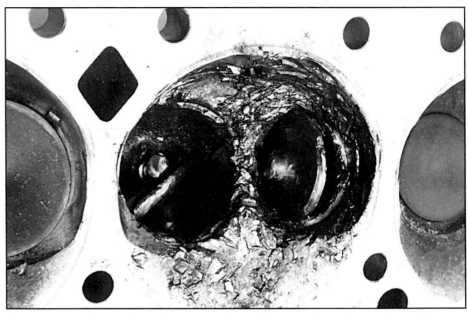

Close up of the damage shows how severe the environment of a racing engine can become. Both seats are gone and the valves are actually embedded into the head.

The cylinder head has the greatest effect on power of any other component in the engine. Because an engine is not much more than a glorified air pump, the head is always the restriction to airflow in and out of the engine. Cylinder head theory could take up an entire library of books, so I will limit this discussion to the important details and get right to the point—spend as much time, effort and money on the cylinder heads as possible. Cubic inches don't mean anything when compared to cylinder heads. Look at it this way: the heads (and other induction path components) determine *how much* power the engine produces while displacement determines *where* it makes this power.

Note: In all of the following illustrations that have two heads, the bottom head in the photo is a stock production head. I've included it for comparison.

BASIC HEAD THEORY

It is very easy to select a set of heads that are not the best for your engine. There are several heads available for the B engine that range from mild to wild. Performance and budget will be the most important criteria used to select the right heads for your application. There are also many different factors that must be considered, like port flow, combustion chamber size, port volume, port size and valve size. All of these things are important and should be compared carefully.

Port Flow

Port flow has the greatest impact on power production while port size and volume impacts rpm range. If the ports can flow more air, the engine will be able to move more air through its cylinders and therefore make more power. Similar to sizing a carb, the easiest solution to getting more air into the engine would be to make the heads very large. While this would allow more airflow, the resulting velocity would be very slow, thus causing poor throttle response and power. The port opening directly determines the velocity through the port. If the airflow is kept equal, a smaller port will generate more velocity. The formula on page 150

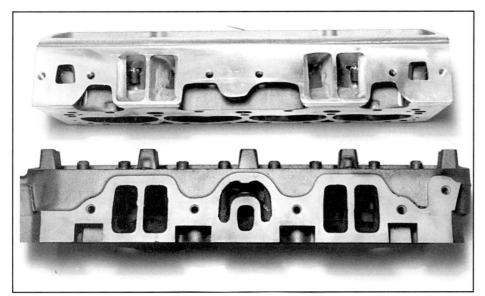

Notice that the port layout and size of these two heads are very similar; however, actual port volume and opening size on the upper head are actually larger and it flows better as well. This top head, which is a Brodix small-block Chevy head, illustrates the limitations of a stock Mopar head.

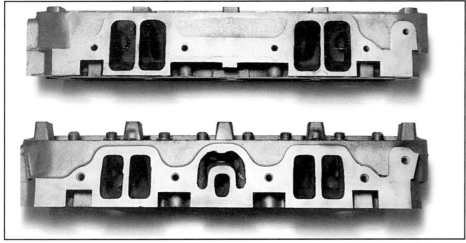

Original Max Wedge head has a much larger intake port than a regular production head. Though the Max head has a larger port, it is not a raised port design.

will allow you to figure out the relationship between port opening size and rpm range. If the engine has a large port volume, the available "column" of air that is available when the intake valve opens can be larger.

Port Area vs. Volume

While this is good, larger port volumes usually mean larger port openings, which mean lower velocity. There is a balance between these two and it is usually due to the physical area that the head must fit into. If the head had small port area but large volume, it would need to be physically larger, meaning it would have to have a longer port, and therefore it may not fit on the engine. Imagine if the port were the size of a drinking straw. The area is very small but the volume could be made large by making the straw very long. Obviously it would have to be so long that it wouldn't even fit under the hood! While this is an extreme

illustration, it should help you understand the relationship between area and volume.

Exhaust Port—The Wedge head has a strong exhaust port that usually doesn't require too much work. Because the exhaust gas leaves the head under pressure from the cylinder it is not as important as the intake port, which has to rely on Mother Nature's atmospheric pressure. The cam timing can be altered by adding more exhaust duration if the exhaust port is weak. Generally the exhaust port should flow in the area of 70% of the intake flow. If it is much more than this, the head has a weak intake port. If it is less than this, some additional duration can be added to the exhaust lobe of the cam.

Flow Numbers

On the subject of flow numbers, keep in mind that every flow bench is different. Do not take any flow number as an absolute. Always be sure that the flow bench test pressure is the same in any comparison. Consider the entire flow curve, not just the peak number at .850" lift. Remember that even a big cam spends much more time below .500" lift than above. A head with a very broad flow curve will make the best overall power.

Porting

Porting heads is something that everybody with a hand grinder thinks they can do. Most people wouldn't bore their own block or balance their own crank but they don't think twice about porting their own heads, which is usually a mistake, because head porting is the single most sensitive power-producing modification in the entire engine. Porting without a flow

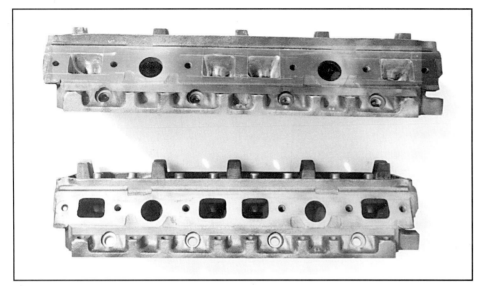

Ported production head on top shows how the exhaust ports have been raised slightly and enlarged for more airflow. Do not gasket-match the exhaust port floor. If that is done, the head will flow worse than stock.

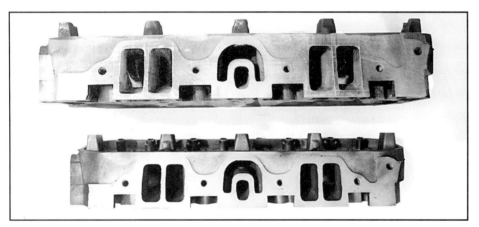

Ported production head (top) shows what gasket matching is supposed to look like. Port size is increased, allowing more airflow.

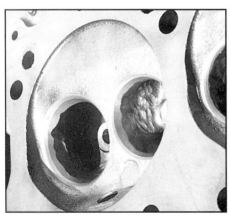

A bowl area that has not been ported correctly. This head looks like the Mopar templates were used, albeit incorrectly. Airflow is the most important part of making horsepower. If you can't do it right, leave it to the pros.

A close-up of how not to do porting. All surfaces must be smooth for maximum airflow.

bench is like honing without a dial bore gauge. How do you know how much material to remove? What flow figures do you have to know if the porting is increasing flow, and by how much? Without a flow bench, you can't tell, certainly not visually. A cylinder wall looks the same at .030" over or .033" over.

So if you are building a high performance racing engine, leave the porting to the pros. If you want to do some mild porting and polishing on your own, go slow and remove as little as possible. This way there is something left for the pros to work with if you decide to have the heads done at a later time.

STOCK HEADS

The first heads to look at are the stock head family. I will only give some background on Max Wedge heads because they are so difficult to find, so do not base your engine plan on the Max Wedge head unless your class rules specifically require it.

The 1962–1964 Max Wedge heads are popular because of their larger intake and exhaust ports as well as a larger 1.88" exhaust valve. While these things were a low-tech move in the right direction at the time, as soon as the 426 Hemi appeared in 1964, all wedge head development stopped. The lowly wedge was relegated to street duty, where it quickly established itself as a contender. The good flowing, small ports added up to large amounts of usable torque, which was perfect for the street. In fact, many Hemis were embarrassed by their wedge cousins.

Significant factory development on the wedge head did not start until the early 1990s. In the meantime, the

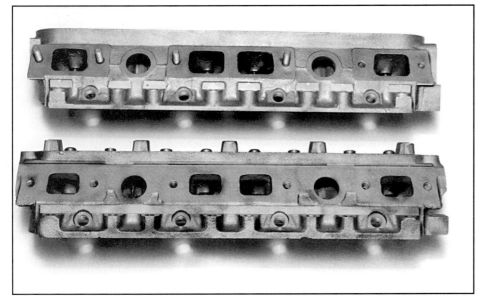

The production Max Wedge head on top shows how much larger the exhaust ports are compared to a "stock" head on bottom. The Max head also uses a 1.88" exhaust valve size. Do not attempt to enlarge the smaller ports on the stock head to the Max Wedge port size.

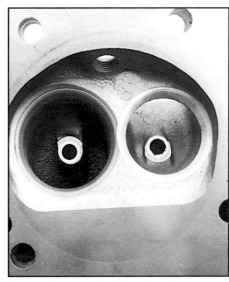

Due to its large 1.88" exhaust valve, an unleaded seat installation in a Max Wedge head will overlap into the intake seat. This will not cause any problems.

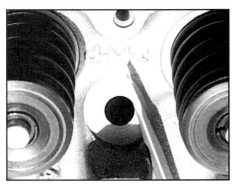

A factory Stage 4 or 5 head can be identified by this logo cast into the head. The Stage 5 head also features a milled valve cover gasket surface.

aftermarket companies discovered the potential of the wedge engine and began producing high horsepower heads for it. Currently there are over 10 different types of heads available for the B block, which is quite a change from the not so distant past when we were stuck with only factory iron heads. But before we discuss what's available in the aftermarket, let's continue on with the stock heads.

Layout & Features

The B engine has "decent" stock heads. With a 2.08" intake and a 1.74"

exhaust valve size on all 1967-up heads (which are the most common), the heads are on par with other domestic heads like those from GM and Ford. Because the ports in the heads are relatively small, these engines produce long, broad torque curves that are ideal for racing. The stock port size eventually becomes a limiting factor in high rpm power, so a larger port becomes necessary.

All of the other production heads share similar port layouts and features. With the exception of the pre-1964 heads, all production heads have cast in rocker support pedestals and six-bolt valve covers. The early heads should be avoided since the aluminum rocker stands are not very strong and finding replacements for them as well as the required four-bolt valve covers is nearly impossible.

Stock Head Recommendations

Now that you know what to avoid, what do you actually want? It depends on your requirements. All of the

1967-up heads can be made into strong performers. Some castings are more desirable for certain specific features, like the 1967 915 head with its closed chamber, or the 1976–'78 452 head with induction hardened exhaust seats. If the cam lift is kept below .500" lift, every casting can be made to flow virtually the same. There may be myths and rumors, but the flow bench doesn't lie. So if you're keeping lift to below .500", then don't sweat the casting numbers—any will work fine. The early '70s heads, like the 346, 902 and 213 heads, have partially hardened seats that should hold up well with unleaded fuel. Only the 452 had true induction hardened seats and all the pre-1972 heads will require exhaust seat inserts for use with unleaded gas. This is a better (cheaper) way to go in the long run as compared with fuel additives.

Stock Heads For Racing Only

For an engine that will only be raced, the two best heads to use are the 1968–1970 906 casting and the

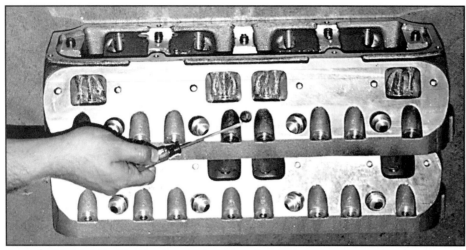

This hole can be installed between the center exhaust ports to provide additional cooling to this area. A water line (into the return side of the cooling system) is run from here into the cooling system to allow the water to circulate through this hot area. This part of the head runs the hottest since there are two exhaust valves next to each other. This modification is a must for heavy nitrous use.

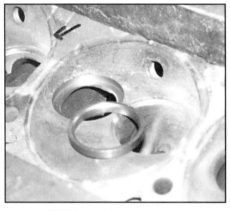

If a pre-1974 head is going to be used with unleaded fuel, a hardened exhaust seat must be installed to prevent damage to the head. These seats must be installed by a good machine shop with good equipment. Only the exhaust seats need this, the intake seat is fine as is since the valve runs much cooler.

If a cam much over .550 lift is used with a production head, the valve guides will have to be shortened to prevent the retainer from hitting it. This guide has also been cut for the smaller PC style Teflon seals to fit inside a double valve spring. The spring pads have also been cut down for use with the double spring.

aforementioned 452 casting.

906 Casting—The 906 head has a combustion chamber size of approximately 83cc as cast. The 906 (and the closed chamber 74cc version, the 915 casting) head has the best floor of any of the production heads and as such can flow the greatest amount of air at high (.650+) lift. To gain the flow at the high lifts requires a considerable amount of work to the floor of the intake port. Though the usual talk is not to touch the floor of

the port (which is true for a medium set of heads) big flow numbers at high lifts will only come from pushing the floor back. This is very difficult to do correctly and should not be attempted unless you have access to a flow bench.

452 Casting—The 452 head, on the other hand, has a fairly flat floor that's easy to port and flows almost as well as the 906 head. If you're building a bracket car and want to try your hand

at porting, use the 452 head. Remember that the 452 has about a 90cc combustion chamber as cast, so figure on a big dome or a lot of milling to get good compression.

If the cam lift is under .550" lift, gasket matching the intake port will have very little effect on flow. Granted the heads may look racier with the gasket matching, but they will not really flow any better. This is not to say don't do it, because it won't hurt flow either. The point is, if it helps at .600" lift and you are only opening the valve .484" what have you gained? For higher lift cams, by all means, do it.

However, do not gasket-match the exhaust ports. If this is done, the flow will usually be worse than stock. The roof of the exhaust port can be raised slightly, but leave the floor intact. The 452 also seems to be more resistant to cracking in the area under the center two exhaust ports than the 906.

General Stock Head Modifications

All production heads should have bronze guides installed because the factory guides are probably long since worn out. If the guides are sloppy, the valve will move around and wear out the valve job quickly. This will make the engine less consistent as well.

If double valve springs are going to be used, the step in the spring seat will have to be cut flat. The guide top will have to be shortened for lifts over .550" to provide adequate clearance to the bottom of the retainer. Always check for retainer to seal clearance when using a high lift cam.

Valves—For performance use, all the valves should be replaced with new one-piece stainless steel units. The factory valves are a two-piece

Mopar Stage 6 head (top) features a raised exhaust port with 1.81" valve for increased flow and straight spark plugs.

The Mopar Stage 6 head (bottom) has a heart-shaped chamber of 78cc and straight spark plugs.

Max Wedge engines use a unique 1.88" exhaust valve. This size is not recommended for the stock head because the port is too small for it.

AFTERMARKET HEADS

If you are building a serious racing engine, you will have to consider a set of aftermarket performance heads. If your budget is such that you can only afford to spend money in one area, this is it. Fortunately, the aftermarket has produced quite a few high performance heads for the Mopar big block.

Mopar Performance

Mopar Performance, Chrysler's racing and performance parts division, offers a few high performance heads for the B engine. They are the cast iron Stage 5 and the aluminum Stage 6 head. Their catalog actually features more than just these two heads but the others are produced by Brodix, so they will be covered in the Brodix section.

Stage 5 Head—The Stage 5 head is basically a stock 452 head with slightly revised ports and more material around the intake port to allow for more porting. Because it is so similar to a stock head, its performance potential is only slightly better. For this reason, this head is not a very cost effective way to go, unless you just want new castings. If you happen to get a set at a swap meet or your class rules require them, they are a direct bolt-on replacement for a stock head.

The intake ports can be made larger than a stock head but I do not recommend opening them up to Max Wedge size because the rest of the port will still be small, and the flow

design with the head and stem conically welded together where they meet. With aggressive cams and heavy springs, these valves can fail. Also it's common for the exhaust valve stems to be worn out so they will require replacement anyway.

With the cost of good valves being so reasonable, they are well worth the investment, especially when you consider that the common oversize of 2.14" intake and 1.81" exhaust are usually the same price as stock size replacements. It's like getting power for free! These larger valves allow for new seats to be cut into the heads which re-establishes the valve height

in the bowl area. A wedge head likes the valve as high as possible in the bowl. After lots of use or valve jobs, the valves will sink, which will hurt flow. There also are 2.19" intake and 1.84" exhaust valves available for using in heads that have worn seats with the 2.14"/1.81" combo. The ports are really not large enough to effectively use these super big sizes; you will gain little or no additional flow, so start out with the 2.14"/1.81" valves and only go larger if the seats become worn out. These larger sizes will allow a set of heads to be saved without having to install valve sets in the head.

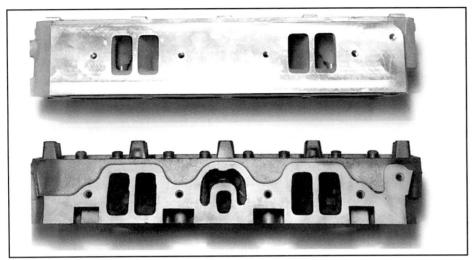

The Stage 6 (top) head has a stock size intake port but it's been raised to gain flow. The amount it has been raised is equal to the difference of a raised block over a low-deck block. What this means is that a Stage 6 head on a low-deck block actually uses a raised block intake manifold. For use on a RB block, intake manifold spacers are required.

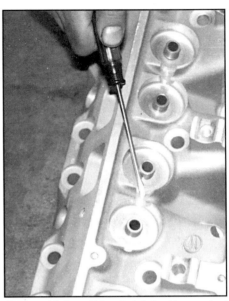

By machining this slot into the spring pockets of a Stage 6 head, oil drain back will be increased and the valve stem seal will have an easier time doing its job.

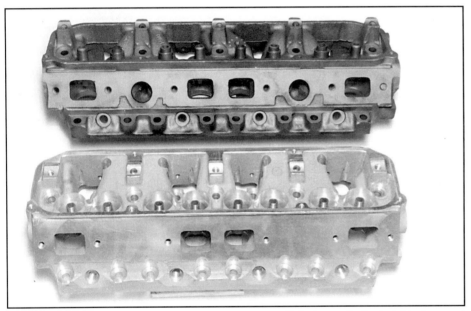

Stage 6 head (bottom) has raised exhaust ports but still features stock straight plugs and rocker pedestals. This head can also use all stock-style components. It is the easiest aluminum head to upgrade with.

increase will be slight. The additional material around the intake port will require the use of special intake rocker arms with additional pushrod offset to move the pushrod away from the port wall. This is also true of the older Stage 4 head. These heads have 452 head type combustion chambers which are around 92cc.

Stage 6—The Mopar Stage 6

aluminum head has been out since the early 1990s and has been controversial among Mopar enthusiasts since. The quality of the heads made during the first few years was so poor, that it was not uncommon to have them leak water and oil. To their credit, Mopar was quick to act, and completely changed the casting process to correct the

problem, so any of the new heads purchased today are much higher quality and will provide many years of trouble-free service.

However the head still can't seem to shake its bad reputation, which is unfortunate. The Stage 6 head is well-suited for racing use especially on low-block engines of 475 cubic inches or less. It is a true bolt-on replacement for a stock iron head because it uses production valves, springs, pushrods, valve covers, oil system and rocker arms. As such, the Stage 6 is an excellent replacement for a stock set of heads (especially if the stock ones are cracked!) because all of the parts can be taken from the stock heads and installed in the Stage 6 heads. This can save quite a bit of money.

The intake ports are the same as stock, but they are raised to give a straighter shot at the valve. Because of this design, this head can flow over 40% more than a stock head if properly prepared. The intake ports are raised the same amount as the raised block is over a low deck block.

The Stage 6 head had some porosity problems early in its production. These early heads can be identified by its larger foundry symbol shown on right. This head should be avoided. The newer heads (left) are all checked for hardness and have a much different foundry symbol. Note the giant crack as shown by the dark line in the dye in the exhaust face of the older head!

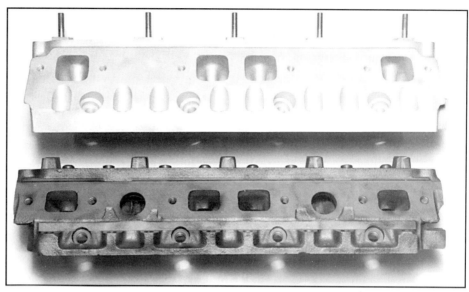

Indy 440-1 (top) has all the typical features found in a good head; thick decks, raised ports and angled plugs. With its 1.81" exhaust valve size, it will flow enough to produce excellent power. Stock head is at bottom.

So if you are going to use Stage 6 heads on a low-deck block, you will need a raised block intake manifold, which will fit without any spacers. If the heads are being used on a raised block, they will require the use of intake manifold spacers to make the high deck intake manifold fit.

The stock valley pan intake gasket on the Stage 6 will not work on low deck blocks (since the ports are raised) so some type of valley tray will have to be fabricated or purchased. This will, however, allow the manifold to be removed without having to open up the valley. On the raised block, the valley can be sealed by using an old stock valley tray gasket with the intake ports cut off to leave only the valley part of the gasket behind. This remaining gasket will seal the valley and the very edge that seals to the head will fit in a machined groove that's in the spacer plates.

To seal the intake ports, use a Fel-Pro 1216 intake gasket. If you are using the spacers, use a gasket on each side. The stock valve seats are cut for 2.14"/1.81" valves. Since the exhaust port is basically production size that's raised slightly, don't worry about going with a larger exhaust valve. These heads have a good exhaust port that needs little work to be able to flow well. The stock intake seat can accept up to a 2.19" valve, and because the port is better than stock, it will respond with a little more flow from the larger intake valve. The port can support a 2.25" valve in the intake if maximum power (and porting) is what you are trying to achieve, but this requires the stock seat to be replaced with an oversized one. This is very costly to do, and if you reach this point, you should go with a larger set of heads.

Because the Stage 6 head flows so well from a stock size port, port velocity is high, and as a result they make excellent low and mid-range torque and power.

Other than the problems described with the intake manifold, these heads bolt on directly without any extra parts. The newer Stage 6 heads feature a heart-shaped combustion chamber of about 78cc's while the older heads have 90cc chambers. Avoid the older castings for the reasons mentioned previously.

As this is being written, Mopar is putting the finishing touches on a new version of the Stage 6 dubbed the Stage 6B. This head is the same as the original Stage 6 in all areas except the intake port, which is the size of the Max Wedge ports.

This will allow the head to support more cubic inches and/or rpm than the original head. These new Stage 6B heads will require the use of special offset intake rocker arms to clear the larger intake ports.

Indy Cylinder Heads

In the early 1990's Indy Cylinder Heads, in Indianapolis, Indiana, recognized the need for high output B engine cylinder heads. The first two heads they developed were the 440-1 aluminum and 440-c iron heads, which were high quality and well

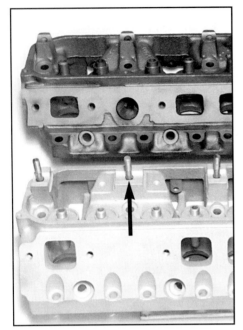

Indy 440-1 head (bottom) has cast-in rocker pedestals. Stock-style shafts can be used but special rockers are required. Note the extra beef around the pedestals.

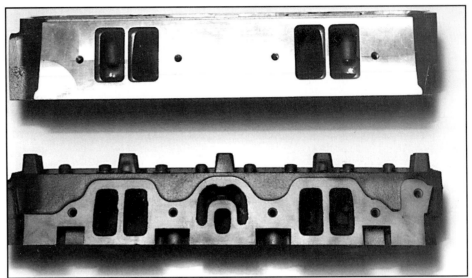

The Indy 440-1 head (top) features a Max Wedge intake port size that is also slightly raised for increased airflow over the original design. Notice that more of the valve guide is showing in the port. This allows for a straighter shot at the valve further increasing airflow. Stock head (bottom) pales in comparison.

received by Mopar performance enthusiasts and racers. After this initial success, Indy developed two other wedge heads, the 572-13 for larger (4.500") bore engines and the S/R head, which uses a stock intake manifold.

440-1 Heads—The 440-1 heads could be best described as a set of modified Max Wedge heads that have been ported. Indy essentially incorporated all of the best design features found in a stock head and improved them.

For example, the intake port on a stock iron head has a slight dogleg right past the port entry to clear the intake pushrod. Indy straightened the port out in this area by widening it, which required two changes. First, the pushrod had to be moved out of the way, which required a special offset intake rocker arm, and second, the stock oil passage that feeds the rocker shaft had to be eliminated. Indy solved the oiling problem by feeding

Indy 440-1 head (bottom) has 75cc combustion chambers as cast and angled spark plugs. Note the smooth contour of the head around the valve guide area. This makes for easier porting and more airflow.

the oil to the heads externally from the oil pressure sender passage on the top of the block in the rear. Both of these two modifications allowed the port to have a much straighter shot at the valve, resulting in more flow. The valve sizes are 2.19" intake and 1.81" exhaust to allow the for the use of existing pistons and bore sizes. A 2.25" intake valve will fit the stock seat with no problems but should only be used on large bore engines.

While they were at the drawing board, Indy specified a lighter 11/32" valve stem size to save weight and increase performance. The only other modifications are a slightly raised exhaust port and angled spark plugs to

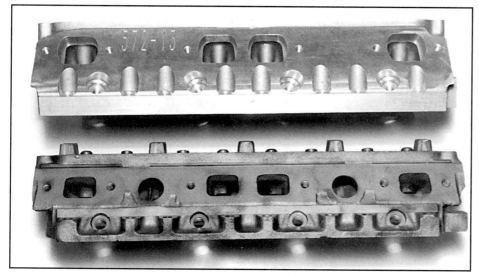

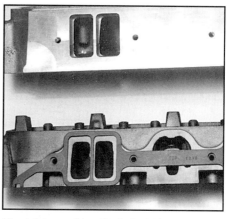

The intake port on the Indy 440-1 (top) and 572-13 head is based on the production Max Wedge. A Max Wedge gasket laid on a stock 906 head (bottom) really shows the difference.

Indy 572-13 head (top) has huge, raised exhaust ports with a 1.88" valve size. Note the angled spark plugs. A new version of this head dubbed the 600-13 will use even larger valves and ports but requires a special 4.840" bore spacing block. Stock head is shown at bottom for comparison.

prevent the plug from getting washed out by the intake charge. A separate block valley tray seals up the engine and allows for easy intake manifold removal without opening up the engine at the same time. The bottom line is that Indy Cylinder Heads identified all of the problems and limitations of the stock head design and corrected them in the 440-1.

In fact, the Indy 440-1 heads can be used as a replacement for a set of original Max Wedge heads. A stock Max Wedge cross ram intake will bolt right up to an Indy head and on the opposite side an Indy intake manifold will bolt on to a set of Max Wedge heads.

The basic design of the 440-1 Indy head enables it to be bolted on to a stock block with a no modifications. In fact, all Indy heads (except the 572-13), can be used with no block or piston modifications since the valves are at the stock 15 degree angle and location. The stock 75cc combustion chamber can be cut even smaller if desired. Because the head is taller than stock, special head bolts (or head

studs) and longer pushrods are required.

Indy has several intake manifolds available for both the low block and the raised block, and for "regular" Holley carbs or Dominator type carbs. As a note, for engines under 500 cubic inches using a Dominator carb, you'll get better performance by using the regular manifold with an adapter plate for the Dominator. Overall the Indy 440-1 head is the best head package to use at the moment for bracket racing with a larger (500 cubic inch or more) engine. The head is easy to use, all the parts fit and they are reasonably priced.

S/R Head—The Indy S/R head has most of the features of the 440-1 head except for a stock port size and location. This smaller port makes the head more suitable for smaller engines and allows for the use of the existing intake manifold. Because the intake port is in the stock location (complete with the stock heads inherent slight dogleg) production rocker arms can be used. This can save some money since your old

rocker arms and intake can be used on these heads. But the oil line kit, head bolts, valley tray and pushrods will all have to be changed to use them. The valve and chamber size remains the same as with the 440-1 heads. These heads can be easily opened up to Max Wedge size if needed.

572-13 Head—With the advent of the 4.500" bore blocks, there became a need for even more flow. In keeping with the theme of improving an existing design, Indy improved and modified their 440-1 head to create the 572-13 head. These modifications include: Angle milling to change the valve angle to 13 degrees; moving the exhaust valve away from the intake .050" to allow a 2.300" intake valve; larger 1.88" exhaust valves; and milling off the stock style rocker arm shaft support pedestals for use with the superior Jesel or T & D rocker arms.

Because the valves in this head are so big, it requires a block with a minimum bore size of 4.500", and revised valve notches in the pistons. And because the rocker pedestals are removed, the rocker arm system has to be different. For these heads, the

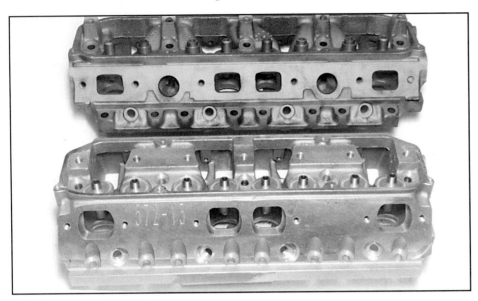

The Indy 572-13 head (bottom, stock head is at top) has the rocker support pedestals machined for a race rocker system from Jesel or T&D. When this setup is used, either spray bar oiling from the valve cover or through pushrod oiling must be used. The exhaust ports are larger on the 440-1 to work with its larger 1.88" exhaust valve.

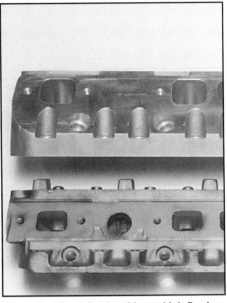

Brodix "original" B-1 head has a high flowing, raised exhaust port and angled plugs. It's interesting to note that this head uses only a 1.77" exhaust valve but still flows well. This small exhaust valve is required by its large 2.30" intake valve while still retaining the ability to bolt on to 4.350+ cylinders. A new version of this head the "B-1 MC" moves the exhaust valve .050" away from the intake to allow even larger valves when used only on large bore engines.

rockers are mounted on individual shafts (one small shaft per cylinder) that are attached to a special steel holder that is bolted to the head. This allows for the removal of a pair of rockers at a time if something breaks instead of having to remove an entire shaft. While this system is easier to work on and very strong, it does not allow for rocker arm oiling to be done through the shaft, because there are four separate shafts per head.

To oil the valvetrain on this 572-13 head, Indy uses a spray bar mounted in the valve cover (supplied by the oil pressure sender passage in the block like the 440-1 head) to literally spray the rockers and springs with oil from above. While this system is adequate, these rocker arms can also be pressure-fed with oil from the pushrods. This is also easily done by using the special "pushrod oiling" lifters that are available. Solid and hydraulic cams can use AMC lifters while roller cams can use special Competition Cams roller lifters made just for this purpose.

Pushrod oiling also requires lifter bores in the block to be bushed or too much oil may reach the heads. As such, drill an oil feed hole of .040" in the bushing to feed the pushrods with oil. Both oiling systems will work but the pushrod oil system has the advantage of delivering pressurized oil to the rockers instead of just spraying oil everywhere. Other than this modification, the 572-13 heads use and require all of the other Indy specific components like their other heads.

Brodix

The Brodix B-1 head was the first commercially successful head for the B engine. Developed in the early '80s, the release of this head coincided with the development of higher output Mopar engines. There were other attempts at making an aluminum head during this era (the Zeeker head is an example), but none were very successful and soon disappeared. Since Brodix was already in the aluminum head business, it was easy

for them to produce a quality head. As with the Indy line of heads, the B-1 family eventually grew into five separate cylinder heads as demand increased and more Mopar engines were raced. The B-1 family also powered Mopar's Pro Stock drag race effort for several years and powered them to three world championships.

B-1—The first head was simply called the B-1. This head design was based on the premise that "bigger is better." This head has the largest intake ports of any bolt-on wedge head. With these huge ports and 2.300" intake valves, the B-1 is capable of some impressive flow rates. Unfortunately though, these flow rates through the giant ports come at the expense of velocity. The exhaust ports are similar to the stock design, but are raised for more flow. An interesting note here is that the

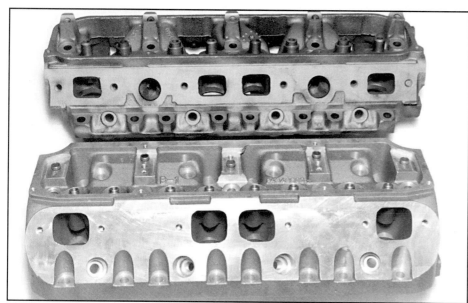

Overview of the original B-1 head (bottom). Note the machined pads for the rocker arms. Double bolts are used on the three center rocker supports making the rocker assembly very strong. Angled plugs and raised exhaust ports are typical for such a race head. Stock head is shown at top for comparison.

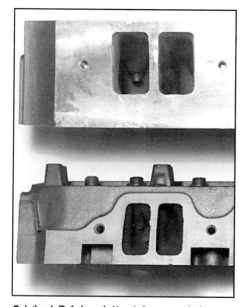

Original B-1 head (top) has much larger, raised ports. This head can be made to flow almost double the amount of air of a stock production head (bottom).

exhaust valve size is a relatively small 1.77". This smaller size exhaust valve allows the head to bolt on to blocks with relatively small bore sizes (4.350"+) without a problem. A larger exhaust valve would have required a larger bore block (as with the Indy 572-13 head), which wasn't readily available at the time unless you purchased an ultra-expensive aluminum blocks. Nevertheless, the exhaust port is still capable of flowing nearly 70% of intake flow (which is fine) and with great velocity since the valve is small.

Though the head can make a tremendous amount of power, the slow intake velocity made for weak bottom-end power, especially on smaller (440 range) displacement engines. For this reason, the "original" B-1 is really not recommended for engines under 500 cubic inches unless you like twisting the engine to 7000 rpm or more. The combustion chamber has angled spark plugs and a volume of 72cc. This can be reduced to less than 50cc if needed. Because of this, high compression with a flat-top piston is not a problem for these heads.

On the subject of pistons, stock valve pockets will not work. A custom set is required with B-1 valve pockets.

The only off-the-shelf intake for these heads is a single four-barrel (Dominator style) for the low-deck block. Spacers are available to use this intake on a raised block. Any other intake configuration will have to be fabricated.

B-1 MC—With the availability of larger bore blocks, there is a new B-1 head on the market, the B-1 MC head. This head is the same as the original except that the exhaust valve is moved away from the intake by .050" to allow a 2.400" intake valve to be used. As a result, this head can flow about 10% more air than the original B-1, but this head can only be used on the 4.500"+ bore blocks. Slightly different rocker arms and piston valve pockets are required. For the larger bore blocks the B-1 MC head is the one to use. It is easy to install, and the 2.400" intake valve makes it an attractive option for increasing power on larger displacement engines.

B-1 PS—The Brodix designers realized that the big ports on the basic B-1 design were causing low-speed torque problems on the smaller engines, so they developed the B-1 PS head. This head is very similar to the original head but with a much smaller, raised intake port. Think of it as an original B-1 head with the floor of the intake port filled in. This head was one of the first efforts at making a serious Pro Stock head for the B engine and it was fairly successful. However, these heads are not very common, so your chances of finding a set or using them is slim. Although no longer mass produced, Brodix will still custom-make a set of these heads upon request; however, you'll need a custom-fabricated intake manifold. Both of these facts obviously make it an expensive option.

B-1 TS—When Brodix pulled the plug on the PS head, they went back

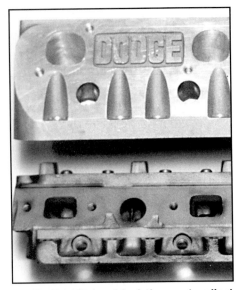

Brodix B-1 TS head had the most radical exhaust ports of any wedge head. Almost D-shaped and much higher than stock, they will flow the most of any head with its 1.90" exhaust valve. Plugs are only slightly angled. Stock head is shown at bottom for comparison.

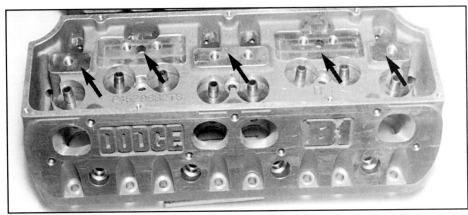

Rocker gear on Brodix B-1 TS head is about as complex as it gets. Using individual rocker shafts for each rocker arm, this head uses five different support blocks! All of this is required due to its canted valve arrangement. It is complicated but it still works great.

The B-1 TS head has a wild chamber with a centrally located spark plug for good combustion. Finished chamber size will vary depending on application.

to the drawing board and designed a completely new head. All of the previous Brodix designs had been based on their ability to bolt on to a stock block. However, it was apparent in the late '80s and early '90s that stock-based technology wasn't going to win Pro Stock races. Brodix went all-out and the TS head is the result. This head is a radical departure from anything they or anyone else had ever done before. This head features non-siamese intake ports (like a Hemi), canted valves and radically raised exhaust ports. The exhaust ports are designed like the stock head's because NHRA rules at the time required Pro Stock heads to have the same valve layout as their production counterpart. The TS head took the stock layout to the limit. The equally spaced intake ports require a different block bolt pattern and lifter spacing.

There are several versions of this head that are tailored to specific blocks. There is a version for use on a stock Hemi block that uses 2.325"/1.900" valves, a version for the "Wayne County" 4.840" bore spacing block with 2.400"/1.94" valves, and the newest version for 4.900" bore spacing blocks for use with even larger valves. In addition to the block requirements and modifications, this head uses special rockers from Jesel or T & D, all mounted on six individual support blocks per head. The rockers are oiled through the pushrods by special Pro Stock-style roller lifters. In keeping with the Pro Stock theme, a sheet metal intake manifold must be custom-fabricated.

As you can see, using this head requires some complicated modifications, so you shouldn't even consider it unless you are "totally serious" as the name (TS) suggests.

Currently, Keith Black and Indy make blocks that can be used with this head. It's doubtful that any of the old C&S Development Pro Stock blocks are around in good shape for you to use.

However, despite the extra work involved, don't be afraid to use these heads. While they have some special requirements, most all-out racing heads do. Parts like Jesel rockers may

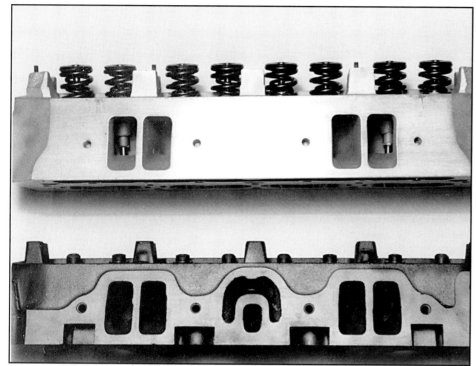

Brodix B-1 BS (top) head has stock size ports in the stock location. This allows a stock intake manifold to be used. With its 2.200" intake valve, airflow is greatly increased over the stock head (bottom).

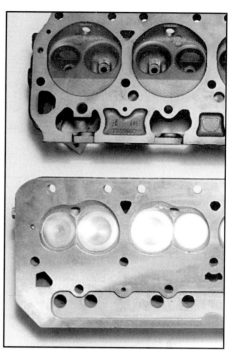

Chamber of the B-1 BS head (bottom) is a small 65cc as cast. This allows for high compression even with flat-top pistons. The 2.20" intake and 1.81" exhaust valves may require valve pocket relocation in some pistons.

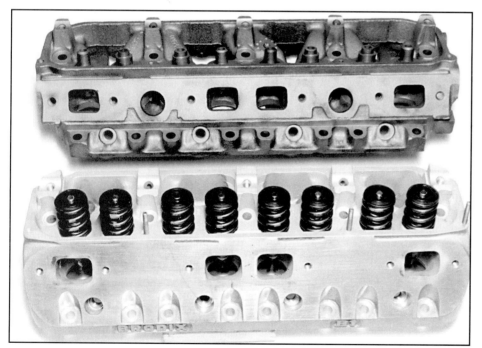

Brodix B-1 BS head (bottom) has stock-style cast-in rocker pedestals allowing easy shaft installation. This design is simple and strong.

seem strange to Mopar guys; they are normal to the GM racers because this head is very similar to what they use.

The TS head will flow more air than any other head for the big block, and the fact that it ran successfully in Pro Stock is proof that it is up to the task of just about any type of drag racing.

B-1 BS—After putting so much development into Pro Stock racing heads, Brodix decided to produce a milder head for less competitive racing applications, specifically the amateur racer. The result is the B-1 BS head. This is a bolt-on head that uses a stock intake manifold but BS specific rocker arms on a stock-style continuous shaft that is oiled like a production head. The head has 2.200"/1.81" valves and a 65cc chamber with straight spark plugs. This small chamber is nice for getting high compression on a smaller engine with flat-top pistons.

The BS head flows about the same as other stock port, big-valve heads; however, likewise, there is a limit as to how much as head can flow with the stock configuration. These heads make a good bracket or street head, are easy to use, and are priced inline with other "small port" aluminum heads.

As for modifications, slightly

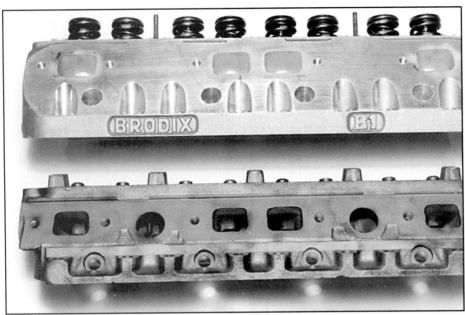

Brodix B-1 BS head features a raised exhaust port with a 1.81" exhaust valve and a thick deck for strength. Spark plugs are slightly angled. Stock head is on bottom for comparison.

The combustion chamber of the Brewer head is a high swirl design. Note the large bowl area and the straight shot from the port into the bowl. Plugs are angled toward the exhaust to prevent them from being washed by the incoming fuel charge.

The B-1 head requires oil return lines back into the pan. Make sure to route the oil lines to clear the frame and starter.

different valve pockets are required and the 65cc chamber may require some piston adjustment; you may even have to go so far as to get a new set to obtain the correct compression ratio. As with all other B-1 heads, the castings are high quality and very durable.

Brewer Heads

Another aftermarket high output head worth considering are those produced by Fred Brewer Sales. These Brewer heads have been produced since the early 1990s, but in very limited quantities. The Brewer head is similar to the B-1 PS head since it has relatively small, raised ports. The general layout of the head is very similar to an AMC Pro Stock head from the early 1970s.

The Brewer head features a stock valve layout but with radically raised intake and exhaust ports and 2.250"/ 1.81" valves. There is a large bore version with 2.375"/1.86" valves for larger engines.

The Brewer head is a direct bolt-on replacement for a stock cylinder block. The intake ports are raised so much that the valves are even longer than in a TS head. This port will flow more than any head other than the TS and do it with a smaller port. The intake ports are very close to a stock-size Hemi, so the port velocity is still very high, while the raised, D-shaped exhaust can flow more than some of the smaller aluminum head's intake port!

The Brewer currently uses rocker arms by T&D Rocker Arms in Carson

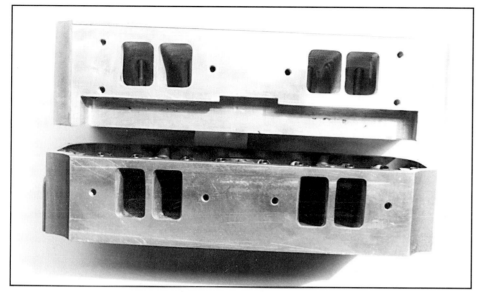

The Brewer head on top gains part of its flow advantage over the B-1 head (bottom) by its raised intake ports. The higher the port the more gradual the transition is from the floor of the intake runner to the head, which results in more airflow.

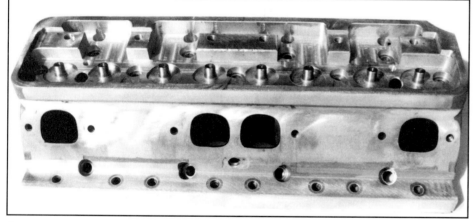

Brewer wedge head has a true D-shaped exhaust port that is raised and used with a 1.86" valve. Note the different deck design and the raised and angled spark plugs. This port will flow more than any other inline wedge head for use on a standard-style block.

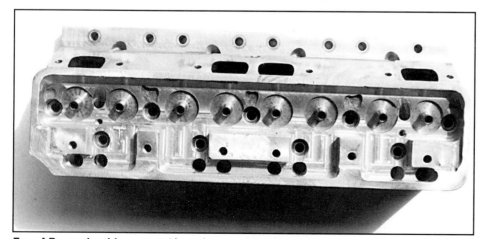

Top of Brewer head has no cast-in rocker supports. The rocker arm system uses a machined holder that runs along the head. In this way, each cylinder's rocker arms is on it own short shaft making it easy to service.

City, Nevada, and are a continuous holder design, with separate shafts for each cylinder. As such, they must be oiled through the pushrods, so you'll have to bush the lifter bores and use special lifters as well.

There is a low-block single Dominator intake available (with spacers for the raised block) at the moment, and sheet metal tunnel rams are also available. The head has angled spark plugs with a 62cc chamber as cast. Because the chamber is so small, most engines will need a dished piston to get good compression, which puts some of the combustion chamber right into the piston and gives slightly better thermal efficiency.

The valve covers are unique too in that they only use two bolts through the center to fasten them to the head (like a new-style small-block Chevy), and an integral O-ring on the sealing surface which requires no valve cover gasket.

As I mentioned, these heads have been produced in very limited numbers. The few sets that have been released have performed extremely well due to the high flow and the small port. My real world, on-track testing has shown that the heads make maximum power at about 500 rpm less than any of the larger port heads. Unfortunately, most of the early head casting produced in the early 1990s were poor quality and tended to leak. However, Brewer has contracted with a major head manufacturer to produce a new version of the heads with high quality, leak-proof castings. These heads have been produced since mid-1998. If you're looking for a used set, I don't recommend any produced before this date.

For an all-out race engine with

Close up of professionally gasket-matched intake port shows what it's supposed to look like. Straight lines with tight corners are the goal. Small chips in edges of ports are factory casting flaws.

tremendous bottom end torque, these are an ideal head. They would be very well-suited for faster brackets and smaller, competition-eliminator-style engines.

GENERAL RECOMMENDATIONS

Overall, if you are bracket racing or cruising on the street with a smaller engine of 475 cid or less, use one of the "smaller" heads like the Stage 5, B-1 BS or Indy SR. All of these heads will give virtually the same flow and power. Since they all have slightly different features, choose the ones that best fit into your plan based on cost and what existing components you might want to use over.

For larger engines 500–540 cube range, a larger head like the B-1, Indy or Brewer is recommended. The larger engines can use the additional airflow and port size of these larger heads. For engines larger than 540 cubic inches, only the largest heads like the B-1, Indy 572-13, TS, or Brewer large valve should be used. These engines will require the largest airflow to make maximum power. There is always a trade-off between port size/flow, engine size and rpm range. Use the formulas on page 150 to calculate the port window area and airflow requirements for your engine size. This is not to say that an Indy 440-1 won't work on a 572 cid engine or a B-1 BS won't work on a 500 cid engine; They just won't produce maximum power. A head that is "too small" for the displacement will produce a ton of low- and mid-range torque, which in some applications may be better. The opposite is true for a head that is "too large"—it will be a high rpm screamer.

HEAD GASKETS

All factory stock engines were equipped with a steel shim head gasket. As the name implies, this gasket consisted of nothing more than a thin (.017") stamped piece of steel. Because of this design, they are not recommended for racing use. Although they can be used to gain some compression with an iron head, they are very prone to failure.

When an engine is running, the head is always bouncing up and down on the block a tiny amount, because the force of combustion is trying to blow the head off. This bouncing is a normal part of the engine running. When power is increased, so is this combustion pressure, and the demands on the gasket are high; the shim gasket can allow this pressure to leak.

If you are using aluminum heads, steel shim gaskets are definitely out because of the different expansion and contraction rates.

Composition Gaskets

The alternative is to use some type of composition head gasket. Since these gaskets are thicker (about .040"), they can absorb more bouncing and twisting before they begin to leak. Most are coated with Teflon to allow the head to "move around" without causing a failure or having to re-torque the head bolts.

Because these gaskets are thicker, the compression ratio will be reduced slightly. Depending on the type of head, the compression drop can be over .5 points. You can account for this drop by designing it into your piston and engine combination. That gets back to what I said in Chapter 1

engine and it does a great job.

For 4.500" bore blocks, Fel-Pro has a new gasket, #1039, which is similar to #1009 except for having a 4.590" bore. This gasket is .051" thick and will seal larger, high compression engines very well. It will also fit the 426 Hemi.

Copper Gaskets

Most all of the composition gaskets can withstand 13.5 compression before they can't hold the seal any longer. If this is the case, the next step up is a copper gasket. Properly used, the copper gasket will seal virtually anything. A simple piece, the copper gasket is nothing more than a sheet of copper with the correct holes punched in. Most copper gaskets are about .042" thick, but they can be obtained in many different thicknesses. While they are very soft to allow for good sealing, they should be used with an O-ring in the block or head to help seal the cylinder. Do not use them if you don't plan on O-ringing.

A drawback is that the copper gaskets are very prone to water leaks, so use some type of gasket sealer (Fel-Pro BLU4) to help prevent this problem. For this reason, copper gaskets aren't really recommended for street use.

Be sure to check the bore opening in whatever gasket you use to be sure no part of it hangs into the cylinder.

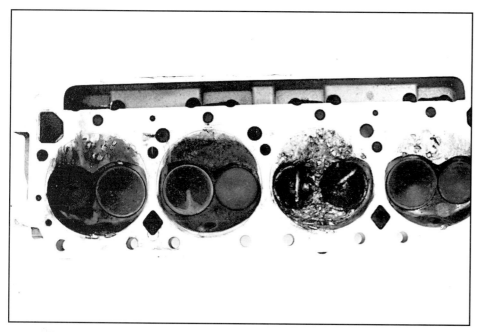

Ka-boom! A broken intake valve caused this damage in a Mopar Stage 6 head. Since the head is aluminum, it can be welded and saved. Notice the nicks in the other chambers. They are from shrapnel from the damaged cylinder transferring throughout the intake manifold to the rest of the engine.

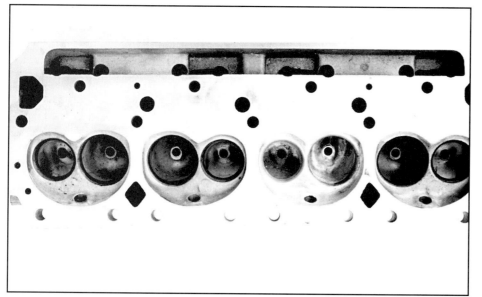

This is actually the same damaged head, ready to do battle again. Hopefully, with Chevys and Fords, not valves and seats!

on planning.

Fel-Pro—The most popular composition gaskets are those made by Fel-Pro. These "blue" gaskets, as they are called, come in three styles: #8519 PT-1 is the stock-style gasket with a 4.520" bore, tin sealing ring and no O-ring. This gasket will work up to about 12:1 compression and can be used with a 4.500 bore engine with low compression.

The race version, #1009, has a 4.410" bore, stainless sealing ring, and an integral O-ring to help sealing. This is by far the most common racing gasket for the big-block Mopar

10

CAMSHAFTS

A roller (left) cam has much more aggressive lobes than a flat-tappet cam. Because of the roller lifter, the valve can be opened and closed much faster while at the same time reducing friction on the cam. They are expensive but they are the ultimate camshaft. It just depends on the level engine you are building.

If the oil is considered the lifeblood of the engine, then the camshaft is the heartbeat. Except for the cylinder heads, no other component can have as great an effect on how the engine runs and how much power it will make. Even with a killer set of heads, the wrong cam will limit the amount of power the engine can make.

The camshaft is one of the more popular "bolt-on" items that most people put on their car. Even a dead stock, low-performance engine can be greatly improved just by slipping in a larger profile cam. Other parts, like bigger carburetors and lighter pistons all contribute, but a larger cam is the quickest, easiest and cheapest way to gain power.

CAM BASICS

All stock Mopar B engines were equipped with hydraulic camshafts, except the Max Wedge engines. These race-only engines were equipped with

solid lifter cams to produce more rpm and power.

There are many design variables that go into making a camshaft. Most racers are only concerned with the lift and duration of the cam as a measure of its performance potential. However, factors such as lobe separation, overlap and ramp speed are variables that can make two cams of the same lift and duration operate quite differently.

The ratio of duration @ .050" of lift to advertised duration determines the ramp speed and performance characteristics of the cam.

The three choices currently available are the hydraulic, solid, and roller style cams. These cams are listed in order of performance and cost. The old rule used to be that you selected hydraulic cams for street use, solid lifter cams for street and race use, and roller cams for racing only. This is definitely not the case anymore. Many street cars have solid lifter and roller lifter cams, and in

The hydraulic lifter (right) has a much higher pushrod cup than the solid lifter. For this reason, solid lifters must use longer pushrods.

fact, most new factory production cars are equipped with hydraulic roller cams. These new hydraulic roller cams have the "no maintenance, no noise" features of a normal hydraulic cam with the reduced friction and high ramp speed lobe of a roller cam. But before you get excited about buying hydraulic roller cam, there are currently none available for the Mopar big-block B engine.

The best cam would be one that could instantly open and close the valve with no wasted motion in the middle. Think of the motion of a shutter in a camera. It can almost accomplish this "instant motion" feat but a design like this would never be able to hold up in an engine. For this reason, we are stuck with a normal valve for now. It is still the best overall design when all factors are considered. Maximum power will be made with the cam that can come closest to this ideal theory. Currently this is the roller type cam. Since there is a wheel on the end of the roller lifter, it can follow the fast ramps of a

roller cam and do it with very little friction. Fortunately, Chrysler engines have the largest lifter diameter (.904") of any domestic V8 engine. This allows the ramps of a Chrysler cam to be faster and more aggressive than the competition. While this is not a big advantage for roller cams, it is very important to the hydraulic and solid cams. If the cam lobe is designed to take advantage of this fact, the engine will make more power as a result. There are several cams on the market with .904" tappet specific lobes on them. Try to use one of these designs in your engine.

Hydraulic Cams

Because the hydraulic (which is not the same as a hydraulic roller) cam is the cheapest and simplest to use, it's no surprise that it is the most popular type of cam for performance use. The larger Mopar tappet allows even the hydraulic cam to have fast ramp speeds that will make excellent power.

***Design & Operation*—**A hydraulic cam is so named because the lifters

are actually full of oil during operation. Unlike a solid or roller lifter, the hydraulic lifter body itself does not push on the pushrod. Inside a hydraulic lifter, there is an oil-filled plunger system that actuates the pushrod as the lifter moves. As the body of the lifter moves upward, the oil supply to the plunger system is cut off and the pressure inside the lifter builds because the internal volume decreases when the body moves up. Eventually the pressure inside the lifter becomes great enough to overcome the force of the valve spring and the pushrod begins to move up with the lifter. Since there is no "direct" connection with the pushrod cup and the lifter body (the oil is in between them) this system can take up any slack in the valvetrain and automatically adjust for wear or deflection. This is why hydraulic cams do not need adjusting and are quiet during operation.

Unfortunately for racers, it is also why they are limited in their performance capability. Because the pushrod movement is always lagging slightly behind the lifter body movement, the cam ramps have to be "fatter" to compensate. This is partially why a hydraulic cam will have less duration at .050" than a solid or roller for any given profile.

The other reason is because of the limitations of the valve springs due to the fragility of the lifter. Because these lifters have moving parts, they can fail if valve spring pressure is too great. Most hydraulic cams use spring pressures of about 120 lb on the seat and around 300 lb when open. By contrast, some rollers use over 300 lb of seat pressure. Lifter "pump up" is another limiting factor to performance as well. This happens when the

When installing solid or hydraulic lifters, only put the break-in lube on the bottom of the lifter. Do not put any on the sides; use oil instead. This will allow the lifter to spin freely in the bore to allow for quick break-in.

motion of the lifter is too fast for the pressure inside the lifter to control. When the lifters pump up, the engine will not be able to rev any higher. For all of these reasons, rpm with a hydraulic cam should be limited to under 6500.

Problem Solving—Because these cams do have some advantages, there are ways to correct or minimize their problems. Lifter pump-up can be minimized by using special anti-pump-up lifters. These lifters will usually extend the rpm range of a cam by about 500 additional rpm.

The preload adjustment can be changed too. Most Mopar cams are set up with about .050" preload. This means that when the valve is closed, the lifter plunger is depressed .050" into the lifter body. If the valve system wears more than this amount, the preload will be gone and the lifters will begin to clatter. The factory preload is set up to allow for long life without clattering after many miles. If the preload is lessened to about .020",

the lifters will operate at a higher rpm before they pump up. This will require adjustable pushrods or rocker arms to accomplish and they will require periodic adjustment for wear. If you have adjustable rockers, .020" preload is possible by tightening the adjusting screw of the rocker 1/2 turn past zero lash. If you have stock-style rockers and want to reduce the preload, try some rocker arm shaft shims. These shims go between the shaft and the pedestal and space the shaft up, which reduces the preload of the lifter. If any lifters clatter after you have done this, reduce the thickness of the shim. If you want to cheat, try old washers from spark plugs under the shafts. This is a quick way to see what thickness you can get away with without lifter clatter.

Lift—Most hydraulic cams are made with fairly low lift specs. Generally, cams with over .520" lift have so much duration due to their design that they are pretty low on torque. Because of the tappet size,

some cam grinders have high-lift designs with relatively short duration. Try to run under 310 degrees duration with a hydraulic cam. If lift is no problem, run as much as the heads will support, because lift rarely causes driveability problems or reduced bottom end power.

Try to find a cam that has a duration @ .050" lift of at least 85% (.85) of its advertised duration. Anything less than this means that the cam has a slow ramp speed. Remember, the faster that valve opens, the more power the engine will make. Generally, 10° of duration in a hydraulic cam will equal 20 horsepower.

The Mopar 509 Cam—The mainstay of B engine performance cams is the Mopar "509". This cam has 292° of duration (248° @ .050") and .509" lift with the stock 1.5 rocker arm ratio. While this cam is an old design, it is still a good baseline cam for performance use. It has adequate lift to work the heads and sufficient duration to make 500 hp from a 440 cid engine. Duration @ .050" is 85% of the advertised duration (all the Mopar cams are 85% cams) so it has good ramp speed. Engle Cams has many designs for Mopar engines that are fast ramp designs.

General Recommendations— While it's impossible to list every cam for each engine combination, use the chart on the next page as a general guide.

This is a very broad, general guide and based on the common 440 cubic inch engine. For smaller engines, use smaller duration and vice-versa. After a duration range is selected, pick the cam with the most lift and duration @ .050" of lift. This should be the best performer within a group of cams.

GENERAL CAMSHAFT RECOMMENDATIONS

Towing RV:	266–272° duration/.450" lift
General Performance:	272–285° duration/.470–.500" lift
Street/Strip:	285–305° duration/.480-520"
Maximum Performance:	305°+ duration/.520"+ lift

Many things will affect your choice, like transmission type, rear gear, overall vehicle weight, etc. Do some research and call cam grinders, Mopar engine shops, and other racers for their opinion. It never hurts to ask around, but try not to get confused. Remember my advice: "The easiest way from point A to point B is to copy someone at point B."

Solid Cams

If one of these big hydraulic cams won't give enough power, switch to a solid cam. Since there is a direct connection between the lifter and the pushrod (and the lifter is solid with no moving parts), a more aggressive lobe and valve spring can be used. The solid cam was the first type to be used in an engine and today it is probably the most popular type of cam for high performance use. Again, due to the large tappet size, the Mopar engine has a camshaft advantage. Because the spring pressure can be increased to about 135 lbs on the seat and 350 lbs open, and there is no lifter pump-up to worry about, the rpm range of a solid cam can be well over 7000 rpm. Therefore, for most bracket racers and dual-purpose street/strip cars, a solid cam is the way to go.

Selection—Again, due to the large Mopar tappet size, a solid cam can be very aggressive and make a lot of power. All of the same cam selection rules apply to solid cams as hydraulic cams. Try to find a cam that has at least 85% of advertised duration at .050". This should not be a problem with most solid cams, and in fact, some are available with near 90%.

Ported Heads—If you can get the heads on a flow bench, pick a cam with enough lift to work the heads. In short, if you are paying for ported heads, at least open the valve enough to use it! For most heads this lift range will be in the .590"–650" area. If any more lift is required, switch to a roller cam. There are many solid cams on the market that are in this range. This is a good lift range to use, because it will work the heads, won't kill the valve springs, and will make good power. If a solid cam is going to be used on the street, use something in the .550"–.590" range to get some better driveability out of the engine.

General Recommendations—There is no need to go nuts with super large cams for street use. Usually a slightly smaller cam won't go all that much slower and it will be much easier to cruise the streets with.

As most solid cams are going to be used for bracket racing, I would recommend the Mopar .590, the Ultradyne .640, and the Comp Cams .650 as good starting points. The Mopar .590 has proven itself to be a good performer for many years and is a very cost-effective way to go. The Ultradyne .640" is a Mopar tappet specific grind that features a tight .016" valve lash. This tight lash design allows for more duration at the valve and for less noise and wear in the valvetrain. It is a state of the art design. If you need the absolute largest solid cam available, use the .650" Competition Cams solid. It features a whopping 290° duration @ .050", and with 324° advertised

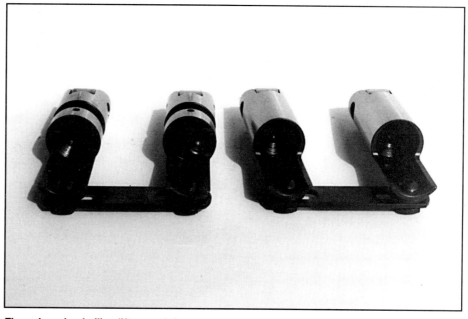

Through-pushrod oiling lifters on left also have an offset intake pushrod cup to help straighten out the pushrod for spread port heads. Captive guide bars will not come loose during operation like some types can. Both pairs of these lifters are from Competition Cams.

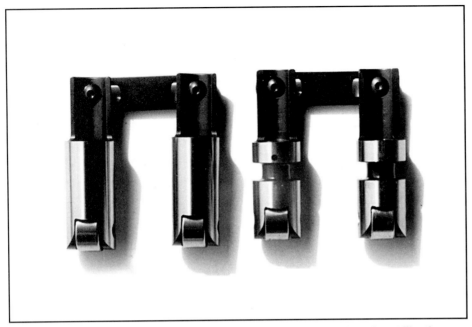

If using a roller cam, try to use a solid body lifter instead of one that is undercut like the ones on the right. The solid body will contribute to better oil control and less aeration of the oil since they move perpendicular to the oil flow in the galley. The two exceptions to this rule are if the lifter bores are bushed, it doesn't matter which type are used, and if the engine is going to use through-pushrod oiling, it will require the lifters on the right. Note the oil passage in the lifter body.

duration and .650" lift, it will wake up any engine.

While all of this duration will produce a lot of power, it will only do so at higher rpm levels. If you have a small engine or a heavy car, do not use this cam. For large engines and light cars, especially with four-speed or trans-brake-equipped automatics, this cam will come about as close to roller cam performance as is possible.

The older mushroom tappet cams are not very popular any longer, so the chances of finding one are slim. While a mushroom cam will allow for a very aggressive ramp, the newer style cams available come close enough without having to go through the hassle of spot-facing the bottom of the lifter bores and holding the lifters in with clothespins while trying to install the cam itself. Though some people still swear by them, the mushroom cam is outdated and I wouldn't recommend one.

Roller Cams

If maximum power is the goal, the only way to go is with a roller cam. The roller cam is unique, in that it uses a special lifter that actually has a roller wheel on the end of the lifter to follow the cam. Because of this, the friction at this point is drastically reduced, and there is no danger of flattening the lobe or having a ramp so aggressive that it damages the lifter. Roller cams usually need around 175-225 lb of seat pressure to work properly, although there are some drag race style cams that use over 300 lb of seat pressure.

Roller cams are currently available with just over 1 full inch of lift. These mega-cams will wear out a set of valve springs in only a few drag racing events. Most Mopar roller cams are in the .700" lift range. For engines using stock heads, this lift area will work the best. Keep in mind

that stock heads will rarely flow significantly more at .800" lift as compared to .700" lift. For this reason, there is no need to break things all the time with a huge cam. For larger, more modified engines with aftermarket heads, the practical lift range is about .800" while still keeping a good degree of reliability in the valvetrain.

Street Use—Don't rule out the roller cam for street use either. Though they are the most expensive way to go at about three times the cost of a solid cam and lifter setup, they will still make the most power and have the best idle quality of any style cam. For street use, select a milder cam like in the .575"/290° advertised duration range and use some type of endurance (circle track style, not drag race) valve spring. With this setup, good reliability can still be achieved. Some smaller spec roller cams will idle better than a hydraulic cam and still produce much more power. Drag cars like at least 270° duration @ .050". When equipped with an 8" torque converter, a 440 cubic inch engine can use a cam with approximately 283° duration @ .050" and about .700" lift. Larger engines (those in the 500 cid range) can use up to 290° duration and over .700" lift. The largest (550 cid and above) engines can go over 290° duration with nearly .800" lift. There are many cams with even higher lifts available but valve spring life will be greatly reduced.

Obviously there are many, many variables that have to be taken into account such as engine size, head type, vehicle weight, use, rpm range, etc. The best thing to do is gather all the information about your engine combo and call some cam grinders and see what they recommend. Once

The #4 cam journal can be grooved to provide more (and full time) oiling to the valvetrain. This is not required but can be done if there are problems with burned pushrod ends or galling rocker shafts. Do this only if necessary as more oil to the top means less to the bottom end.

armed with all the facts about your engine, you can make a better decision about a cam.

CUSTOM CAMS

Most racers are going to buy a cam off the shelf instead of having one custom ground. Generally, they are going to take the advice of their favorite cam grinder or a racer buddy. But while these methods will work, more information is needed in order to choose the absolute best cam for your particular engine.

Determining Lift

To determine what lift is best, have the heads flowed on a flow bench with the manifold that you plan on using and get an idea of how much and how well the heads flow. If the heads are not ported correctly, you may be in for a surprise, especially with stock iron heads. If the porting is

done incorrectly, stock heads have a tendency to fall off dramatically above .450" lift. I have seen "ported" stock heads that flow better at .400" lift than they do at .700" lift. If you have a set of heads like this, you are wasting your time and beating up your valvetrain by running a .700" lift cam. Granted, power is made more from

duration than from lift, but if you are paying for porting or for a very trick set of heads, at least open the valve enough to take advantage of them. Get the heads on a flow bench and then select the cam lift based on where the heads fall off in flow.

Choosing Duration

After this, choose the duration that will produce the power and rpm range that you want. If the exhaust-to-intake flow as measured on a flow bench is less than 70%, consider a cam with more duration on the exhaust than on the intake. This is commonly called a "split pattern cam." This type of cam will be better for heads that are lacking exhaust flow. Since the B engine has good heads available, usually straight pattern cams will work better because almost all of the heads can flow 70% on the exhaust side. If the exhaust flows more than 75%, it means that the intake port is weak and needs more work, so don't be fooled into thinking that you have the world's best exhaust ports!

Large displacement (500+ cubic inch) and nitrous engines will usually work best with a split-pattern cam. It

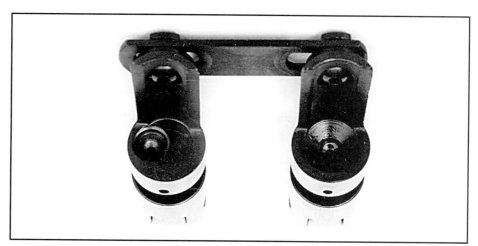

Close-up of offset lifters. This type is required with B-1 TS and Brewer wedge heads due to their spread intake ports. Other race heads like the original B-1 and Indy heads can also use this type of lifter to help with the pushrod angle but they don't require them.

If a roller cam is used with a timing chain, a thrust button is also required. This is due to the fact that the roller cam isn't ground with any taper on the lobes, meaning the lifters don't spin to keep the cam from moving forward. Installed correctly, the cam should have only a small amount of movement. The thrust button also acts to prevent the cam bolts from loosening.

is not uncommon to have 15° or more of extra duration on the exhaust side in a big nitrous engine, because the massive power and exhaust generated by these engines needs an outlet. These types of cams usually have less lift on the exhaust (even with the extra duration) to create a higher velocity in the exhaust port for better scavenging. A split-pattern cam will generally run at higher rpm, because it is larger overall than a straight-pattern cam.

Lobe Separation

Lobe separation will affect how much overlap the cam has with the higher number having less overlap. Most Mopar B engines like a 107°–109° separation. Larger engines should use 109°–112°, and nitrous engines should try 112°–114°. This is something that your cam grinder can help you with.

Intake Centerline

Do not confuse this lobe separation with the intake centerline degree measurement. This number describes where the intake lobe is relative to the piston at maximum lift. Since most cams have an intake centerline of 102°–110° also, this number is easily confused for lobe separation. When the cam is degreed in, the intake centerline is what is being measured and changed. If the installed centerline is lower than the design centerline, the cam is said to be *advanced,* and if the installed centerline is greater than the design, it's *retarded.* Advancing the cam will produce more low-speed power and retarding will make more high-speed power. The installed centerline can be changed, the lobe separation can't. Higher lobe separation means less overlap which is better for low speed power and idle quality. Huge cams have more lobe separation to help them make some low speed power since they are so big to begin with. Before purchasing a custom cam, call around to cam grinders and Mopar engine shops to see what they recommend. They have probably built your combo before so use their vast experience to help you pick the right cam.

If you want to experiment on a dyno or at the track, change the valve lash on the cam from your normal settings. More lash will have the effect of making the cam smaller and less lash will make it appear larger. Don't change it too much either way, usually .005-.007" will be enough to show a change. After you have run all the combinations of tighter and looser on both valves, you should have a handle on what cam is right for your combination. Don't run the cam with a lash other than what the cam grinder recommends since damage to the valvetrain can result. Take this information and have the right cam ground.

Fitting the Cam

There needs to be at least .090" clearance between the valve and the piston. With some of the new high tension springs available, minimum clearance has been reduced somewhat, but to be sure, keep .090" as a good minimum for a general-purpose race car.

Checking Clearances

Most B engines will clear about .550" lift with no valve pockets in the piston. Any more than this will require some valve pocket in the piston. Also, any decking of the block or milling of the head will reduce the piston-to-valve clearance. There are many methods used to find this clearance, such as using clay in the valve pocket or tightening the lash down .090" from normal and turning the engine over by hand.

These methods work well if you

already have the cam, but if you don't have it yet, there is a simple method you can use to figure out what cam will fit. Bring the piston up to exact TDC and put the head on. Pick one cylinder on the head and remove the valve springs on both valves. With a dial indicator on the valve stem, measure the clearance as you push the valve down until it hits the piston. This number should be in the .250"–.400" range depending on valve pocket depth, head milling, valve size, etc. Add the head gasket thickness if you didn't use it. After you get this number, look in the catalog of the cam you are considering. There should be a lobe specification chart somewhere in the catalog. Find your cam on the chart and look up the "tappet lift at TDC" number. Take this number (it will depend on installed degree position but use the largest number to be safe), multiply it by the rocker ratio, and subtract the lash. This figure will be how much the valve is off the seat when the piston is at TDC. Once you get this number, subtract it from the measured number of the valve clearance and you will have the piston to valve clearance. Keep your measured figures handy so that if you want to change cams in the future, you can see if it will clear before you buy it.

CAM DRIVES

Once you have decided on a cam type, you need to choose some way to drive it. The most common and traditional method is to use a timing chain, but there are also gear and belt drives available. Each system has certain advantages: The chain is the cheapest, the gear is the most accurate, and the belt is the easiest to

Rollmaster timing chain is about the best there is. With steel upper and lower gears and a 9-position crank sprocket, it is state of the art for timing chains. Cam timing changes are easy while the engine is on the stand, with no gear bushings required.

adjust. Consider the drive method carefully, because ignition timing will be affected as well as the cam timing. If the valve openings and closings and ignition spark don't occur at the right (or same) time, power and consistency will suffer. There is no use in worrying about degreeing the cam perfectly if a sloppy chain is going to allow it move around 10 degrees or so.

Timing Chains

The timing chain has been around as long as the internal combustion engine. Simple, cheap (usually under $100) and reliable, the timing chain usually does its job for years with no problems. The stock engine uses a link chain with a cam gear made of nylon-covered aluminum. This is done to keep the chain quiet during operation. After many years of use, the nylon eventually falls off and the chain becomes sloppy enough that it

can jump teeth on the gear, resulting in engine failure. These chains should be avoided for performance use.

Double Roller Chains—The factory knew about this fact too, and fitted some high performance engines (notability the 426 Hemi) with double roller chains to correct this problem. The double roller chain has also been the standard for racing engines for many years. These special chains have two rows of links that fit into special sprockets on the crank and the cam. Chain jumping is virtually eliminated, but noise isn't. These chains will make some noise while running, however, it is music to the ears of most performance enthusiasts. While these chains won't jump in timing, they will stretch after a long period of use, which will eventually result in a timing variation at high speed.

Selection—If you are going to use a timing chain, select one that is of a true roller design for less friction and

Rollmaster chains can also be fitted with a Torrington thrust bearing on the back of the upper gear. This cuts down on friction and wear at this point.

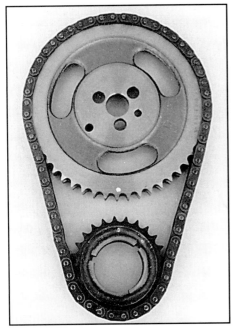

Cam timing changes can also be made with a multiple position crank sprocket. Note that there are 2 dots on the crank gear for each installed position. Make sure to note that the dot on the keyway is NOT the one used to line up with the cam gear. Always double-check the cam timing with these chains, as some are not accurate.

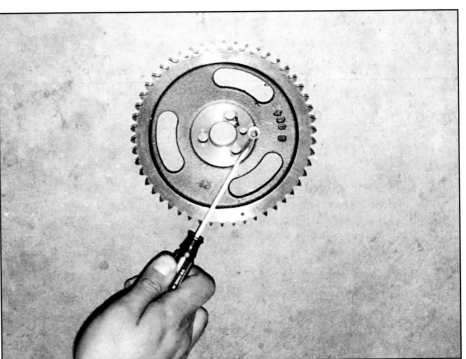

To advance or retard the cam with a timing chain, a special offset degree bushing can be installed in the upper gear. This will move the locating pin in the cam relative to the sprocket thus changing the cam timing. The stock pin hole in the gear will have to be drilled larger to fit the bushing.

wear. Some chains have multi-position crank gears to help with degreeing the cam. Always check these different positions with your degree wheel because they are rarely accurate. I have seen some chains that claim +/– 4 degrees and they were actually more like 7 degrees.

If you do not have a degree wheel, don't move the cam around with the sprocket, use the dowel pin bushings in the upper gear because they are much more accurate. The one exception to this is the Rollmaster chain. This chain has a 9-position crank gear that is extremely accurate. It also features a steel upper gear (most are cast iron) and an available Torrington bearing for the top gear to reduce friction and wear where the gear contacts the block. Some chains are available now that are slightly shorter to make them fit tighter. This is important if the block has been line-honed, because this process actually moves the crank closer to the cam by a few thousandths of an inch.

Installation—The chain should fit tightly. If it is loose it will allow the cam to move around. If you are running a roller cam, make sure to use a thrust button in the cam gear, or the cam will move from front to rear in the block. Hydraulic and solid cams don't need a button, because the taper that is ground into the lobes to spin the lifters keeps the cam in the block.

If you are running a roller cam in a racing engine, check the chain every year to see if it has loosened up, and if so replace it. Check the timing at a high (5000+) rpm occasionally. If it is moving around, either the chain or the distributor (or both) is causing it. Check it out and fix it. It is costing the engine performance and consistency. Also note that this engine has both a single and a three-bolt method of attaching the cam gear. Usually all hydraulic cams are use the one-bolt

The gear drive provides for the most accurate cam timing available. There is no chance of any movement or slippage with one. They also allow for easy cam timing changes.

Backside of Milodon gear drive shows why it is the standard. The large fixed idler gear provides strength as well as rock solid cam timing. Avoid gear drives that have floating idler gears as they are not nearly as accurate.

The 7-bolt attachment of the upper gear makes cam timing changes easy by moving the upper gear around on the mounting plate. All the holes have a very slight offset between each other.

chain while solids and rollers use the stronger three-bolt method. Check your cam before buying the wrong chain.

Gear Drives

For maximum accuracy, a gear drive is the way to go. With a gear drive, the cam is driven by fixed gears instead of a less accurate chain, so the cam timing will always be perfect. The only problems with a gear drive are that they are noisy, expensive (usually over $400), and if improperly set up, can transmit vibrations from the crank to the cam, which can cause broken valve springs.

Selection—Always use a type of gear drive with a fixed idler gear instead of the kind that has a floating pair of gears in the middle. The fixed gear system is much more accurate. The most common gear drives are those made by Keith Black and

Milodon, and they are standard equipment on just about every Top Fuel car.

The gear drive can also be set up to run a fuel pump for fuel injection units that work off the cam gear. Most gear drives allow for easy cam timing

changes by removing the upper gear cover and moving the gear to another hole. This is easily done in a few minutes.

Installation—Installing a gear drive can be confusing because most drives don't have timing marks on the gears.

The Jesel belt drive is the newest method of driving the cam. Its all-external design makes cam timing changes very easy and its lower friction actually frees up a few horsepower.

The belt drive allows for cam timing changes of +/– 10°. These easy-to-use markings keep track of the cam timing. This cam is set 2° retarded.

Actually it's very easy to work around. To install, bring the engine to #1 TDC with the gear drive installed and rotate the cam (with its gear off) until both lifters for #1 cylinder are "up" the same amount. This is called "splitting the overlap" and it should occur right at or near TDC. At this point, install the upper gear on the cam (don't turn the crank) by choosing the holes that line up the best between the gear and cam plate, and then check the degreeing. This should get the cam degree in the ballpark and allow you to change the cam timing by the gear drive

manufacturer's instructions. Always follow the instructions, especially with respect to gear backlash to ensure that the gears will move freely. The gear drive has a thrust button built into the gear cover for use with any three-bolt cam.

Belt Drives

For the ultimate drive system, consider a belt drive. These are more expensive than even the gear drive at over $650, the belt drive has two advantages: easy, external cam timing changes and a belt to absorb vibrations from the crank. Since the belt can't run in oil, all the sprockets and the belt run externally. The oil is kept inside the engine by a special plate with Teflon oil seals. Since the upper sprocket is on the outside, it is

very easy to adjust the cam timing by loosening four nuts and moving the sprocket the desired amount. The belt will absorb vibrations (like a supercharger belt does) but it is still subject to some stretch although less than that of a chain. They are easier to install than a gear drive and both sprockets have timing marks. At the moment belt drives are only made by Jesel and are only made for three-bolt cams. Generally the belt drive is worth a few horsepower, but it should be considered a luxury item unless you are planning to change the cam a lot in the future. Although changing the cam timing can be a useful method to compensate for different track conditions, there are many other areas that can give more power for the same amount of money.

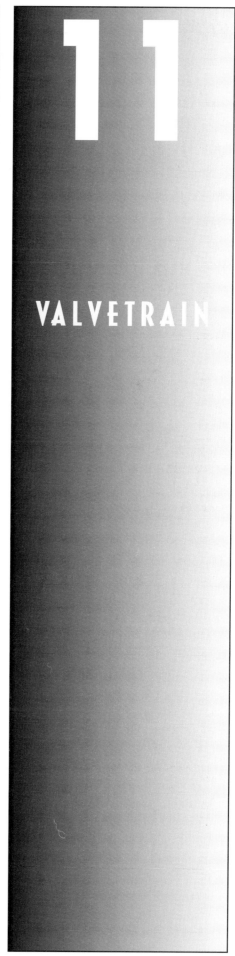

11

VALVETRAIN

Stock head with the old reliable ductile iron "Max Wedge" rockers and stock valvetrain. These rockers are great for all but the highest output engines. They can be used with any type of cam.

The valvetrain on a B engine is very unique from most other domestic engines. Due to its design, it is very well suited for racing with little modifications required. The valvetrain incorporates a fixed rocker shaft attached to the head at five points. This is much stronger than individually mounting each and every rocker because once the shaft is bolted to the head, it strengthens the entire system. The rocker arms pivot on the shaft and are spaced in such a way so they can't move around. Unless something breaks, the rockers are always held in alignment with the valve stems. Because the pivot point of the rocker arm is fixed, the rocker ratio will be constant over its range of motion. The valvetrain is oiled from small holes in the bottom of the shaft under the rocker arms. The oil arrives at the shaft from a passage in the block from the number four cam bearing. The supply of oil is not constant, but it comes in pulses. During operation, this pressurized oil is thrown all over the valve gear, keeping it well lubed.

The strength of a shaft rocker system is well known, as proven by the many aftermarket shaft conversion kits available for other brands of engines. Fortunately for Mopar enthusiasts, we get it for free!

Your choice of valves and rocker arm system will depend mainly on what heads you plan on using. For specifics on these components, refer to the chapter on cylinder heads. There are many other valvetrain components that we can take a look at here.

VALVETRAIN WEIGHT

One of the biggest shortcomings of an "underhead cam" engine is the valvetrain weight. When you consider all valvetrain parts—rockers, pushrods, lifters and such—the weight adds up pretty fast. The only way to significantly increase horsepower is to turn high rpm, which in turn is limited by how much the valvetrain can handle.

A quarter placed on the valves from a **B1 TS** head shows how huge the 2.400" intake and 1.900" exhaust really are. A set of "oversize" stock-style 2.14" and 1.81" valves are shown at right for comparison.

Valve Float—Most of us are familiar with the term "valve float." Simply put, this happens when the spring can no longer control the valve motion and keep it on its seat during the closed period of the cam. The valve is literally bouncing off the seat. When this happens, the engine will not be able to rev any higher. If allowed to happen for long periods of time, it will result in component failure in the form of broken valves or springs. The only way to increase the valvetrain speed capability is to use heavier load valve springs or use lighter components that can get away with less spring pressure. An all-out racing engine must use both of these methods to be successful.

Reducing Weight—The valve, retainer and locks comprise the sprung weight side of the valvetrain, and as such, have the most bearing on maximum rpm. Reducing the weight of the unsprung side, i.e. pushrod and lifter, will not have as great an effect on increasing the rpm potential of the valvetrain. Not to say that the unsprung side is unimportant, but concentrate more on reducing the weight of the valves and retainers.

VALVES

The valves in these engines will vary with the head type. If your heads have 3/8" stem valves (stock heads) do not go through the expense of changing to custom 11/32" stem valves. The stock heads have a fairly short valve, so their weight is not too much of a problem. And these engines will not have enough cylinder head flow to turn enough rpm where the valve weight becomes a limiting factor anyway. I'm sure there are some builders using stock heads that think they need to twist the engine to 8000 rpm, but the engine has long since stopped making power before this point. Airflow will not increase much with a thinner stem valve, since most race 3/8" valves have undercut stems that are the same diameter in the port as an undercut 11/32" valve.

Titanium Valves

With aftermarket heads that have 11/32" stem valves already, the only way to reduce valve weight is to use titanium valves. These valves are

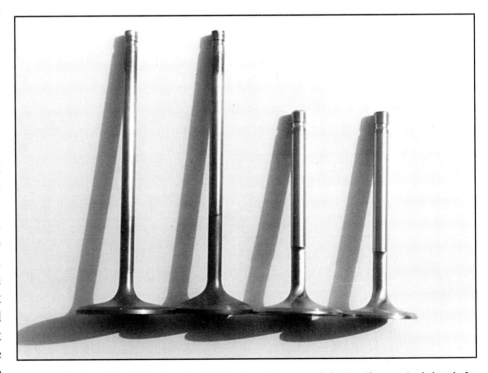

The **B-1 TS** valve also illustrates why the head works so much better than a stock head. An extra long valve is needed because the head is tall to allow for longer, straighter ports. An old racing saying is that a wedge head is only as good as its valve length. Stock length valves on right pale in comparison.

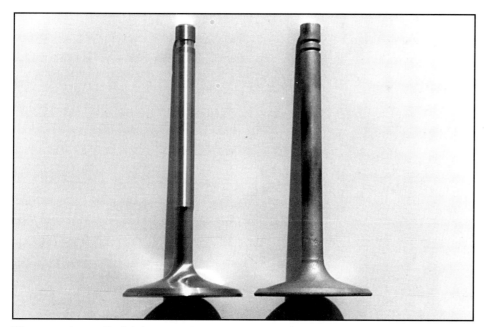

The race valve on the left has many improved features over a production valve. The single-lock groove design is stronger and the undercut stem provides more flow. It is also made from a one-piece stainless forging instead of a two-piece design welded together, like the stock valve.

are of a one-piece design. The raw blank is forged into a valve, making them much stronger than a production welded valve. If you are considering buying stainless valves, make sure you ask the manufacturer if they are one-piece.

The most commonly used one-piece valves in Mopar engines come from REV, Manley, and Ferrea and they all work great. Make sure you use one-piece valves in any engine that is more than an inexpensive stock rebuild. If a valve head breaks off, it causes considerable damage to many other expensive components. One-piece valves are not very expensive and very durable, and provide some cheap insurance.

If the valve spring pressure is increased for a roller cam, then you have no choice but to use one-piece valves, because a two-piece valve will break very quickly. It all comes down to application and budget, but sometimes a dollar saved will end up costing much more in the long run.

nearly four times the price of stainless valves, so use them wisely. Obviously, the larger intake valve should be the first candidate for replacement especially for any valve size of 2.300" or larger. Generally, just replacing the intakes will extend the operating rpm range enough to do the job. With a very big, aggressive cam, the titanium valves will also extend valve spring life considerably. For this style engine, either you spend the money on the valves or you will eventually spend the money on the springs. At least if you go with the lighter valves you will also be gaining performance at the same time.

The bottom line is until you are running in the low 8's or faster in the quarter, just stick with a high quality stainless valve. Most production and some aftermarket valves are of two-piece construction. During manufacture, the stem and the head are conically welded together. These valves work fine for low rpm engines with wimpy cams, but for racing, they

are not a good choice. In high rpm, racing applications, these valve tend to fail, commonly with the head snapping off from the stem.

One-Piece Valves

Most all aftermarket stainless valves

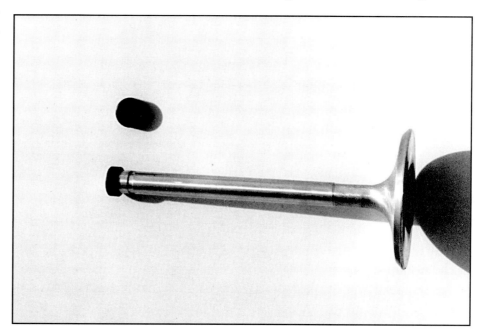

These lash caps fit on the end of the valve to protect the stem from wear. They are not required on most valves since they have hardened tips. They can also be used to correct for short pushrod length.

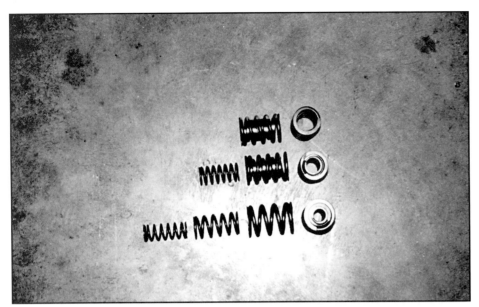

Valve springs come in three varieties: single, dual or triple. Each has its own place and application. Always use the correct spring for your cam and follow the cam manufacturer's specifications.

VALVE SPRINGS

Without doubt, the most important part of the valvetrain is the valve springs. They are responsible for keeping the valve motion under control in a racing engine, which is virtually impossible. Valve springs must condense a tremendous amount of pressure and strength into a small size that can fit on the head, and do all of this without breaking.

Because the springs operate at cam speed (1/2 the engine speed), the valves are another component that has a 50 per second cycle time at 6000 rpm. Without significant advances in valve spring technology, the performance levels of today's racing engine would not have been realized. Today's cams are so aggressive in their pursuit of ultimate power that spring technology has had to evolve quickly to compensate. An aggressive cam is certainly nothing new, but there haven't always been the right materials available to make the springs hold up.

Valve Spring Pressure

To make maximum power, the cam should open and close the valve instantly. Any time spent at low lift is a wasted opportunity for power production. Ideally the best cam lobe would be square with no wasted area. However, since we are living in a world governed by physics, a square cam lobe is completely impossible. Hopefully I didn't need to point this fact out to you! Cam grinders are always trying to develop a cam that is as close to a square lobe cam as possible while still allowing the engine to be operational. An object that is at rest tends to want to remain at rest. Because of this, as the acceleration rate of the cam lobe and/or the rpm of the engine increases, the spring pressure must also increase. Mopar engines have a tappet size of .904", which is the largest in the industry, so the acceleration rate of their cams can be very high. Because the larger tappet allows for more contact area, even with a high acceleration camshaft, the

load on the lifter and the lobe can be held to an acceptable level.

The choice of valve spring will be determined by the type of cam you are running. The general rule is that the more radical the cam profile, the stronger the spring has to be. High seat pressures will force the valve closed on the closing ramp of the cam, while high nose pressures will prevent the lifter from flying off the cam at the top of the opening ramp, like a ski jumper.

Seat Pressure—Seat pressure can be easily adjusted. If the pressure is too low, you can shim the springs; if it's too high, use special retainers to decrease it. Always follow the cam manufacturer's specs.

Open Pressure—The open pressure really can't be changed on a set of springs since it's determined by the spring rate and the lift of the cam. The rate of the spring is expressed in pounds per inch (lb/in) and is the fancy term for how much pressure is required to move the spring down a certain amount. Use this formula to figure it out:

open pressure = seat pressure + (lift x spring rate).

Obviously, if the springs have more seat pressure they will also have more open pressure. If your springs have too much open pressure do not lower it by lowering the seat pressure. The only solution it to get a set of springs with a different spring rate.

Valve Spring Setup

There are two main theories on how to set up springs on the heads; either by using the height or the pressure method. What most people don't realize is that they have to do it using both methods; it's impossible to do it any other way. Remember that the engine will only see the spring pressure. If the valve has 120 lbs on the seat, it doesn't know if the spring is set up at 1.500" or 2.500". The spring height has little to do with it other than making sure that the spring can take the lift without coil-binding.

When the heads are set up, the proper method is as follows:

• Measure every installed height for each valve
• Determine at what installed height the springs will give the desired pressure and cam clearance
• Adjust each valve installed height to match your desired height by increasing or decreasing as necessary

In this way, all the spring pressures will be equal AND all the heights will also be equal because the springs all have the same rate and thus will give the same pressure at the same height.

Selecting Proper Spring Pressure

Different types of cams—hydraulic, flat-tappet (solid) and roller—all have different spring requirements.

Hydraulic Cams—A hydraulic cam has the mildest lobes, so it requires the least spring pressure. Generally, a hydraulic cam will operate best in these engines with about 120 lb of seat pressure and 300 lb of open pressure. Any more than this and the cam or the lifter can be damaged. With a good set of lifters and proper preload, this pressure will rev to about 6500 rpm with no problem. If you need more rpm than this, you should switch to a solid lifter camshaft.

As a note, the trend in the Stock Eliminator class is to use a hydraulic

cam with about 160 lbs of seat pressure. While some gains have been seen, keep in mind that these vehicles don't make too many passes on a camshaft or lifters without replacement. Always remember that anything will usually work a few times. The key is making it work all the time.

Solid Lifter Cam—The next step up would be the solid lifter cam. These cams are by far the most popular for high performance street use and bracket racing. They will make good horsepower and since they eliminate the pumping action of a hydraulic lifter, they can rev well over 7000 rpm. Because the Mopar tappet size is so big, some roller cams can come fairly close to roller cam performance without all the added expense.

With all of this performance and cam acceleration rate, the spring pressure needs to be increased as well. Usually, a solid cam needs about 135 lb seat pressure and about 350 lb open pressure. Much more pressure than this and you run the risk of flattening a lobe off the cam and/or damaging the lifters. Most cam manufacturers don't recommend much more than 350–370 lb of open pressure for the same reasons. If any more rpm or acceleration capability is needed, consider making the switch to a roller camshaft and lifters.

Roller—The acceleration of a roller cam is so high that a normal flat style lifter would simply not be able to follow the ramps without something failing. A well-designed roller cam can operate at speeds of over 10,000 rpm with "good" reliability. Of course, part of the roller cam's ability to rev this high is due to the valve springs. Usually a roller cam will require at least 200 lb of seat pressure with 500

lb open pressure.

In an effort to increase the aggressiveness and rpm range of roller cams, there are a lot of springs available on the market now with over 300 lb on the seat and close to 1000 lb open! These killers have more seat pressure than a hydraulic spring has at maximum lift. Needless to say, if the engine won't rev to the moon with these springs on it, it never will.

If the rest of the components in the system are up to snuff consider a set of roller springs with at least 230–250 lb of seat pressure since they will still be strong enough to do the job as they get weaker during use. If your springs are at only 200 lb when they are new, they may get too weak by the end of the season.

Drag Racing—For drag racing, the best type of springs to use are some type of tool steel. These springs are usually trade-named H-11, Vasco-Jet, or Pacaloy, depending on the brand. While each may be slightly different in material, they all share the common traits of very high seat and open pressure, and they are all brittle, since the material is so strong and hard. This type of spring will give the best life in drag engines. Usually they hold their pressure very well right up until they break.

Endurance Racing—For endurance engines (street, circle track, or marine) use some type of spring from "silicone steel" material. These springs have high seat pressure but less open pressure and are far less brittle than the tool steel springs. Usually they don't break as easily, but they do lose pressure gradually. As such they should be checked every season.

Titanium Wire—There also are springs made from titanium wire but I

The 10 degree locks (right) offer much more strength than the stock 7 degree style. Since they are not much more expensive than production replacements, they should always be used in any performance rebuild.

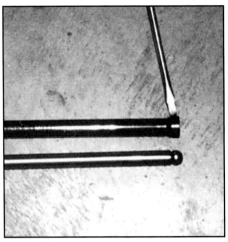

When switching to adjustable rockers, new pushrods that have a cup on one end are required to fit the adjuster. The exceptions are Jesel and T&D rockers, which still use a ball/ball style pushrod

would not recommend them for anything short of professional Pro Stock drag racing. They have great pressure and are light, but when they break, they shatter, sending tiny shards of titanium all throughout the engine. They are the only spring capable of controlling the new style Pro Stock cams that have over a full inch of lift. By the way, they also cost more than $2500 per set!

Retainers & Locks

You will need some sort of spring retainer to hold your new mega-springs on the valve. The production engines use a stamped steel retainer with 7-degree, multi-groove valve lock. These retainers have adequate strength for hydraulic cam engines, but any wilder cam than this should have better retainers.

There are two basic types of retainers: the 7 degree and the 10 degree. By increasing the angle of the lock in the retainer, more holding power can be exerted on the valve stem by the 10 degree set up. The lock grooves don't actually hold the valve in; it is the tremendous force, generated from the pressure of the

valve springs, exerted by the lock on the valve stem.

Single Groove Locks—Most all racing valves are a single-groove lock design for increased strength. The stock multi-groove locks are designed to allow the valve to float in the lock so that it can keep the seats free of carbon by actually spinning the valve slightly. Because of this, this setup is not as strong as a single-groove lock design. Any racing engine should use the single-groove lock valves.

Make sure to always use the correct locks with the correct retainers. The 10-degree and the 7-degree parts are not interchangeable. Since the 10-degree retainer system usually only costs a few bucks more than the 7-degree ones, go for the 10-degree retainers, even for a mildly modified engine. The extra strength and safety margin won't hurt.

Titanium Retainers—If the engine is going to be operated over 7000 rpm, consider titanium retainers. They are lighter than the chrome-moly retainers and can help extend the life of the valve springs and the rpm

capability of the engine. For engine speeds less than this, the titanium retainers are not required, but can be used if less weight is desired. Usually they are about three times the cost of the moly parts. Make sure that the bottom of the retainer has at least .060" clearance to the valve seal or valve guide at maximum lift. If not, it may collide, causing broken parts. To correct, machine the guide down as needed.

PUSHRODS

The pushrods in your engine are a very simple part that usually give years of trouble-free service. The stock Mopar pushrod is a "ball / ball" end design. This means that each end is rounded and fits into a cup in both the rocker arm and the lifter.

If adjustable rockers are going to be used, then a switch to a "ball/cup" pushrod is required. The pushrod will still fit into a cup in the lifter, but the rocker arm end of the pushrod will have a cup that the rocker arm adjuster ball will fit into. The exception to this rule are the Jesel, T&D and Comp Cams Pro rockers, as their adjusters have a cup end.

The cup adjuster is a better way to go, because the chance for it breaking off is much less than the ball type of adjuster. The traditional Mopar ball-type of adjuster can completely break off while the cup type can't. Also, the cup-type adjuster can loosen up some and the pushrod won't come out of its place if the pushrod length is correct. If the ball-type adjuster loosens up, the lash will increase to the point that the pushrod will fall off. All this is due to the fact that the ball adjuster has to stick down from the rocker in order for it to get oil while the cup-

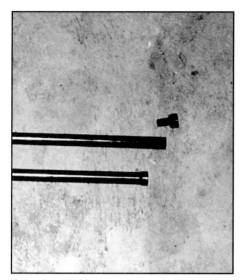

Cut-to-length kits are also available to allow for easy custom-length pushrods. To make one, simply cut the pushrod to the correct length and press in the cup end.

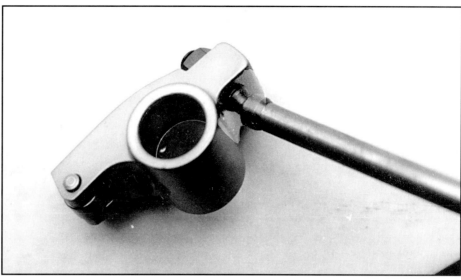

With the correct pushrod length there should be 0 to 2 threads of the adjuster showing under the rocker arm. Any more or less than this and the oil flow will not be directed to the pushrod cup correctly.

style gets oil internally from the rocker itself, and thus doesn't need to protrude from the bottom of the rocker.

Pushrod Length

Correct pushrod length is important for reliable high rpm operation. With the "normal" ball-style adjuster, the correct pushrod length is the length that will leave 0-1 adjusting threads below the rocker arm when the lash is properly set. Any more than this and the angle between the pushrod and the adjuster will become excessive and may lead to adjuster breakage. Any less than this and the cup of the pushrod may be too close to the rocker arm body to get proper oiling. The higher the spring load and rpm, the more critical this becomes. The engine may run great with three or four threads showing, but it will probably be a matter of time before a problem occurs.

Many people refer to this situation as rocker arm geometry but it's really pushrod geometry. The rocker arm geometry can only be changed by moving the shaft on the head. Proper rocker geometry is achieved when the contact point of the rocker is in the center of the valve stem at 1/2 lift of the cam. Changing this is pretty difficult, as the shaft has to be moved. Most of the heads will give acceptable geometry with the shaft in the stock position. Remember that hydraulic cams use a different pushrod, since the cup in the lifter is higher up in the lifter than a solid or roller. Most solid and roller lifters can use the same length. Of course, the raised-block engines use a longer pushrod than the low-block engines since their block is taller. There are also cut-to-length pushrod kits that allow you to build the exact length pushrod you need.

Stronger Pushrods

Each time the heads are off, roll the pushrods on a very flat surface such as glass, and check to see that they roll evenly. If they wobble, they are probably bent, and should be replaced. If a pushrod is bent, it was probably caused by some sort of mechanical interference, such as not

enough valve-to-piston clearance. But if you check this and find you have adequate clearance and are still bending pushrods, they are just not strong enough.

A stronger pushrod has to be larger in diameter and/or thicker in the wall. The most common pushrod size for the B engine is 3/8". This size fits with every head available. If a larger pushrod is desired, the next step up is a 7/16" diameter pushrod. These will fit very close in most heads so if you are going to be using them, make sure to carefully check to be sure they are not contacting the head.

Tapered Pushrod—A neat compromise between these two sizes is the 7/16" tapered pushrod. These pushrods are made from special 7/16" tubing that is tapered down to 3/8" near the ends. This allows the pushrod to fit in the head while putting more material in the center of the pushrod where most of the flexing occurs.

Wall Thickness—Most aftermarket pushrods are made of tubing with a wall thickness of about .050". This thickness works well up to about 200 lb of seat pressure. Above this, they are only marginally strong enough. There are pushrods available for B engines with an extra-thick .083" wall. Any pressure over 200 lb should use these thicker pushrods. If you are using springs with 300 lb of seat pressure, these pushrods are mandatory.

If the pushrods are flexing all over the place, the valve will not be able to get the full design lift of the cam. The stiffer the pushrods are, the closer the valve motion will be to the lobe motion. This will result in more power. If they are strong enough and there are no clearance problems, your pushrods should last for a long time.

If the engine is using through-pushrod oiling, be sure that the pushrods have an oil passage through the entire length. If your engine is suddenly running badly and the oil pressure is down to about 5 psi, you have probably had some type of valvetrain failure. The poor running is caused by the loss of a cylinder while the loss of oil pressure is caused by a lifter coming out of its bore. The lifter

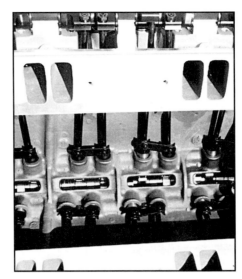

The effects of the wider port and intake rocker offset on these Indy 440-1 heads is shown by the pronounced angle of the intake pushrod.

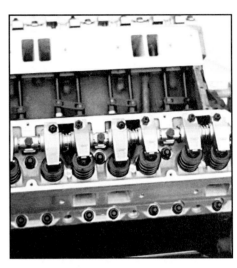

Roller rockers on these Stage 6 heads are the same as used on production iron heads. These rockers are a good investment for durability and performance. Note that the pushrods are all straight since these heads do not have wider or spread intake ports.

can jump out of its bore if the pushrod or rocker breaks. This will cause a huge oil leak in the lifter galley resulting in low pressure to the rest of the engine. Check this first if there is a sudden drop in oil pressure.

GENERAL VALVETRAIN TIPS

With a stock diameter rocker shaft setup, non-roller bearing rockers are

generally stronger than those with roller bearings on the shafts. When the rockers are machined for the needle bearing race, it leaves the rocker with a very thin cross-section in the valve spring relief area. This causes the rockers to split off the shaft. The better needle-bearing rockers use smaller diameter shafts to keep more meat in the rocker body.

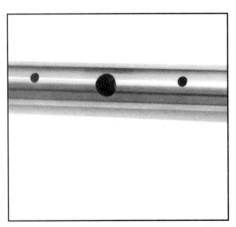

Oil holes in rocker arm shaft are offset slightly to one side. Always install the shaft with the holes down and toward the valve stem.

Stock-style rocker arms work fine for any hydraulic cam. Though they are not adjustable, they work fine for a medium-effort engine. Note the positioning of the pushrod socket as there is a left and a right rocker arm. These are Mopar Performance HD replacements which have additional material in high stress areas.

The oil hole in this Crane roller rocker arm is positioned to spray oil on the adjuster ball and the rocker cup. A similar hole provides oiling to the roller end of the rocker for the roller and valve tip.

Indy 572-13 head setup for the T&D rocker setup. Bar with studs bolts to the head and the rockers mount to the bar. This is a very strong arrangement.

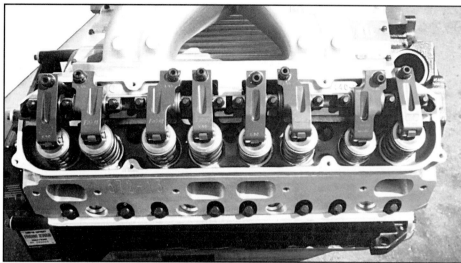

T&D shaft rockers on an Indy 572-13 head. Notice that each pair of rockers has its own individual shaft. This makes it much easier to remove a rocker arm than with the conventional single shaft per head design. These rockers must be oiled either by a spray bar system in the valve cover or through the pushrods.

The needle bearings on the shafts are only a small gain. The rocker arm shaft is pressurized with oil so the friction between the rocker and the shaft is lower than you would expect. If needle bearing rockers are going to be used, make sure that the rocker shafts are hardened or the bearings will tear up the shafts.

Roller Rockers

On the subject of rockers, roller rockers are not as large of a performance gain for these engines as they are for some other brands. Since the Mopar system uses a fixed pivot point (the shaft), the rocker can maintain its ratio throughout its travel. The inferior stud-mounted rocker will vary its ratio as it moves up and down, and as such will respond to the fixed pivot design of a roller rocker. Where the roller rocker has advantages is with strength, valve guide wear and ratio. The aluminum roller rocker is much stronger than the ductile iron rockers that are commonly used. While this is not a problem with

hydraulic or solid cams, it can be with roller cams. These roller cam engines should have roller rockers as standard equipment. Since the roller tip can freely roll across the valve tip instead of grinding into it, valve guide friction and wear will also be reduced. This is also important with heavy valve spring pressures.

Roller rockers are usually made a

little more accurately so their ratios are more consistent. As far as a big power gain over the iron rockers, forget it. Since their cost is not that much more than the iron rockers (once the cost of new shafts are figured in), the roller rockers may be a good initial investment. This way, if you upgrade to a larger cam, you will already have the rockers for it.

Indy head requires this external oil line kit to oil the valvetrain. The factory oil passage in the head is eliminated to allow the ports to be wider and to give a straighter shot at the valve.

Rocker arms for Indy 440-1 head are similar to production but with a few changes for greater strength. Note billet hold down clamps, shaft studs and increased intake rocker offset.

T & D rocker arm set up for B-1 heads is bulletproof even with the largest cams. These rockers feature needle bearings on the shafts and are much stronger than the stock-style B-1 rockers. Note the extra offset of the intake rocker and the extreme intake pushrod angle required by the huge intake ports. On some blocks, grinding may be necessary for intake pushrod clearance.

Valve Lash

There are several different ways to set the valve lash of your cam. Since some cams have a different opening and closing ramp, some methods will not work with certain cams. The best overall method that I have found is as follows.

1. Adjusting each cylinder at a time, set the exhaust lash when the intake valve is at maximum lift and set the intake lash just after the exhaust valve starts to open. This method will work for any type of cam.

2. Make sure that you roll the engine over after adjusting the lash to be sure that the lash never exceeds the correct setting at any point of the cam lobe.

3. Always adjust the lash with the engine warm. This will take into account any expansion of the components.

Lash can be varied a little from the design specification to determine how well the cam is suited for the combination. Increasing the lash .005" has the effect of making the cam smaller while tightening the lash will make it appear larger. If you make one of these changes and performance increases, the engine is telling you that it wants a cam change in that direction.

Here's the ultimate race setup: dual Holley four-barrel Dominator carbs with custom intake.

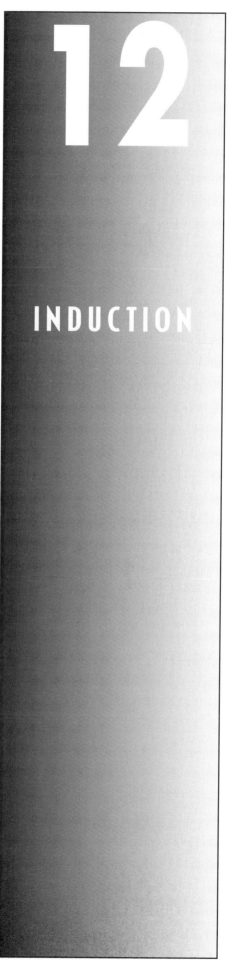

INTAKE MANIFOLDS

One area where the B engine has always excelled is the factory intake manifold. Throughout its history, this engine has been equipped with just about every possible manifold configuration you can imagine. There were dual four-barrel carbs on a long ram-style manifold; cross-ram dual four-barrels on the Max Wedge engines; low-rise dual four-barrels on some 1962 383 engines; three two-barrels on the famous Six Pack engines from 1969–1971; and many different single four-barrel intakes were available on most engines. The aftermarket manifold story is no different, with everything from single four-barrels on dual-plane intakes to custom sheet-metal manifolds with dual 1300 cfm Holley Dominator carbs.

Every manifold has its place depending on application. The intake requirements for a restoration engine are completely different than for a race-only car. Like everything else in a racing engine, the carb and intake must be matched to the other components for maximum output.

Basic Intake Operation

As is the case with the exhaust system, the intake side of the engine does not function in a steady-state condition. That is, there is not a constant flow of mixture inside the manifold. Because each cylinder gets its fuel mixture at different times, the manifold has "charges" of fuel flowing through it. Granted, with eight cylinders in an engine, the amount of time between charges is so small that it may appear to be constant, but it is not.

For example, imagine that the engine only has one cylinder. When the intake valve opens, the fuel mixture begins to flow into the cylinder. Everything goes along fine until the valve slams shut and the fuel mixture is cut off. The fuel, however, has momentum and bounces off the shut valve, causing it to reverse direction. But just as it starts to reverse direction, the valve may open again, and the mixture has to change

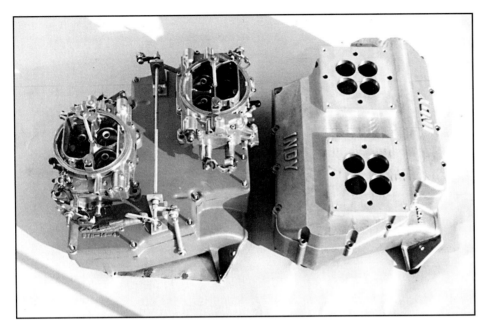

Cross-ram intakes have always been popular on Mopar engines. These descendants of the production Max Wedge cross ram are an old Edelbrock STR intake (left) and a new Indy intake. Both manifolds have a variety of lids for use with different carb setups. The STR hasn't been produced in many years, while the Indy is a current production item.

direction once again. The frequency and intensity of these "waves "is determined by engine displacement, rpm and cam timing.

Tuning Intake Runners—If we can figure out the timing and location of these waves going back and forth in the intake, we can build the intake runner length to take advantage of them. This principle is the theory behind tuning the manifold to produce a "ramming" effect. If everything is timed and sized correctly, it is possible to jam more mixture into the cylinder and thus make more power. The shorter the runners are, the better the intake is at high rpm (since the pulses are much shorter at high rpm), and conversely, long runners produce more power at lower speeds. This is where the long-ram and cross-ram manifolds come from. The long ram intakes are tuned for power at low speeds in heavy cars while the shorter cross rams are tuned for high rpm horsepower. In reality, the cross rams

are just shorter runner versions of the long ram. The runners are short enough to be folded up inside the box which forms the plenum of the manifold. A tunnel ram is similar

except the runners rise vertically to the plenum instead of running across the engine. The engine doesn't really care which direction the runners go; it only sees the length of the runners and the volume of the plenum.

The plenum is the area where all the runners meet under the carburetor. The plenum helps to dampen out the individual pulses from each cylinder and present a smoother signal to the carb. Larger plenums generally favor higher rpm and vice-versa. Without a plenum (say a pair of cylinders hooked up to each barrel) the carb would get very strong, individual pulses and would be very hard to tune. Engineers experimented with these IR (isolated runner) tunnel ram manifolds with a pair of four-barrel carburetors (one barrel for each cylinder) but found that they didn't work very well.

Recommended Manifolds

By far the most common intake

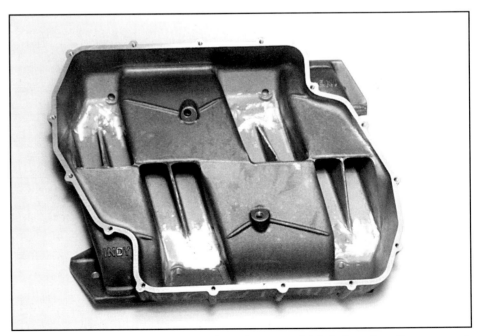

Inside of the Indy cross-ram intake (actually a plenum ram intake) shows how the runners are actually folded inside to achieve their length. This runner length will determine the rpm range of the engine with shorter runners being preferred for higher rpm use.

manifold for the B engine is the single four-barrel manifold. Simple and easy to install, they deliver the most overall power for your racing engine. Generally they are available in two different styles, the single plane and the dual plane. The dual-plane intake is what all of the non-race prepped engines came factory equipped with. In these manifolds, each half of the carb feeds four-cylinders. The manifold is basically divided into two separate halves which effectively makes the runners longer. This helps to produce better low-speed power and response which is what a production engine needs. A single-plane manifold simply has all the runners attached to an open space (the plenum) under the carb. Each runner draws from the entire carb which results in more power at higher rpm. A single-plane intake will have less low-end power but more high end power. Depending on the application, this may not be what you want. Everything with parts in the induction path like intakes, heads, cams, and headers are always a trade-off. You exchange low end power for top end power.

Stock Manifolds—The production Mopar intakes work fairly well, especially for casual racing. As far as the factory race manifolds go, I can't recommend them for use these days because they are so hard to find. The cross rams will only work with Max Wedge size ports, making installation on stock size heads difficult.

Dual-Plane Manifolds—If you want to run a dual-plane intake manifold, the stock iron ones are a good choice. Even though they aren't as trick as an aluminum manifold, the air doesn't care. Most of the dual-plane intakes around aren't much

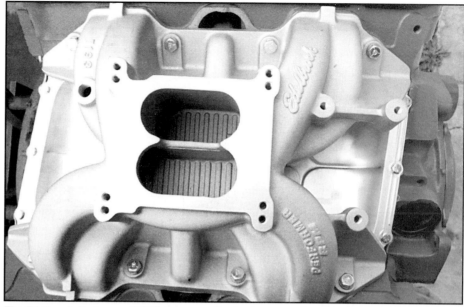

The Edelbrock Performer RPM intakes are the best compromise design between a single- and dual-plane intake manifold. They work great for dual-purpose street/strip engines because their power output is close to that of a single plane, yet they have most of the low-speed torque of a dual plane.

better than a stock one. In fact, the Mopar M-1 dual-plane manifold is just a copy of a production intake cast in aluminum. Granted this manifold will save weight but it will perform just like a stock manifold.

The Edelbrock Performer RPM is a dual-plane intake that features large runners and a large plenum. Because

of this, it can produce good power at a higher rpm than normal for a dual-plane intake with only a small loss in power at low rpm due to its large size. It has proven to be a good manifold for street/strip cars.

Single-Plane Manifolds—For race use, a single-plane manifold is usually the way to go. Most drag cars and

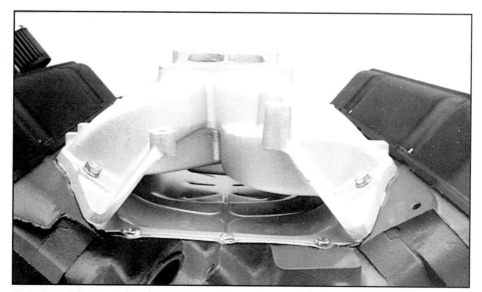

End shot of the Performer RPM 440 intake shows how much taller it is as compared to a standard dual-plane intake manifold. Hood clearance is usually no problem with these intakes.

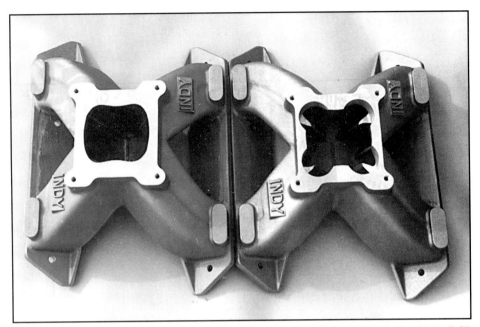

Most intake manifolds like these for Indy heads are available in either a standard pattern (left) or a Dominator pattern.

Holley Dominator carb flange. If you are planning on running a Dominator carb, you would naturally think to go with the second model mentioned. However, in my testing, a car will usually ET faster using the standard flange manifold and an adapter plate (2" high minimum use Moroso or Holley brand) to accept the Dominator carb. This method seems to produce more overall power than with the Dominator manifold. The M-1 Dominator manifold has a huge plenum that is pretty shy on low-end power, which is critical for drag racing. But if the engine is going to be run at high rpm for a sustained period of time, such as in circle track racing, the Dominator manifold is the better choice.

Using the standard flange with an adapter also gives you the flexibility to run both styles of carburetor. However, be sure to check your hood clearance with the adapter plate method because it is pretty tall.

Always check the hood clearance regardless of the manifold used,

circle track cars will benefit from a single-plane manifold. The B engine inherently makes strong low-end power because of its large displacement and relatively good heads with small ports. In reality, it doesn't need a big boost in low rpm power. There are several single-plane manifolds on the market for these engines and some work better than others. Try to select a manifold that has its runners aligned with the ports in the head. Some B engine manifolds have runners that enter the head port at an angle. Remember that the fuel charge has mass and because of this it doesn't like to change direction. Make sure that the plenum isn't too big for your rpm range and engine size.

Mopar M-1 Manifold—My testing has shown that the Mopar M-1 intake manifold will give the best overall performance in a single-plane manifold for production-sized (iron, Stage 6, B-1 BS, Indy SR) head ports. The Indy 440-1, and Brodix B-1 heads have to use their own special intakes. The Indy 440-1 can use an

original Max Wedge cross-ram if desired. The M-1 produces acceptable low-speed torque and makes strong top-end power.

The M-1 comes in two forms for both the low-block and raised-block engines. One model comes with a standard square bore/spread bore flange and the other has a larger

Side view of the Indy cross-ram shows its overall height.

A variety of tops are available for the Indy intake so it can be used for different applications.

especially with the M-1. These intakes are pretty tall and may not fit under the hood of some cars.

Edelbrock Torker II—If you can't fit the M-1 intake, the next choice would be the Edelbrock Torker II manifold. This intake manifold is not the same as the old Torker 440 or TM-7 Tarantula. The Torker II is almost as good as the M-1 but it isn't quite as tall. It doesn't make as much top-end power as the M-1 but it can fit where the M-1 won't. There isn't a Torker II for the low-deck engines but since these blocks are lower, hood clearance is rarely a problem with them. Use the taller M-1 on the low-deck engines.

Manifold Tuning & Modifications

Manifold air/fuel mixture distribution is something that is hard to check. The best way to check it is by measuring the exhaust temperatures during a test run on the track or on the dyno. Try to get the temperatures as close to each other as possible, hopefully within 50 degrees

or so. Do not modify your intake for distribution purposes until you know there is a problem. If you don't have access to equipment to monitor all eight exhaust temperatures at the same time, try to read the spark plugs to see if there is any variation from cylinder to cylinder. If one area looks different than the rest, try changing the jets in that area of the carb to try and equalize the mixture. If you don't

have access to a dyno, leave the manifold alone.

Gasket Matching—It is a good idea to gasket-match the runners to make sure they match the heads. The tops of the runners can be radiused more where they meet the plenum to smooth out the airflow. Make this radius as smooth as possible, with no flat spots.

Alignment—The only other thing to do is to check for port and bolt hole alignment. Sometimes the manifold doesn't line up well with the ports or bolt holes, especially if the heads or block have been milled a lot. However, do not get out the grinder and wallow out the bolt holes until it "fits," because this doesn't correct the port misalignment. Have the manifold milled at a machine shop until it fits correctly.

Blocking Exhaust Crossover Passage—All factory iron intakes and some aluminum intakes have an exhaust crossover passageway to circulate exhaust under the carb to help warm it up in cold weather. While this is okay for a stock engine, this additional heat is not what we

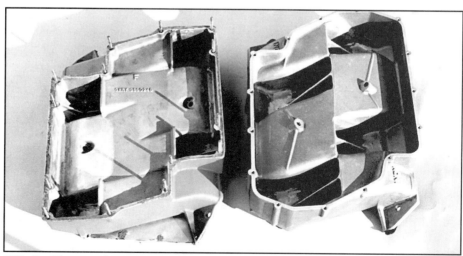

With the lid removed you can see that these intakes are basically a regular tunnel ram intakr with the runners folded up inside. The Indy runners (right) are much shorter, which produces more high rpm top-end power. At left is the Edelbrock STR, which stands for "street tunnel ram."

End shot of a sheet metal-style tunnel ram on a 596 cid engine with B-1 heads. This style of intake will produce the most power for an all-out racing engine. They are very expensive (usually about $2000) and require a lot of hood clearance to accommodate the extra height.

are many fast Mopar race cars that run only one carb, and if they can do it, so can you. Two carbs are twice the cost, hassle and aggravation of a single carb. A single carb will be more consistent, because there are fewer things that can go wrong or change with only one carb.

Tunnel Ram Manifolds—Most of the off-the-shelf tunnel ram intakes are too restrictive. If a tunnel ram is what you want, invest in a custom-fabricated one. These manifolds are designed and custom-built for your particular engine combination and will out-perform any other generic manifold. The runners are usually tapered out larger where they enter the plenum and are spread apart to locate them right under the carburetor barrels. Additionally, the carburetors can be twisted on the top to precisely locate the barrels over the runners.

The B-1 head has a cast aluminum tunnel ram kit that works okay, but it is hard to put together if you don't have access to a machine shop. Indy has tunnel rams for their heads and

want for a racing engine. It is a common practice to block this passage for high performance applications. This will keep the manifold cooler, resulting in a denser intake charge which will make more power. This deal can also benefit a street performance car but only if the car is going to be used in the warmer months. With this modification, engine warm up will be slower.

The easiest way to block it off is to use a special intake gasket that seals off this passageway. Use Fel-Pro intake gasket #1214 for low-block engines and Fel-Pro 1215 for raised-block engines. The Mopar M-1 manifolds, as well as all tunnel rams, do not have the crossover passage, so there is no need for the special gasket.

Multiple Carb Manifolds

If the engine is a true all-out racer, multiple carbs may be an option. The B engine is capable of over 850

horsepower with a single Dominator carb (and lots of other parts!) on a single-plane intake. If this still isn't enough, multiple carbs are required. For bracket racing up to the 7-second zone, stay with a single carb. There

Sheet metal intake for B-1 TS heads also has two stages of nitrous oxide for added power. One system is a fogger setup that sprays into each runner and the other system is a set of spray bars running through the plenum.

Although carbs on new cars are a thing of the past, in drag and circle track racing, the Holley four-barrel reigns supreme. This 950 HP series carb has many performance modifcations built in. Far more radical modifications are made in classes where carb modifications are not limited. Holley modular-style four barrels are available in a variety of airflow ratings and with either vacuum or mechnically actuated secondaries. Photo courtesy Holley.

Holley's 4500 Dominator carb is available in several size, and is an excellent choice for big-blocks. This is a 750 cfm unit, good for a mildly modified street engine, but for racing, you will likely be looking at the 1050 or 1150 cfm sizes, depending on the needs of the engine. See the sidebar on page 121 to determine carb requirements. Photo courtesy Holley.

Retrotech Performance has CNC-machined tunnel rams for standard and Max Wedge engines.

All of these custom manifolds are considerably more expensive than a store-bought single-plane, with the custom sheet metal jobs usually going for over $2000. Make sure that you can't do anything else to the engine for this kind of money that will give more power. All of these tunnel rams will drastically reduce bottom end torque, so keep this in mind. If your drag car isn't light or doesn't have a trans-brake, I would not recommend a tunnel ram.

SELECTING A CARBURETOR

Once you have chosen the manifold, you need to choose a carburetor to go with it. There are many different sizes, brands and types of carbs available. Even fuel injection is becoming an option now. It all boils down to this:

your engine requires a certain amount of air/fuel mix to produce a certain amount of rpm and power. It doesn't care how it gets it. The mixture can come from a vacuum secondary carb, a mechanical secondary carb or fuel injection—it doesn't matter. What *does* matter is driveability, how responsive the engine is on a daily basis. All of these fuel systems have different levels of driveability. Fuel injection, if properly done will provide the best driveability, because the ratio of fuel to air can be adjusted instantly for any change in load or rpm. Before the advent of computers, mechanical means were used to adjust the air/fuel ratio of fuel injection. This usually resulted in good performance and response, but poor economy since the adjustment method was too slow and archaic.

On the subject of slow and archaic adjustment methods, we have the carburetor. Even when perfectly set

up, the carb is strictly low tech. Any adjustment of air fuel ratio is done by the various systems and circuits inside the carb. These systems are all vacuum and pressure-driven and as such are fairly slow to react. This is why problems like loading up and bogging are common with carbs that are being used on racing engines.

The use of the vehicle will determine what type of carb to use, but the first thing to consider is what brand of carb to use. Most all Mopar factory cars were produced with Carter carbs. While they were fine in their day, Carter is not in the carb business anymore, but they are essentially being built by Edelbrock, so you do have the option of running a Carter carb if you want to. Just check your local auto parts store for the Edelbrock information.

Carb Considerations

At this time, a Holley carb is the way to go. Some people may not "like" them but the fact is that no other carb dominates all forms of racing like Holley. They literally have a carb for every need. Holley carburetors are the most flexible and

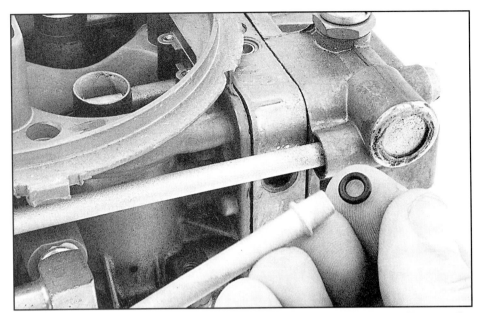

On single-feed Holleys, fuel reaches the secondary float bowl through a tube. Whenever the float bowls are removed, the O-ring seals on each end of the tube must be carefully extracted. Most times, they're reusable, but if you suddenly spring a leak, you know they weren't. Photo by Dave Emanuel.

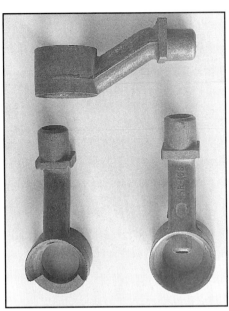

Holley has a number of different booster venturi designs and has used all of them over the years. Down-leg boosters offer less restriction than the straight-leg variety. The cut-out on the underside of one of these boosters was added to alter fuel distribution. Photo by Dave Emanuel.

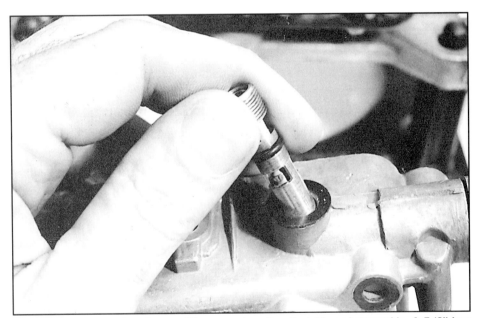

Holley inlet needle and seat assemblies are externally adjustable and removable. A 5/8" hex wrench is used to turn the adjusting nut and a wide-bladed screwdriver is used to lock the assembly in place. Photo by Dave Emanuel.

tunable of any other type. Since most racers use them, parts are no problem to buy or borrow at the track if needed. Remember that the engine doesn't care what brand of carb it has. If it is set up properly, all carbs of the same flow rating will make virtually the same power.

Vacuum vs. Mechanical

The second thing to consider is to use a vacuum secondary or mechanical secondary carb. The major difference between these two carbs are the way the secondary barrels are opened. With the "double pumper" type carb, the secondaries are opened mechanically by a linkage attached to the throttle cable. The term "double pumper" actually only describes a mechanical secondary Holley carb. There are many other mechanical secondary carbs that are "single pumpers." The vacuum secondary carb opens its secondaries by way of a vacuum diaphragm that pulls them open. Because vacuum is an indication of engine load, this diaphragm can automatically adjust the amount that the secondaries are open.

For maximum performance, you want maximum power instantly, especially in drag racing. Everything has to be full blast for the entire quarter-mile. A mechanical secondary carb is a full-blast carb. As soon as you mash the pedal, all four of those barrels are going wide open. This will give maximum performance immediately if everything is working

Dialing in secondary diaphragm opening rate is considerably easier with this two-piece cover. Part no. 20-59 is for single carbs, 20-73 for dual four-barrel installations. Both covers in part no. 20-73 have a nipple so that two covers can be connected with a tube to balance the opening signal. Photo by Dave Emanuel.

An old trick for instant secondary opening on Holley four-barrels is to put a screw in the secondary throttle link slot. This effectively turns a vacuum-secondary carburetor into a mechanical secondary model. This only problem is that with no rear accelerator pump, the engine is sure to stumble when the secondaries pop open. Holley offers a selection of secondary diaphragm springs (kit number 20-13) for tuning secondary opening rate. Opening rate is affected by spring stiffness and overall height. Photo by Dave Emanuel.

and set up correctly.

Bogging—If things aren't working right, instead of maximum performance you will have maximum *bogging*. If you're a racer, you might know what bogging is. It is when you nail the pedal and the engine falls flat for a second before it takes off. Meanwhile, the guy in the other lane is five car lengths ahead of you. This happens because of how the carb adjusts to varying loads. Because the carb only works off pressure and vacuum, it sometimes can't adjust quickly enough. When you are idling, the carb is using its idle circuit to run the engine. At full power it uses its main system. The problem and cause of the bogging is the transition from idle to main. When all the barrels snap open, the air speed inside the venturis of the carb suddenly slows. Unfortunately for the poor carb, the main system only responds to airflow (and therefore speed) in the venturis.

When the air speed falls momentarily, the carb thinks that the engine has basically stopped running and doesn't dish out any fuel. The engine would actually stop running if not for the carb's accelerator pump. This pump shoots some raw fuel directly into the venturi of the carb to keep the engine running long enough for the main system to realize that it needs to start working. In other words, the accelerator pump covers up the air speed drop and the resulting lack of fuel delivery. Is this primitive or what? If the pump can't squirt enough fuel to keep the engine running, it will bog. Most carbs only have one accelerator pump, usually on the primaries. This is why most mechanical carbs are prone to bogging. What makes the Holley carbs unique is that they have an additional accelerator pump for the secondaries. This drastically helps to increase response. These accelerator pumps can be adjusted with different

opening cams and nozzle sizes to help to reduce bogging.

Vacuum secondary carbs on the other hand use the engine's air speed to open the secondaries. The carb has a vacuum diaphragm that senses the load and air speed to determine the secondary opening. Because of this, it's almost impossible to open the secondaries too fast and cause bogging. If the carb senses that the engine isn't ready for the additional air flow, it won't open the secondaries too soon and cause a bog. There are diaphragm spring kits that allow the opening rate to be adjusted depending on engine size and use. However, since the secondaries usually won't open very fast, power is lost. The trade-off here is that the mechanical secondary carb will be bogging, trying to make max power instantly while the vacuum secondary carb will be moving the vehicle instantly, albeit not at max power!

Try to figure out where your

Holley carbs equipped with mechanical secondaries usually employ a link (arrow) from the primary throttle bracket for activation. Many times, this link must be bent (to shorten it) to ensure that the secondaries open fully. Photo by Dave Emanuel.

performance goal lies relative to the two above-mentioned scenarios and pick the one right for you. If it's a casual street car, use the vacuum carb. It won't bog and its fuel economy will be better. If it is a real race car, use the mechanical secondary carb. These carbs will deliver max power when you want it, not when your carb thinks you want it. Though it may bog at first, the mechanical secondary carbs are very adjustable and with some tinkering, they can be made virtually bog-free.

The acceleration rate of the engine is important. With a big engine and decent converter (or manual transmission) the engine should be able to rev quickly. This inherently reduces bog too. If the carb is sized properly, bog should not be an issue. Holley knows that carbs are prone to bogging. This is why there are so many different sizes of Holley carbs. It allows you to put a carb on the engine that's just big enough do to the job but not too big to be a bogging

pig. Most racers think that bogging is caused by a carb that's too big. This is generally true but it's important to understand the theory and reason behind it. Remember that bogging is caused during the time that the main circuit is catching up to the engine and the air speed is slow. A bigger carb simply needs even more airflow to get the main circuit working. This is why bigger carbs are more prone to bogging. It's just air speed (or lack of it) that makes it all happen.

Carb Size

The last thing to consider is the size of the carb. This is measured in terms of flow rate (cfm, cubic feet per minute). For maximum power, there should be no restriction in the induction path. Ideally, Mother Nature's atmospheric pressure should jam in as much air as the engine can handle with nothing getting in the way. If the carb is too small, it will be a restriction. If it's too big, it may be hard to get the bogging out of it. Carbs do not force mixture in, the atmosphere just pushes in a certain amount of air in response to the pressure changes in the cylinders as the pistons move. You could put 50 carbs on your 440 and it would still run. Max power would be great because there would be no restriction. However there would also be negligible air speed through each carb and it would be impossible to prevent bogging, even with an accelerator pump the size of a garden hose!

Fortunately there is a formula that determines minimum carb size for an engine at a given rpm, and we cover that in the sidebar listed nearby. Use it to figure out your requirements. Generally it's better to have a carb that's on the smaller side because it

Whenever Holley float bowls are removed and reinstalled, or whenever the accelerator pump cam is moved, the pump override spring may need to be readjusted. There should be the slightest of preloads on the pump lever. Any clearance between override mechanism and the pump lever will delay the pump shot which may cause a hesitation. Photo by Dave Emanuel.

will be more responsive and easier to tune. On the other hand, a drag car with a transbrake can benefit from a carb that's larger than the formula figures. Since transbrake cars usually leave with the carb wide open (the ignition rev-limiter keeps the rpm down on the starting line), there rarely is any bogging and the accelerator pump is not of much concern. Because of this, the larger carb won't be a problem to launch and it will deliver the best top-end power. Remember that carbs always require some tinkering to get them to work well. It takes testing, time, and patience to get one sorted out.

General Carburetor Tips

Power Valves—All carbs have some sort of power valve. This valve is controlled by vacuum and serves to enrich the mixture with more fuel when the engine is under load. Without a power valve system, the carb would run too rich at partial

Power valves for Holley carbs are available from a variety of sources, but not all are suitable. The valve at left is a genuine Holley part, the one on the right, an aftermarket replacement. Note the difference in the opening, and it's not surprising that the replacement valve doesn't have the same fuel flow potential. It's unsuitable for performance use. Photo by Dave Emanuel.

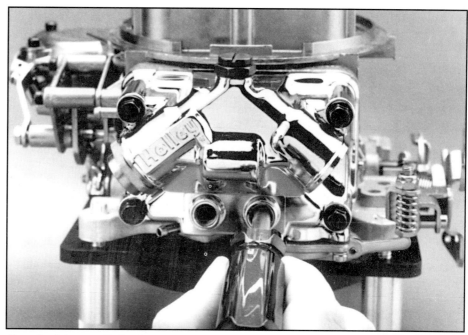

Changing jets on a Holley is a relatively simple task, requiring removal of only four fuel bowl screws. Once the bowl is pulled off, the metering block, which holds the jets, can be separated from the carburetor's main body. However, if you really want to get with the program, get this recent addition to Holley's line of parts–Quick Change float bowl kits. Two plugs in the front of the bowl allow jets to be changed without removing the bowls. Each kit is supplied with a dual feed type bowl, fuel bowl, gaskets, plugs and a jet removal tool. Quick Change bowls are available in standard and chrome finish for Model 4150/4160 and 4500 carbs.

throttle, resulting in poor fuel economy. Under load the vacuum in the carb drops. Once the vacuum falls below a certain point, the power valve will open and more fuel will flow through the carb. Most carbs have some type of spring-loaded power valve where the loss in vacuum will overcome the spring and allow the valve to open. The problem lies in the fact that an engine with a big cam has low vacuum at idle. Sometimes the idle vacuum is below the power valve opening point and the power valve will actually begin to open at idle. Needless to say, this will cause too much fuel to flow since the power valve thinks that the engine is under a heavy load but it is not. This is the main reason why racing engines "load up" at idle. The carb will begin to flow too much fuel and will actually drown out the engine.

The trick is to select a power valve that has an opening point just below the lowest vacuum reading at idle. In this way, the power valve circuit will not kick in at idle and the idle quality will be much better. Unfortunately, only Holley carbs have power valves that are easily changed to one with a different opening point. For most other carbs, the power valve spring

tension has to be adjusted in some way. Racing carburetors don't have power valves because they aren't meant to go cruising around town.

The opening point of a power valve can be a small source of inconsistency in performance. If you have a Holley carb with a power valve, it can be eliminated by plugging. This will require the jet size to be increased by about seven sizes to compensate for the lack of additional enrichment. Carefully check the plugs or exhaust temperature to be sure that the carb is rich enough for proper operation. By blocking off the power valve, the car may become more consistent but idle quality may suffer.

Fuel Lines—The best carb in the world won't make much power if it doesn't have a good supply of fuel. The stock fuel lines and an HP mechanical pump are adequate for

street use and casual racing but are too small for real race use. If the car is going to be competitively raced, replace the factory fuel line with 1/2" tubing. Make sure that the inlet in the tank is replaced with the larger tubing as well. You don't want any restriction there. Some books recommend using 3/8" tubing, which will work fine, but the 1/2" stuff is only slightly more expensive and just as much effort to install. Besides, the 1/2" system will always be there if you decide to step up to a bigger engine in the future. Run an electric fuel pump in the rear and some type of regulator mounted somewhere near the engine. From the regulator, run a 3/8" line to each float bowl of the carb and you will be set.

Fuel Pump—Having a fuel pump with enough capacity is important for two reasons. First the engine needs a lot of fuel (about .5 pounds per hour

A high capacity fuel pump is required to feed your high output engine. This Barry Grant 400 pump will supply enough fuel for a 600 cid engine with nitrous oxide.

A high capacity regulator will also be required to keep up with the demand. There are many new regulators on the market that fit the bill nicely.

per horsepower) to produce big power. Second and less obvious is the fact that the pump has to pump the fuel up to the engine against the force of acceleration trying to keep it in the back of the car. This is why the fuel pumps on the market have such high capacity. They must have reserve power to overcome the force of acceleration. Obviously the faster the car, the more force and therefore more pump is required. Observe your fuel pressure gauge at the top end of the track. If the fuel pressure falls off at all, your fuel system isn't adequate to supply the demand from the engine. Update it before damage results from leaning out the engine. If you are using nitrous, put the largest capacity fuel system that you can afford on your car. You can't lean out a nitrous engine too many times without damaging something. If you don't spend the money on a fuel system, you will be spending it on new engine parts.

Jetting—Jetting the carb is a question that most engine builders get several times a day. Unfortunately for most racers, the answer they most often here is "whatever jets make the

car go fastest." This may not be the most helpful answer, but it is the correct one. There are so many factors to consider here that it would be impossible to just spit out some jet numbers that are correct for every engine combination and track altitude. Always start with the stock jet size for your carb and go from there. After the car has a baseline established, bump up the jets 1 size all the way around and see if there is a positive change. If so, continue in that direction until there is no more change. If richening up the carb causes a negative change, then go leaner.

Always keep the stagger in the carb from primary size to secondary size the same as it is from the factory. The difference in jets sizes within the carb are usually from the fact that the venturis are a different size. For a drag car, always tune for maximum mph as this is a truer indication of engine power. The relationship of E.T. to mph is more of an indication of chassis efficiency. If you have access to a dyno, do some tuning there to find out at what exhaust gas temperature (usually around 1300 degrees) gives best power. At the

track, tune to duplicate this best temperature. Don't fall for the old myth that goes like, "I have an 850 cfm carb but it's jetted down to a 750 cfm." The only thing that can change the airflow potential of the carb is the size of the barrels, not the jets. Remember to always give the engine what it wants even if it goes against what you (or your buddies) think it wants. An engine speaks a language all of its own; it will tell you what it likes, it's your job to listen!

Modified Carbs—All the racing magazines have ads for tricked out Holley carbs. My experience has shown that if you have the correct carb for your application, having your carb modified will not show a large performance gain. However, you will most likely see an increase in consistency and idle quality. Both of these things are especially important for a drag car. Don't neglect idle quality for a drag car since it is important to have a consistent idle for staging the car on the starting line. For the money, a modified carb can be a good investment toward winning races.

SELECTING THE RIGHT CARB FOR YOUR ENGINE
by Dave Emanuel

Air Capacity

Choosing a performance carburetor amounts to somewhat more than purchasing the largest model your budget allows. The first step is to determine the maximum airflow potentially demanded by the engine that is to receive the carburetor. On the surface, this appears to require no more than converting cubic inches (engine size) to cubic feet, multiplying by maximum rpm (to determine the engine cfm requirement), and selecting a carburetor that offers a corresponding airflow capacity. However, intended usage, engine efficiency, engine operating range and the total number of throttle bores must also be taken into consideration.

The basic mathematical formula for relating engine size and rpm to carburetor airflow capacity is:

cfm = Engine cid x Maximum rpm/3456

By way of example, consider a 440 cid engine with a maximum engine speed of 8000 rpm. By working it through the above equation, the cfm works out to 1018 cfm. Therefore, a carburetor with near a 1018 cfm (1050 is likely) capacity would appear to be ideal.

Volumetric Efficiency

However, no adjustment has been made for volumetric efficiency (V.E.). Simply stated, volumetric efficiency is how many cubic inches of air and gas are consumed by an engine every two revolutions. Theoretically, a 440 cid engine with a 100% V.E. will consume 440 cubic inches of air and gas every two revolutions. However, except for well-prepared race engines, few engines reach 100% V.E. Also, volumetric efficiency is not constant throughout the rpm range, although it is usually highest at the engine speed where maximum torque is produced. According to Mike Urich, former vice president of engineering at Holley Carburetors and co-author of HPBooks' *Holley Carburetors, Manifolds & Fuel Injection*:

"An ordinary low-performance engine has a V.E. of about 75% at maximum speed; about 80% at maximum torque. A high-performance engine has a V.E. of about 80% at maximum speed; about 85% at maximum torque. An all-out race engine has a V.E. of about 90% at maximum speed; about 95% at maximum torque. A highly tuned intake and exhaust system with efficient cylinder-head porting and a camshaft ground to take full advantage of the engine's other equipment can provide such complete cylinder filling that a V.E. of 100%—or slightly higher—is obtained at the speed for which the system is tuned."

Urich goes on to recommend that you assume a V.E. of 85% for high performance street engines and a V.E. of 110% for all-out, highly tuned racing engines. As an example, consider the 440 racing engine running at 8000 rpm:

cfm =   440 cid x 8000 rpm/3456 x 1.1 V.E.

cfm = 1120

Theoretically, a carburetor with an 1150 cfm capacity would be ideal. The 1.1, by the way, is 110% converted to a decimal. To calculate the street carb cfm, use the above equation, only multiply by .85 (85% converted to a decimal) to arrive at a theoretical cfm.

These percentages of volumetric efficiency really mean that instead of consuming 440 cubic inches of air and gas every two revolutions, a 440 engine will use that percentage thereof. In other words, an engine with an 85% V.E. will only use 374 cubic inches of air and gas every two revolutions (440 x .85).

The laws of physics prevent these percentages from changing very dramatically. Intake manifold efficiency, valve and port size, camshaft timing and exhaust manifold configuration are a few of the more readily identifiable factors affecting the volume of intake charge that will reach a cylinder prior to the power stroke. Since the low pressure created by a piston moving downward in a cylinder (during the intake stroke) is not sufficient to draw in 100% of the volume required to completely fill that cylinder (with the piston at the bottom of its travel), the effect of inertia is needed to keep the incoming air/gas mixture flowing after the piston has started moving upward (during the initial stage of the compression stroke). The inertia or "ram" effect increases with rpm, which is one of the reasons that internal combustion engines produce maximum horsepower in the upper rpm ranges.

This all-out race engine is plumbed with nitrous and requires a lot of extra spark. The distributor shown is a Mopar Performance race unit.

The only type of ignition to use in your racing engine is an electronic one. The days of point ignition are long over for anything other than a street engine that has been restored to factory original condition. Chrysler began using electronic ignition systems in 1972 for passenger cars (an industry first) and actually had semi-electronic systems (point-triggered electronic box) for race cars in the '60s. Not only will a good electronic ignition make more horsepower than a point ignition but the engine will start easier, run better and consume less fuel. Maintenance will be virtually eliminated as well, because the electronic systems have nothing to adjust or wear out. They are much more reliable than points, so your chances of ignition failure are reduced. Racing ignition systems can have many extra features like rev limiters, timing retards, starting line controllers, etc. These things can be very helpful to your racing program as will the extra consistency that a good

ignition can provide. Because there is no parts that will wear out like the point-type ignition, the electronic ignition can perform the same function over and over again, making the engine more consistent in its power output.

IGNITION BASICS

The basics for the ignition of a racing engine are not much different than for a stock engine. The compressed air/fuel mixture needs to be ignited at the right time to produce maximum power. The main difference in ignitions is that a high performance ignition system has to be able to fire at a much faster rate and with a hotter spark. At 6000 rpm, the ignition must be able to produce a spark 400 times per second. Everything in the system has to be up to task or the spark will become weak, because the recovery time for the components is so short. If this happens, the spark will eventually become too weak to ignite the fuel and the engine will not be able to rev

A 440 distributor is longer due to the higher block height. A 440 distributor can be made to fit in the low deck block by simply using this Mopar Performance spacer. If you are buying a new race distributor, get one for the 440 block even if you are using a low block engine. By doing this you will be covered for both block types with the addition of the spacer.

A race distributor usually has "sharper" points on the reluctor to minimize misfiring at high rpm.

any higher. With things like high compression and nitrous oxide, the spark must be very strong at all times or it can actually be "blown out" by all the pressure. Obviously if this happens, the engine won't produce much power or rev very high since the mixture won't be able to burn thoroughly enough.

Trigger

Most electronic ignitions use some type of magnetic triggering mechanism in the distributor to signal the control box that it's time to make another spark. The Mopar system uses a spinning reluctor (magnet) with eight spikes that spins near a pickup coil. When one of the reluctor spikes comes close to the pickup coil, a small current is generated in the coil. This current is fed to the control box which then zaps the ignition coil, making it

fire the spark plug. A hotter spark is produced by the coil because it is zapped with much more voltage than a point ignition can generate. A point ignition can only hit the coil with battery voltage because that's the only source for electricity in the car. An electronic ignition can actually generate a higher voltage in the control box due to its circuitry.

Capacitive Discharge

Most control boxes have a special circuit that charges a capacitor which then rapidly discharges into the coil. This is where the name capacitive discharge ignition and the terms "CD" or "CDI" come from. It's not uncommon for these systems to put 200 volts or more on the primary side of the coil instead of the usual 12 volts as with a point ignition. This is why electronic ignitions have a hotter spark than their point counterparts. This hotter spark is much more resistant to being blown out under high compression.

Distributor

For maximum power, the spark also has to occur at the right instant each and every time. Since the trigger of the electronic distributor simply consists of a spinning magnet, the timing can be much more accurate. Nothing ever wears out, so barring some kind of mechanical breakdown, the distributor should provide years of trouble-free service. A good distributor is a lifetime investment purchase so buy a good one. The best ignition box in the world won't do much good if the voltage doesn't get to the plugs at the right time. The low-block engines use a shorter distributor than the raised-block engines. As a tip, buy a raised-block distributor even if you are currently using a low-block engine, because the RB distributor can work in a B engine by using a Mopar Performance spacer kit. This way you are covered for both block types, with only one distributor.

Distributor Drive

Remember that the distributor is

The street distributor has less pronounced points on its reluctor.

driven off the camshaft via the oil pump driveshaft. If any of these components are worn or sloppy, the ignition timing won't be accurate or consistent. Make sure that the timing chain is tight when you install it. If it jumps around, the timing will also jump. The easiest way to test it is to check the timing at a high rpm like 5000 or 6000. Don't worry about the myth that "free revving" the engine this high will blow it up. If it won't rev to 6000 rpm in the pits, it certainly won't go to 6000 rpm under load on the track. If the timing marks are anything but steady, you are losing power and consistency. Figure out where the problem is and correct it.

MOPAR CONVERSION KITS

The first level of a racing ignition would be the Mopar electronic conversion kits. The kits have been around for what seems like forever and they work great.

Orange Box

The basic vacuum advance kit with the orange control box is a good street and track ignition system. This setup works well to an rpm maximum of about 6500 rpm. Above this and the output of the box begins to fall off. The engine will still rev over 6500 but maximum power won't be realized.

Chrome Box

If the engine is going to be used for more serious racing, simply replace the orange box with the chrome one.

The chrome box will produce enough output for virtually any racing engine. They can be wired the same so the swap should take about one minute to do. The chrome box is the most popular Mopar ignition for race track use. Mopar sells a race ignition conversion kit that comes with the chrome box and a mechanical advance distributor that also has provisions for a tach drive. The tach drive part is kind of neat to have but the days of mechanical tachometers has long since been over. This distributor is a better one for racing, though, because it has a better reluctor design than the vacuum advance distributor. The race reluctor design has more pronounced "spikes" than the vacuum unit. These spikes allow for more accurate timing and less chance of false triggering. As a quick note, I have personally used this distributor in engines that make over 1200 horsepower and run in the high 6-second zone in the quarter mile. They really work great.

Both distributors have fast advance

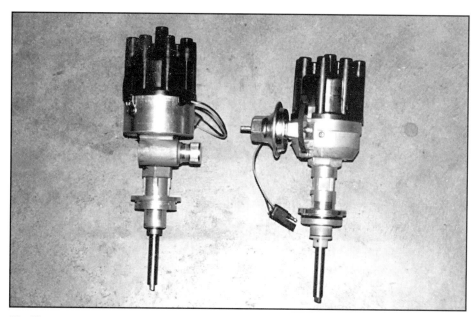

The Mopar race distributor (left) has the provision to run a mechanical tach, while the street unit has vacuum advance. Both work well in their respective applications.

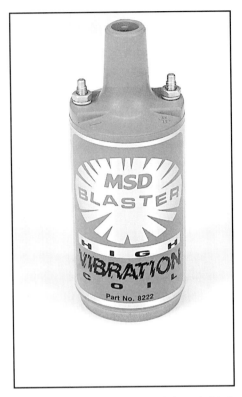

There are numerous models of high performance coils, but not all coils are compatible with all ignition systems. Be sure to verify compatability before installation and also make sure a coil is rugged enough for your application. This MSD coil is specifically designed to withstand a vibration-intensive installation, like racing.

curves that will bring in all the advance by 2000 rpm with the vacuum distributor and 1500 rpm with the mechanical advance distributor. The vacuum unit can be used for street use, but make sure that the engine does not detonate when the vacuum advance is hooked up. For racing use, mechanical advance is the preferred way to go.

Super Gold

If you want the ultimate factory Mopar electronic ignition system use the "super gold" box and the mechanical advance distributor. This unit will give the highest output of any of the factory boxes and will supposedly fire cleanly to over 10,000 rpm. Hopefully, your engine will not

be exceeding this rpm level. The gold box is intended for short-term use only so it is not recommended for street use. If the ignition will be used on the street, don't use the gold box. The chrome box is the most advanced system you can use for the street.

Coils

Make sure that the coil used will be able to handle the extra energy from these high output boxes. A points-type coil will work in an emergency but an electronic ignition coil should be used. As with everything else in a race car, the ignition will only be as strong as its weakest link. Don't make the weak link the coil. The coil has to have the ability to produce a strong spark at a rate of over 400 per second. There are many coils on the market, but the two that work best are the Accel chrome race coil #140306 (not the big yellow ones) and the MSD Blaster 2. These coils will keep any engine happy.

Ballast Resistor

Make sure to use the proper ballast resistor with any of the Mopar systems. Use only the two-wire ballast, not the four wire. The two wire will make the box output more, but only the three Mopar high performance boxes noted above should be wired with it. Use the 1/4 ohm ballast P2444641 for maximum output. Many people don't know what the ballast resistor does any way; Chrysler cars seem to be the only ones that use them.

Operation—Basically, a resistor limits the voltage input to the coil. A 12-volt coil is not meant to run on 12 volts. It is meant to run on about 9 volts. I'm not crazy here, read on. The hardest time for a coil is during

The Ultra Coil from Jacobs is a take-no-prisoners unit that delivers up to 1950 watts of spark power.

engine starting, especially when it's cold outside. Under these conditions, the engine is turning very slowly and it really doesn't want to start. The battery voltage is low due to the load of the starter and the cold temperature. The battery voltage is actually down to around 9 volts (surprise!) during this time. Because the poor coil is only getting 9 volts, the spark during cranking would be too weak to fire the engine if it were set up to run on 12 volts. Because it's made for 9 volts, it fires clean and hot during starting. Unfortunately for the coil, once the engine starts and the alternator kicks in, the voltage goes up to near 14 volts. This would be too much for the coil to handle and it would quickly fry. This is where the ballast resistor comes in. It is switched into the supply line to the coil when the key is in the "run" position and drops the voltage down to prevent damage to the coil. When the key is in the start position, the ballast resistor is bypassed. Other cars do have a similar setup but it is usually in the form of a resistor wire instead of the more familiar (to Mopar enthusiasts) white resistor. Because these things get hot and occasionally fail, Chrysler figured

Multi-spark discharge systems can be connected to virtually any type of distributor. These systems put a fat spark across the plug gaps, which not only makes for excellent power output, It also is very effective at preventing plug fouling when an engine is run a lower speeds. You can also add quite a few racing accessories. Courtesy MSD.

under high pressure too, which turned out to be correct.

Just like any other fire, the fuel only needs one spark to ignite if everything is running properly. Unfortunately things are rarely running properly inside a racing engine. Big cams with long overlap cause loading up due to mixture contamination. High compression pistons generate more pressure. Nitrous oxide brings more fuel to burn. High rpm leaves less time for the fuel to burn. All of these things combine to make ignition difficult. A multi-spark system will usually be able to fire the air/fuel mixture under all of these conditions because there are more sparks available.

Advantages—At idle some multi-spark boxes can produce twenty sparks per plug, and at 8000 rpm about three sparks per plug. This is truly amazing. But unless you have some real problem in the combustion chamber the multi-spark ignition will rarely make much more power than a conventional ignition. Remember, one

that it would be easier to replace the little resistor than trying to rip the wiring harness apart to find the resistor wire. For racing, the lower resistance ballast will put more voltage on the coil and make it produce a hotter spark. This will cause the coil to run hotter, so try to mount it where it can get some ventilation.

MULTI-SPARK IGNITIONS

During the energy crisis of the early 1970s, car manufacturers were experimenting with very lean fuel mixtures to try and improve fuel economy. They were using such lean mixtures that the ignition couldn't even fire them. A new ignition was developed by Autotronic Controls and called *multi-spark discharge*, or MSD the trademark it is commonly known by. The MSD brand by Autotronic Controls is definitely the more popular brand, but Accel, Jacobs and Mallory also make high performance systems as well.

The early multi-spark ignitions had the ability to produce multiple sparks

each time a plug needed to fire instead of the normal one spark per plug. These extra sparks had the ability to fire the super lean fuel mixtures since there is more chance of a spark igniting something if there are more sparks present. As the quest for better fuel economy continued, racers began to look at this ignition for their use. If it could fire lean mixtures so well, maybe it could fire rich mixtures

Jacobs Electronics offers a number of Energy Pak ignition systems for street, race and marine applications. These patented systems tailor spark intensity and duration according to engine requirements. Photo by Dave Emanuel.

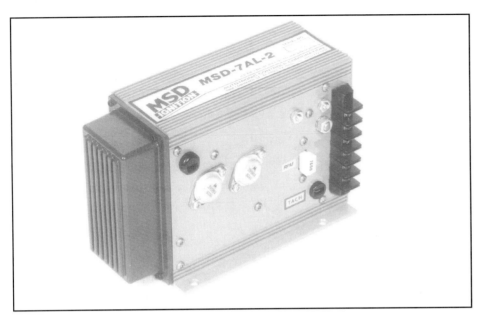

MSD's 7AL-2 is designed for drag racing and provides a tremendous amount of spark energy. The unit also includes a built in rev limiter; maximum rpm is controlled by a plug in chip.

GENERAL RACING IGNITION TIPS

Use the following general tips for racing engines.

Distributors

Mopar distributors sometimes have a problem with high rpm timing flutter. To prevent this, weld the advance mechanism so that it's locked down. This is easy to do by taking the distributor apart and tack-welding the pins in the advance plate. If you do this, the distributor will not have any advance at all—the timing will be fixed. Start the engine and set the timing to what your maximum advance will be. This modification makes triggering much more accurate but will make starting difficult, especially with high compression and a hot engine because the timing is

spark is all it takes. It will however, prevent plug fouling, promote better idle quality without "loading up," and aid in starting.

What makes a multi-spark system so good for a racer are all of the accessories that can be added on to a basic ignition box. There are automatic timing retards, rev limiters for everything from starting line rpm to blow-up protection, rpm activated switches, shift lights, etc.

The list of things that can be done with a multi-spark ignition is almost immeasurable. Make sure that the coil is compatible with the multi-spark ignition box—not all of them are. These systems usually put at least 350 volts on the coil and need a coil with a fast recovery rate because it will be producing many more sparks. For dual-purpose engines used on the street and track, use the MSD 6AL box with a Blaster 2 coil (from Autotronic Controls). For track only (or limited street driving) use the MSD 7AL box and a Pro Power coil. The 7AL system is pretty much the

standard for professional racing. The MSD catalog has many different wiring plans for all the accessories, so get a copy if you plan on using their system.

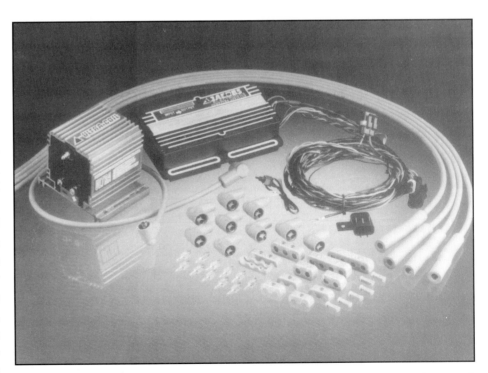

The Jacobs Ultra Team is a complete ignition system featuring high output coil, control module, plug wires and separators. Independent dyno testing has shown this system capable of increasing power output compared to other race type systems.

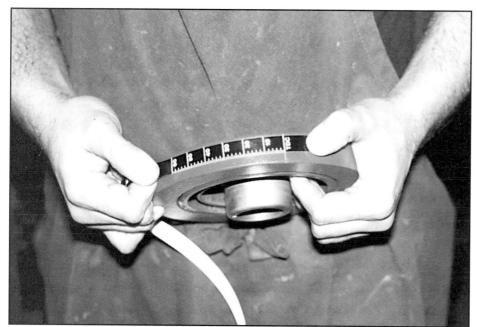

A timing tape can be added to a stock damper to provide to allow for easy reference points for total timing and valve adjustments. After gluing it on, spray over it with clear paint and it won't fly off at high rpm. Make sure to install it in the correct direction!

the contact in the cap for the cylinder that needs to be fired. All this is done obviously while the engine is not running. If absolutely no timing variation is your goal, go with a crank trigger. As a note, the welded distributor trick comes pretty close to a crank trigger in accuracy at a fraction of the cost.

Timing

Proper ignition timing is extremely important for proper operation and reliability. Not enough advance will result in poor performance while too much will result in engine damage. Most B engines are happy between 33–37 degrees of advance for maximum power. This is dependent on many, many variables, such as head type, cam profile, compression ratio, rpm range, etc. Experimentation at the track or on the dyno is the only way to find the best setting for your engine. Generally start at 34 degrees for your baseline and adjust from there. Make sure that your distributor gives maximum advance at about 1500 rpm. Don't be afraid to check the timing at higher rpm as it's the only

now locked at full advance. Only do this if you have a separate "start" and "run" switch. Get the engine cranking first and then hit the run switch. Either the engine will start or it will stop cranking. If you have an MSD, there's a start retard of 20 degrees built into the timing controller accessory box and into the new 7AL-3 box. This more accurate timing will result in much more consistency in the engine.

Crank Triggers

For the most accurate triggering of the ignition box, use a crank trigger system. This system uses a special wheel that mounts on the vibration damper to trigger the box. This wheel has four attached magnets placed at 90 degree spacing around the edge. The magnets trigger a pickup coil that is fixed to a bracket mounted on the block. The principle of operation is exactly the same as in the stock distributor except with no variation in timing caused by timing chain stretch or distributor shaft flexing. Ignition

timing is set by adjusting the pickup coil on its mount to get the desired timing. The distributor at this point just "distributes" the sparks and does no triggering. The rotor needs to be phased to the correct point in the cap though. This is done by aligning the trigger magnet exactly with the pickup coil after the timing has been set. At this point align the rotor with

Mopar offers a lightweight starter that can solve tight chassis installations. Not only is it much smaller than a stock one, it cranks faster too. They are a must for high compression engines.

Spark plug on left shows what can happen during a nitrous oxide system malfunction. If the timing is too far advanced or the correct amount of additional gasoline is not injected damage like this can occur. In this engine, both the cylinder head and the piston also suffered some heat damage. Both plugs are from the same engine, on the same quarter-mile run. The power of nitrous is shown by the fact that this dragster still ran a 6.73 ET on this run with three other melted spark plugs! The culprit was a stuck fuel solenoid.

way to see what is going on. Always set the timing by the total timing method, meaning set the timing for 34 degrees at the point where all the advance is in.

If you are running a vacuum advance distributor, disconnect the vacuum advance when setting the timing. As a note, this distributor seems to give the best performance if the vacuum advance is left disconnected at all times.

Spark Plugs

Spark plugs are the topic of many questions to engine builders. Let me go out on a limb here, and say that like oil, any spark plug will do the job. The plug companies spend lots of money on advertising to try to convince you that their plugs are the only ones for you. This is simply not true. My racing experience has shown that any brand of plug will work fine. Conventional-style plugs work just as

well as the new split electrode plugs. Do not overpay for your spark plugs.

Heat Range—A racer should primarily be concerned with the heat range of the plug. Plugs are available in many different heat ranges, from hot to cold. The heat range actually means how hot the business end of the

spark plug will run in the combustion chamber. A hot plug has a slightly longer nose and because it sticks into the chamber a little further, it will run hotter. This is needed for a stock engine that must be able to idle in traffic without having the plugs foul. A hotter plug will be more resistant to fouling, especially at low speeds, than a cold plug. However, this hotter running plug is not desirable in a racing engine. The hotter tip of the plug may actually cause detonation and pre-ignition since it may ignite the fuel simply by virtue of the fact that its tip is so hot. Because you are trying your best to suppress any and all detonation, you don't need the spark plug to cause it. Therefore, try to run the coldest plug possible in your racing engine. If the cold plugs foul too easily, go up one step at a time until the fouling stops.

With Nitrous—If you are using nitrous oxide, make sure to run the coldest possible plug. When the engine is on the nitrous, the combustion temperature soars very rapidly and the engine is very susceptible to detonation. A cold plug

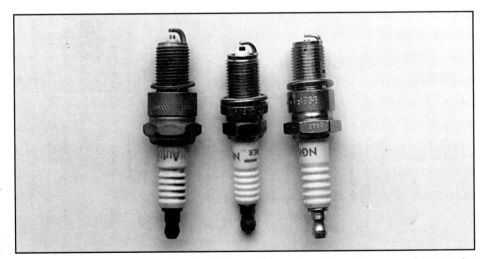

Spark plug heat range is very important in a racing engine. Generally you want to run the coldest plug that will not foul out. A stock plug on left may cause pre-ignition in a high compression engine. A colder one (center) will cure this problem. Special plugs (right) are available with recessed electrodes to clear domed pistons.

If a spark plug has too cold a heat range, it will foul. If it's too hot, the plug may self-destruct. This warm-up plug was accidently left in an engine during dyno testing and the center electrode was completely burned away. Photo by Dave Emanuel.

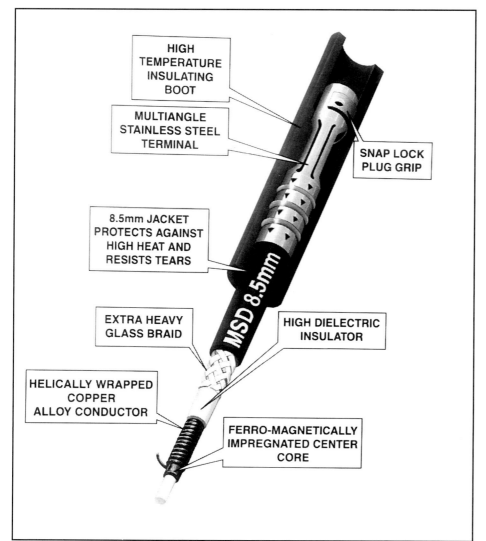

Spark plug wires look simple enough, but it takes careful selection of conductor, insulating and jacketing materials to ensure that wires survive in the hot and hostile underhood environment. Exhaust heat is a plug wire's biggest enemy.

will help prevent detonation.

Spark Plug Gap—One of the benefits of a high output ignition is that it has the ability to fire a larger gap in the plug. If the spark is larger, there will be a greater chance for ignition and hopefully the fuel will burn more completely. The old points ignition usually couldn't fire a gap much over .035" reliably, especially under high load. With the newer style ignitions, gaps of .060" or more aren't uncommon. If you are running a Mopar ignition, use a plug gap of .040" and with an MSD system use a gap of .060". For use with nitrous, shorten the gap to .035" with either ignition. The additional fuel and nitrous in the chamber make the plug very hard to fire. A reduced gap will prevent any misfiring with nitrous.

Wires

The spark plug wires should be in good shape, free of any cracks or breaks. Use a good quality wire with at least 8mm insulation. A solid copper core wire will deliver the most power to the plugs but will also cause too much electrical interference to run many of the on-board electrical accessories that are popular on today's race cars. For this reason, choose a heli-coil type wire to prevent ignition interference. Make sure to loom the wires nicely and keep them off anything metallic. This is especially important around the headers. Due to the spark plug location on a wedge head, the plug wires have to run very close to the header pipe. More than one race has been lost due to a burned plug wire and the resultant loss of one cylinder. Don't let it happen to you.

Huge 2 3/8" primary headers help this nitrous 596 cid B-1 engine make big power.

For maximum performance the big-block Mopar needs a set of exhaust headers. The factory exhaust manifolds simply won't cut it. It doesn't matter if they are the factory high performance versions or not; throw them away. This sounds like a strong statement and frankly it is. It's not necessarily an airflow problem, as much as it is a matter of tuning. The stock manifolds don't have any primary tube length at all since all the exhaust ports simply dump into the same space. Because of this, there is no chance of picking up the scavenging effects that a properly designed set of tube headers can give. While it's true that headers have a few negative side effects, the advantages more than outweigh them.

HEADER DESIGN

For headers to work with maximum efficiency they need to be properly designed. The four main areas of header design are: primary tube diameter, primary tube length, and the diameter and length of the collector. It is possible to design the ultimate set of headers for your engine.

Unfortunately, the ultimate set of pipes may not fit in your vehicle, which effectively makes them useless. Generally, the headers that are available from the aftermarket header manufacturers are the ones that you will be using, because most people can't build their own set. These designs are dictated more by the chassis than by ultimate performance, which is a good compromise, because you actually have to use them in your car!

Theory

There are many different theories floating around as to why headers work. Let's dispel the myths and go for the truth. Because the exhaust gases are coming out of the engine in the form of pulses instead of a continuous flow, all sorts of pressure waves are moving inside of the header pipe. At certain frequencies of pulsing (amount of pulses per second, determined by engine rpm) the pipe will begin to resonate similar to the pipe of a pipe organ. If the length and diameter of the pipe is changed, this resonance point will also change. Where and how this resonance occurs will determine how well the pipe

Big-tube 2" headers for B/E bodies will make the most power of any drop-in headers. A bodies should use fenderwell headers for best performance. Use the formula in the appendix for optimum sizing but remember that they have to still fit in the car!

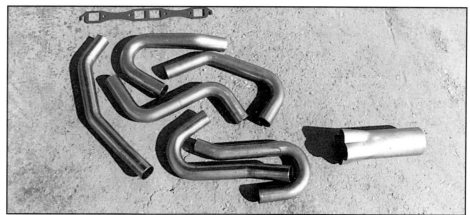

For unique applications, a weld kit will allow you to fabricate your own set of headers. They will take some time to do and are not for the novice mechanic.

works. All this high-brow sounding stuff is where the term "tuned" headers comes from. Inside the pipe, the outward-moving exhaust pressure wave also has a reflected wave of much smaller intensity that actually moves up the pipe. Although it sounds crazy, any open-ended tube that pulsed waves travel through experiences the same phenomenon.

Scavenging & Reversion—Any pressure or frequency wave has a maximum pressure point (a peak) and a minimum pressure point (a valley). If we can time the reflected pressure wave so that a valley occurs at the location of the exhaust valve or the cylinder, it will actually help suck the exhaust gases out of the cylinder and into the header pipe. This is called *exhaust scavenging.*

On the other side of the coin, if the header pipe sizes are wrong and the point of maximum pressure (a peak) occurs at the location of the exhaust valve, some exhaust will enter the cylinder, leading to decreased performance. This is called *exhaust reversion.* The old myth that the pressure wave traveling through the pipe mysteriously had some sort of vacuum wave behind it that was responsible for the scavenging is false. It's all in the timing of the waves.

A perfect header design will ensure that the intensity of the valley (remember this is the low pressure point) of the reflective wave will be maximized at the exhaust valve. Now hopefully you understand all this well enough to notice that the frequency of the pulses determines their location and that frequency is determined by engine rpm. All this leads to one conclusion: Any header design will be perfect at only a specific rpm! Above and below this narrow rpm point the header is a compromise. Attempts to broaden this band include stepped headers of different diameters and expansion chambers. Both of these things affect the waves' speed in the pipe and therefore change the pulse timing. Because everything in an engine moves so fast, many things, especially in the induction path, are a compromise. If you want the ultimate set of headers for your engine use the formulas on page 150 and design your own.

For best overall dragstrip performance, use the point of maximum torque as the design rpm. This point will be different depending on displacement, port flow, camshaft, etc. but will generally be between 4500 and 5500 rpm. If the engine's

application allows it to operate a steady speed, use that rpm. Try to keep the amount of bends to a minimum to ensure maximum flow.

HEADER RECOMMENDATIONS

Now that we have the theory out of the way, it's time to get back to reality. As discussed before the headers that you will probably use will be determined by your chassis more than anything else. Without doing all the math, a smaller primary tube will give the best low- and mid-range power. The same is true of longer primary pipes. For maximum high rpm power, a larger, shorter pipe is best. Using these guidelines, a general recommendation is a follows:

Street 383–440 cid: 1 3/4–1 7/8"
Street/Strip 383–440 cid: 1 7/8–2"
Strip Only 440–500 cid: 2"–2 1/8"
Strip Only 500–550cid: 2 1/8–2 1/4"
550+ cid: 2 3/8"

These are only general guidelines. If your car is heavy, go with the smaller tubes and conversely, if you have a light car like a dragster, use the larger tubes.

Giant 4" muffler on left dwarf the already huge 3" muffler on right. Dual 3" size should be the minimum used for any serious street car.

To gain more torque and power from an exhaust system, a crossover tube can be installed between the two exhaust pipes. This original idea was used by Mopar in the 1960s.

Collector Length

If you are buying off-the-shelf, you are stuck with whatever collector length will fit in your car (you don't want the exhaust blowing out into your tire for example!), which is why I didn't recommend any particular length. If you are building a set, run the numbers in the formulas and figure out what's best. Collector size will usually be determined by primary tube size with the smaller pipes having a 3" collector, the mid-sizes a 3 1/2", the larger sizes a 4", and the huge 2 3/8" pipes a 4" or even 5" collector. The optimum collector length will depend on the vehicle. Generally the longer the collector, the more low-end torque the engine will make.

The best length is best found by trial and error. Start with about a 12" collector and shorten from there. An old racer's trick is to put a paint stripe down the length of the collector and run the car a few times down the track. Cut the collector off at the point that the paint stops being burned off. What most racers don't know is that they are making the collector the correct length for all the waves. The point where the heat is lower in the collector (where the paint is not being burned off) is probably the point of a drop in the intensity of the waves!

Exhaust System

If the car is being used on the street, some type of exhaust system will have to be used. Any exhaust system will reduce the power output of the engine. However, it's a little impractical to drive around the street with open headers all the time. Over the last few years there have been many advances in the exhaust and muffler department. The new high-flow mufflers on the market are so good that there is very little loss of power. Recent dyno testing of a 572 cubic-inch Mopar wedge engine by Dynomax has shown that even a small 2 1/2" turbo-style muffler reduced power output by only 40 horsepower. This is on an engine that made over 850 hp and 750 lbs-ft of torque.

Their larger race-style mufflers showed much less reduction in power. In fact, the giant 4" straight-through-style mufflers showed only a 10 hp drop. My recommendation would be to run the exhaust pipe the same diameter of your header collector if possible. If this is not possible, try to run a minimum of 3" exhaust pipe.

A 3" pipe is pretty common these days on production trucks, so most exhaust shops have the equipment to bend it correctly. Choose the mufflers based on your intended use. If the car is for street racing, use a straight-through-style of race muffler. If not, go with a turbo-style for less noise.

Remember, with the new technology that is available, even the worst of the new-style mufflers will reduce power only a few percent. As an added measure, fabricate a pipe that connects both sides of the exhaust together somewhere between the headers and the mufflers. Try to use the same diameter pipe as the rest of the system if possible. This H-pipe, as it's called, will give more torque and less noise. The Mopar engineers designed the first H-pipes back in the early '60s for their muscle cars. It's a good idea to run one and they're easy to install. Try to run tailpipes of the same diameter to prevent fumes from entering the vehicle. The best exhaust will have as few bends as possible.

After all of your hard work, don't rush things now! It's easy to rush at this stage because the engine is so near to completion. But assembly is a very detail oriented process, and you must proceed methodically and with care. If you don't, chances are you'll be rebuilding a blown motor.

In this chapter, I am only going to give you some assembly tips in photos that I have learned in the 15 years I've been building Mopar engines. This section presumes that you know something about bolting an engine together, so it is not a complete "step-by-step" assembly process that you would find in a basic rebuild book or shop manual.

The key to successful engine assembly can be summed up in one word: cleanliness. An engine is a precise machine with close tolerances, and dirt or foreign objects (like metal shavings) that become lodged between components can quickly lead to disaster.

Assembly requires a certain amount of knowledge and special tools. If you don't have both of these things, consider having a professional assemble your engine. Experienced engine builders develop a "feel" or sense for how the components are

fitting together, and learn to spot a potential problem that an inexperienced builder may miss. While this may cost you some extra money initially, if it saves the engine from breaking, then it is money well spent.

GENERAL ASSEMBLY TIPS

The actual assembly process is not all that difficult, but it does require attention to detail. Make sure that when you are bolting the engine together that you give it your full attention and patience. One overlooked nut or bolt can easily cause engine failure.

I'm not trying to scare you into not doing your own assembly. There is a tremendous amount of personal satisfaction derived from seeing something you have built go down the track successfully. On the other hand, if you need to buy $500 worth of special tools to assemble just one engine, you might be better off with the professional.

If you do decide to dive in, make sure you have a clean, well-lit area to work in. After washing all of the parts, lay them out on a clean workbench so that you can see what you are working with. Set out all the rings and bearings to be sure that you don't forget to install one. Don't laugh, I've seen it happen!

I recommend washing all the parts with soap and water first and then with some type of solvent right before assembly. Always use paper towels to wipe down or dry parts, because any traces of the paper that work their way into the engine will dissolve, unlike cotton rags.

Torquing Fasteners

Always follow the recommended torque for the rods, main caps, and cylinder head fasteners. Make sure that you use the correct lube on the threads, as it will affect the torque readings. The fasteners need to be stretched to ensure their holding power. If they are stretched too much (tightened too tightly) or too little (tightened too loose) they can fail. The fasteners will usually specify a tightening torque usually with oil or moly on the threads. Never tighten them dry or with Loctite® on the threads. When tightening, don't take it to the final torque in one shot. Use three-step increments of, for example, 25, 50, 75 lbs-ft for the head bolts. This gradual tightening will stretch the fastener better, resulting in more strength.

Always clean all threads and threaded holes with solvent before assembly. This too will ensure better

holding power.

Rings

If you are using file-to-fit piston rings take your time and go slowly. This is where inexperienced engine builders usually make the most mistakes—by over-filing the rings. It takes time to develop a feel for gapping the rings. If you overgap by a few thousandths of an inch, don't sweat it, because it will not show up as lost power. If the gap is too small, the ring may seize in the bore, causing a big problem. So remember, when in doubt, a larger gap is preferable to a tighter one. If you are unsure about the whole process use pre-gapped rings or have your machinist do them for you. When installing the pistons make sure that none of the rings get out of their groove as they enter the cylinder.

Camshaft

Make sure that the camshaft turns freely in the block. Since each cam bearing is a different size in these engines, camshaft installation can be tricky. The cam should turn by hand with little effort. If it's too tight, clearance the tight bearing slightly with a bearing knife or a Scotchbrite® pad.

Always use some type of molylube on the cam lobes if you are running a hydraulic or flat-tappet cam. The lobes of the cam are a high pressure spot that is not pressure-oiled. On initial start up there won't be much oil thrown on the cam, This is why the molylube is required.

Engine Break-In

To break in the cam properly, run the engine no lower than 1500 rpm for

at least 10 minutes. I also recommend varying the speed between 1500 and 3500 rpm during this process. You are trying to splash oil on the lobes, but more importantly you are trying to get the lifters to spin in their bores. There is a slight taper ground into the cam lobe and the lifter bottom to make the lifters spin during operation thus preventing them from wearing in one spot. If they do not spin, they will fail. By varying the speed, the lifters have a greater chance of spinning. Roller cams do not need anything more than oil on the lobes and require no break in.

After this short break-in time, set the timing, check for leaks and readjust the valve lash if applicable. Try to get some sort of load on the engine as soon as possible to help seat the rings. If the engine was machined and assembled properly it should be ready to use (or race) immediately. There is no need to baby it for 500 miles or anything like that. That myth is from the old cast-iron ring days. Most drag engines will never see anywhere near that kind of "mileage" in their lifetime, so a long break-in is impossible.

With moly rings and a smooth cylinder wall finish, the rings should seal immediately. Other than the cam and the rings, nothing else is really "wearing in."

Finally, don't be afraid of blowing up the engine either. Nothing will prevent it from blowing up on the 10th pass if you take the first 9 passes easy. The parts don't get stronger with use!

The photos on the following pages illustrate some additional tips.

Checking the ring end gap is best done with a feeler gauge. A good rule to follow is .004" of gap per inch of bore for the top ring and .003" for the second. If the engine is going to be used with nitrous, increase these figures by 20%.

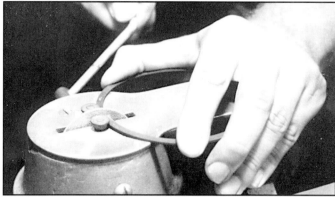

A ring filer is invaluable if you are going to build any quantity of engines. They make sure that the rings are cut squarely and accurately. Always de-burr the rings after filing to remove the burr. This will make sure that the rings will move freely in the piston groove.

A ring-squaring tool makes checking the end gap much easier, and it is more accurate. They are a good investment.

If you don't have access to a squaring tool, a flat-top piston can work. Make sure that it's inserted as squarely as possible.

A tapered ring compressor is the best way to install a piston but a different one is required for each bore size.

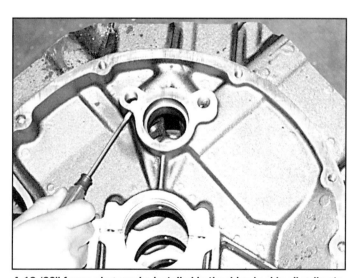

A 19/32" freeze plug can be installed in the driver's side oil galley to block off the oil to the lifters on this side of the block. Install the plug far enough in the galley to block off the oil feed coming from the passage under the oil pressure sender.

Use some type of lube on the bearings before installation. Many products are available to do this.

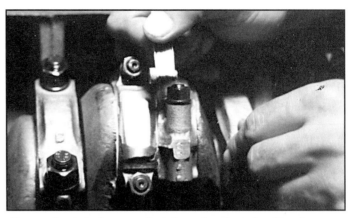

Always check to be sure that there is adequate side clearance between the rods. For a racing engine side clearance should be at least .010". There is really no maximum side clearance, but any over .020" will sling more oil around inside the engine. This, however, is not a problem.

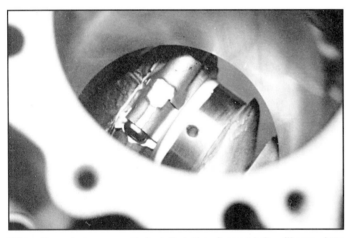

When the rods are correctly installed, the oil spurt hole will spray into the opposite cylinder. All Mopar engines hang the rods with the bearing tangs toward the outside of the engine and the oil spurt hole toward the cam.

If you are using main studs, use 12-point nuts on the rear cap to provide clearance to the seal holder. This will save the hassle of grinding the seal holder.

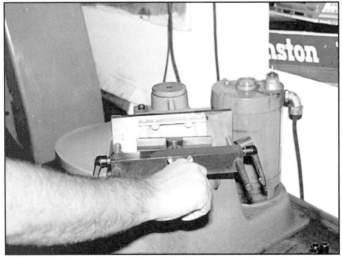

Cutting the main seal holder on a rod cap grinder can solve many seal leaks. It's a good idea to square the holder up on the grinder by about .010" before installation. More cutting may be required to stop some leaks.

Always use some red Locktite® on the cam bolt and torque to spec.

Make sure to correctly install the oil slinger. If it is installed backwards, it will grind into the teeth of the sprocket.

When checking the degreeing of the cam, find the point on the degree wheel that corresponds to .050" before max lift of the tappet. In this example this point is 62 degrees. Always turn the crank in one direction only to eliminate the effects of slack in the chain.

After finding the .050" before point, the .050" after max lift point has to be found. In this case it's 154 degrees. Take this number and add it to the first reading (62 degrees) to yield 216 total, which means the cam is in at 108 degrees (216/2).

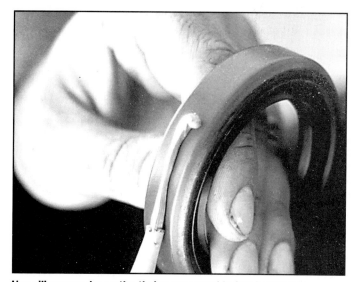

Use silicone sealer on the timing cover seal before installation.

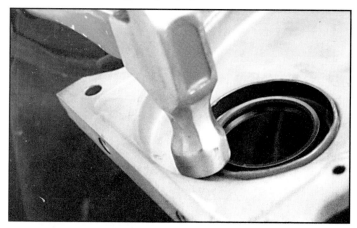

The easiest way to install the timing cover seal is to pound it in directly with a hammer.

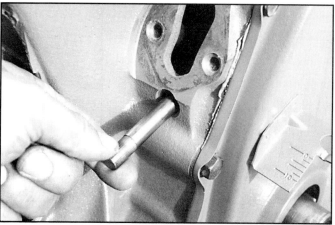

The fuel pump rod needs to be used with a mechanical fuel pump. If an electric one is being used, this rod can be left out. There is no oil in this passage.

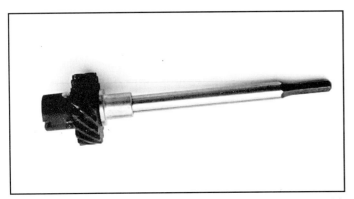

To install the distributor drive bushing use an old drive to pound it into the block. This way the ID of the bushing won't collapse during installation. After it's in the block, work the old drive through it until it fits freely. Check the fit with the new drive to be sure that it also turns freely.

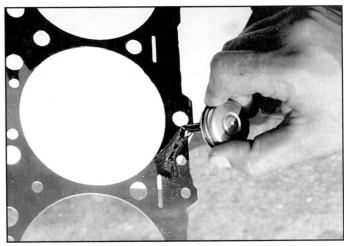

If you are using copper head gaskets, they must have some type of sealer on them to prevent water leaks. Fel-Pro #BLU-4 works the best.

All gasket surfaces need to be completely clean for maximum seal and to prevent leaks.

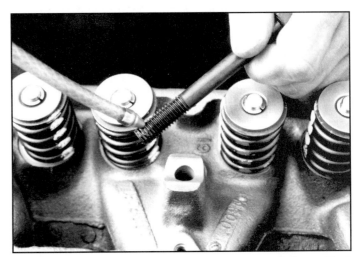

Always follow the manufacturer's torque spec on any fastener. Most torque values are given with 30-weight oil on the threads, but always check to be sure.

Always torque fasteners in slow easy steps. At least 3 increments are recommended.

A neat trick to help hold the pushrods during rocker installation is to prop them up with a piece of welding rod.

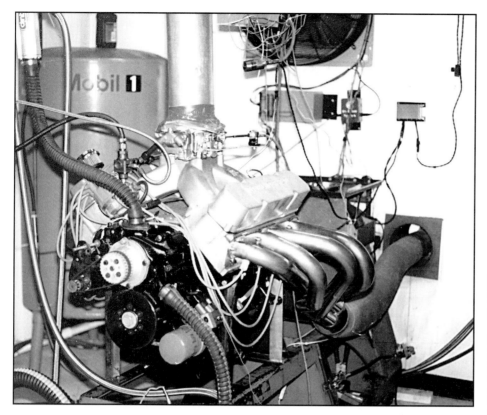

This 572 cubic inch Indy head engine made nearly 840 horsepower and over 740 lbs-ft of torque with a 640" roller cam and 10.5:1 compression. This would be a monster street engine.

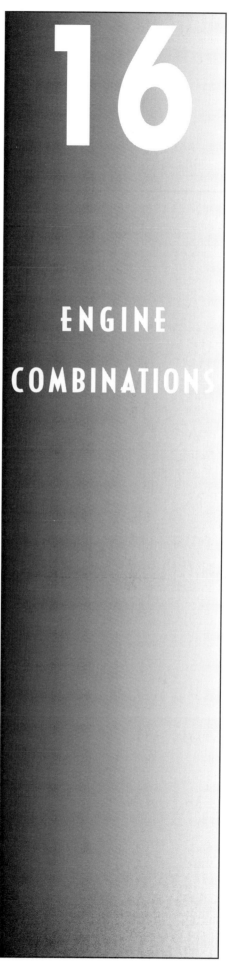

16

ENGINE COMBINATIONS

All this information and theory is fine, but what do you do with it after you understand it all? The answer is to build an engine! The engine that you ultimately build will be determined by your performance goal and your racing budget. In several years of building these engines, I have built or investigated just about every possible combination. With the exception of some wild Competition Eliminator or tame restoration engines, the B engine usually comes in four different forms. They are:

1. "Basic" 440 cid, 440 block
2. 400 block strokers
3. 440 block strokers
4. Aftermarket block, big bore

Sure there may be other combinations out there but these four are the most common and cost-effective ways to go fast. All four types can be built from mild to wild by only changing a few things. They all share the inherent performance and strength that the engine family is known for. While it is impossible to list every possible setup, I'm going to run down what I feel is the easiest way from point A to point B for a track version and a street version.

Since this is a "recipe" type of list, there are some basic things that are going to be implied that you are going to need to have done regardless of use. For example: cleaning, Magnafluxing, honing with a deck plate, balancing, new valve guides, electronic ignition, etc. As a general rule, try to do as much machine work as possible and use as many new parts as possible. This will ensure a long and trouble free life.

GENERAL TIPS FOR ALL RACING ENGINES

For the track versions here's some

BASIC 440 ENGINE PARTS LIST

	STREET	TRACK
Block:	any 440 block, any year	any will work, pre-1975 is better
Bore:	.030"	.060 over is okay in early block
Crank:	stock steel, race prepped	same
Rods:	stock, full prep, HD bolts	stock okay, aftermarket steel or aluminum preferred
Pistons:	Keith Black cast or lightweight forged 10:1 compression	lightweight forged only, 12:1 + preferred
Rings:	moly, file fit	same w/low tension oil rings
Bearings:	all tri-metal, mains fully grooved	same, aluminum rods use babbit
Cam:	hydraulic or solid	Solid or roller
Cam Drive:	chain	chain okay, gear or belt better
Oil Pump:	high volume	same, but ext. if over 7000 rpm
Oil Pan:	min.6 qt, 1/2" pickup	largest pan possible, 1/2" pickup
Heads:	ported stock iron	ported stock okay, alum. better
Valvetrain:	HD stock style okay	adjustable, roller preferred
Intake:	high rise dual plane or single plane	single plane
Carburetor:	750-850 cfm	850-1050 cfm

general suggestions:

• use main studs
• line hone the mains
• deck the block square
• use head studs with over 12.5 compression
• O-ring the block with over 13.5 compression
• lifter bores can be bushed
• fill water jackets for drag use only
• enlarge oil galley to the mains
• use aluminum main caps over 700 hp or 7000 rpm

Some of these suggestions, like the main studs, oil galley enlargement, line honing, etc., can also be used on street engines to get an increase in durability. Obviously some of these modifications are for the race track only. Some things like timing chains and oil systems are not displacement specific, but rather cost and application specific. If something is better for racing, it is probably better for street use too. I suppose if you wanted the Milodon external oil system and Jesel belt drive on your restoration 383 Road Runner engine, they would work fine but your wallet would be $1500 lighter!

ENGINE A: BASIC 440 CID W/440 BLOCK

This combination is by far the most common combination used today. This combo can be used from street to track with good success. It is very flexible and durable as well as inexpensive to build. If correctly built, it can take you a long way into racing.

That's the general recipe for this engine. Below are two examples of what to expect if you build this engine this way:

Street

The street engine with a Mopar .509 hydraulic cam, bowl-ported stock heads with 2.14"/1.81" valves, light pistons, and single-plane intake should put a well set up B/E body into the 11.80–12.30 ET range.

In an A-body, this is a solid 11-second performer. Generally, power is in the 450–500 horsepower range. This setup needs an 11-inch converter and a shift point of about 6200 rpm for best performance. More porting to the heads and a medium lift (.557" to .600") solid cam can be used for more performance in this combo with not much loss of driveability.

Track

The track version with a .640" Ultradyne solid lifter cam (or Mopar .590 "or .620"), more porting on the stock heads, 12.5:1 compression light pistons, steel rods, and a single-plane intake should go 10.80–11.30 seconds in B/E body and mid-10's in an A-body. With the addition of some of the smaller aluminum heads, such as Mopar Stage 6, Indy SR or Brodix B-1 BS, expect about four to six tenths of a second improvement. An 8" inch converter is needed for the track; a 10" for the street.

ENGINE B: 400 CID STROKER ENGINE

Any engine that can be built in a 440 block can be built better in the low-deck 400 cid block. This is due to the 400's shorter deck height, which allows for a lighter piston. Also, the engine is a little lighter and more compact than the 440. All this jazz about the 400 was covered in earlier chapters so there is no need to go over it again.

Generally there are three types of popular low-deck stroker engines: the 451, 474, and 496 cubic inch versions.

451 cid

The 451 engine is built by taking a 440 crank and installing it in the 400 block. This can be done by either grinding the mains down to the 400 size or line boring the block out to 440 size. The most popular and easiest way is to cut the mains of the crank down. It does not weaken the crank to do this and it is a very reliable way to go.

Rod Length—The engine can be built with either the 400 (or 361/383) rod length or the 440 (413, 426W) rod length and a set of special pistons to adjust for the shorter deck height of the 400 block. Generally, the 440 rod is used since there are more off-the-shelf pistons available. The 400 rod length will produce a little more low-end and mid-range power since the rod is somewhat shorter but it isn't a large gain. Either way is fine and will work well. All the rules are the same as for building a 440 in a 440 block with respect to cams, heads, etc. since the engine is still basically a 440 with a lighter set of pistons. As such, expect about a gain of about one to two tenths of a second over the same combination in the 440 block. This engine requires more machine work and a "nicer" set of pistons to work so there will be some additional cost in building one.

474 cid

The 474 cid engine is really the first of what would be considered a "real" racing engine. With the additional displacement and light internal parts, this engine works great. This engine is built just like the 451 cid engine with the addition of offset grinding the rod journals of the crank to produce more stroke. The journals are usually ground to 2.200" (big-block Chevy) and the stroke is set a 3.915". The crankshaft has plenty of material and strength to handle high power after this has been done.

Rods—The smaller rod size requires a non-Mopar rod to work. Stock Chevy rods can be used, but since they are a little on the short side at 6.135", I would recommend going to an aftermarket rod for this combo. The Chevy rod is also narrower by about .022", so there will be an additional .044" of side clearance. While this sounds excessive, it actually works with no problems. There are steel rods available from Eagle that are made for this setup that use the Chevy bearing but are made for the Mopar width crank. They are also longer at 6.385" and use the smaller .990" wrist pin size. This combination with the steel rod actually balances lighter than a stock rod combo at about 2250 grams. Since this is lighter than a stock 340, not only will it rev quick, but internal stress will be reduced. For drag only use, use an aluminum rod of 6.535" and live with the extra side clearance. The aluminum rod version balances at about 1950 grams, so it is a real rpm screamer.

I would suggest a well-ported set of stock heads and a solid cam as a minimum to make it really shine. If these things are not in your plan, stay

with a 440 or 451. The compression can be kept low for street use or cranked up for track only use. Due to the displacement and rpm potential of this engine, it can handle a larger set of heads like the Indy 440-1 or B-1. However, these engines really like the smaller port aluminum heads due to the additional air speed generated by the small ports. In fact, if you do the math, the stock port window is capable of supporting a 7000 rpm engine of 475 cubic inches. Coincidence, no. That is one of the reasons why this short block was developed.

496 cid

This combination is built around an aftermarket crankshaft, most commonly the Mopar 4.150" stroke crank. Thousands of these engines have been built and can be set up with low compression for street use or wildly set up for track use. It works very well either way. On the street, it can produce over 600 lbs-ft of torque with over 650 horsepower, and for the track can produce over 850 horsepower and 650 lbs-ft of torque.

This engine is very popular at the drag strip because it is so easy to build, produces good power, and is very reliable. This combo is capable of running in the 7-second range in a light car, which is enough to satisfy most Mopar racers.

Crankshaft—The heart of this engine is the crankshaft. Forged from steel, the Mopar 4.150" crank has proven itself to be a strong component for many years. The additional stroke produces more displacement and torque and at a lower rpm level over a smaller engine.

Rods—In a 400 block, a stock length 440 rod can be used, but it must be an aftermarket one since a .990" wrist pin is required with the short pistons. Since the pistons are so short in this engine, they are very light, at about 600 grams with pin. Even with the larger Mopar-sized rods, this combo has about the same balance weights as the 474 engines, so they also like to rev.

Oil System—The 4.150" stroke is about the limit with the internal 1/2" oil pickup tube, and the aluminum rod version will require an external oil system. This engine can be run on the street with ported stock heads to build a low rpm torque monster. As with the 474, though, if you don't plan on a good set of heads and a big cam, stay with the 440. The rule with big engines is that if you build a 496 with the same parts as a 440 (other than the displacement), it will only run like a 440. The moral of the story is: don't build a big short block just to build it. An engine is an overall plan, not just a big crank.

For the track give this engine what it needs: big heads, cam and compression. Here's a recipe for the 496 low deck to make about 800 horsepower, which should put a dragster into the 7.90-second range, a tube-chassis doorslammer into the mid-8s and an A-body into the low 9s. This combo is a real workhorse with long life and reasonable rpm range. This is the cheapest way to go real fast with a B engine!

Block: Pre-1974 400, filled, alum main caps
Crank: Mopar 4.150
Rods: BME aluminum, 440 length, .990 pin
Pistons: 13:1, flat top with alum heads
Heads: Brodix B-1 or Indy 440-1 70 cc full port

Cam: roller, 285 duration at .050. .700" lift
Oil System: external, dual line, race pan
Intake: B-1 or Indy single plane
Carb: 1050 cfm

This is the heart of the engine, with all the normal race parts like roller rockers, aftermarket vibration damper, etc., as well as top-notch machine work. This is a good starting point for real racers, because the good heads and oil system can be used on a larger engine in the future if desired. By doing this, you will have a good spare short block as a backup.

BIG BORE ENGINES

With the release of aftermarket blocks for the B engine, we now have the capability to build very large engines of about 600 cubic inches. The tall deck heights of the B engine make it especially well-suited for stroking. Even with the longest crankshaft, these engines can still use a rod length of over seven inches, which still gives a good rod ratio. The cam-to-crank distance is fairly long and will accommodate a stroke of 4.750" if a small rod journal crank is used.

Bore Size

This long stroke will produce a big gain in displacement but a larger bore is also important in gaining cubic inches. A larger bore not only will add displacement without the extra friction penalty of a long stroke, but larger bores allow for larger valves in the head for more airflow. For many years the B engine was limited to production blocks and bore sizes. This put a limit on real large engines. As of

late, there are several new blocks on the market that will accommodate much larger than stock bores. The 4.800" bore spacing will allow a nominal "big bore" size of 4.500". If the block is stretched to the limit, a 4.560" or even a 4.600" is possible. At these extra big sizes, the block will be at the limit, so think about that before you choose your bore size and remember that even when maxed out, you are only going to gain a handful of cubic inches. These mega-engines are capable of producing a great amount of horsepower and torque. I have dyno tested some of these engines at over 800 lbs-ft of torque at only 5000 rpm. As such, they need an equally strong car to work in. Everything like the frame, transmission, rear end, etc. has to be up to snuff or it will fail. If you do not have excellent components in the rest of the car, do not build a mega-motor like this.

Heads Are Key

Though the bottom end on this engine has a lot of displacement, the real key to getting power from it is a good set of heads. If you have small port heads (stock, Stage 6, B-1 B/S, Indy S/R) I would not recommend a mega-motor. These heads are simply not enough to feed it. An Indy 440-1 head would be about the smallest that I would recommend using. Larger is better here, so the best heads to use are the B-1 original, Indy 572-13, and the Brewer head. An intake flow rate of at least 400 cfm is required for max performance. The bottom line is to put your effort into the heads first and the short block second. There are many 500 inch engines that go faster than some 572's. Cubic inches is not a guarantee of performance, but high up to 14:1 compression, but a copper head gasket with an O-ringed block should be used over this or with nitrous. The sealing area between cylinders is reduced due to the larger bore, so this is a critical area to watch.

Block: 4.500 bore nominal, Mopar Mega-Block, Indy Maxx, Keith Black
Stroke: 4.500" (572), 4.625" (588), 2.200" crank pin size
Pistons: flat top will give over 13:1 or more compression, dished pistons required for less
Rods: 6.800" minimum, 7.000"+ preferred
Heads: B-1, Indy 572-13, Brewer
Cam: Roller, .800" lift, 285+ duration @.050 intake, 295+ exhaust
Intake: Single plane w/1050 carb min., tunnel ram with two 1050's optional

Depending on the heads, this combo is good for a minimum of 850 hp and 725 lbs-ft torque. Actually 1000+ hp and 825 lbs-ft of torque are easily possible as well. Low-compression street versions can be built with 800+ hp and 700+ torque possible with 10:1 compression and an under-700" lift camshaft.

This 474 cid engine with Stage 6 heads is an economical way to go fast. This engine powered a 2200-lb car to mid-8 second times.

flowing heads always are.

General Parts

All the general parts, like rings, bearings, timing components, etc., are the same as with any other B engine.

Some other things also go without saying, like a 1050 cfm carb, SFI-vibration damper, roller rockers, external oil system, etc., are required for these engines. The Fel-Pro 1039 big-bore head gasket will work well

17

GENERAL RACING TIPS

The chassis is just as important as the engine in racing, a fact many amateurs overlook. Reduce the weight of the chassis as much as possible, pick the right torque converter, use the proper tires, and get the car aligned—all of these will put you on the fast track to success.

If you get anything out of this book, make sure that it is the knowledge that a race car is more than just an engine. Many racers do not seem to realize this fact. Sure, it's a lot more fun to buy the new trick roller cam than to crawl around on the garage floor measuring your toe-in pattern, but both things are equally important.

The first thing to do is to define and set your racing goals. Do you just want to go out and go fast or do you want to become track champion? To be successful at the game of racing requires a tremendous amount of dedication. If you can't put 100% effort into it, don't plan on becoming a champion. This is not to say that you won't have fun! Racing can be a very rewarding and enjoyable hobby, career or obsession!

CHASSIS

There is no doubt that the chassis is equal in importance to the engine in terms of performance. I like to think of the chassis as everything that isn't the engine. Even the best engine in the world won't work very well with a weak chassis. Do not overlook the safety aspect of the chassis either. Not only will a strong chassis deliver maximum power to the track, it just may save your skin in the event of a mishap. Never do anything to your chassis in the name of speed that compromises strength and safety. A trick set of heads won't do much good after the car is ruined.

Reduce Chassis Weight

If your goal is to go as fast as possible, the chassis should be as light as possible. It is far easier to make a light car go fast than to overpower a heavy car into going fast. A chassis purchase should be considered a long-term investment. If you invest in lightweight parts for your car, like wheels and fiberglass, they should last forever. On the other hand, wild engine parts by definition are usually more fragile than the original parts. If you have a long-term project, invest in the chassis first and the engine later. I know it's a lot more fun to have a monster engine than a chrome-moly tube chassis. However, it is very easy to have more engine than the chassis can handle. If this is the case, all you end up with is a car that doesn't run up to its potential and is inconsistent.

All the ignition for the dragster fits between the driver's feet! Note brake pedal on left and gas pedal on right.

Strategy For Winning

Because most Mopar big-block engines will be bracket raced on the drag strip, consistency is of the utmost importance. With the use of electronic devices in most race cars, most races are won or lost by the slimmest of margins. Since there is a lot of human variation in racing, which we can't do anything about (other than replacing you with a robot), concentrate on improving your car and eliminating any variables there. The prescription for winning races is :

• A strong, stiff chassis that can handle your power level
• A large, low rpm engine that's not over-stressed
• A fresh transmission and torque converter
• Large rear tires in good condition

Torque Converter

Many racers drop the ball when it comes to buying a good torque converter. For some reason they will spend the money in the engine but not on the converter. This is not a good plan. The converter is the only component in the drivetrain that can have a real effect on how the car performs. No other part between the engine and the pavement can be

A strong, stiff chassis is a must for drag racing. Beefy steel tube rails keep the chassis from twisting under acceleration. Space is tight on a dragster: The battery, fuel pump and filter, and the fuel cell all are crammed in between the frame rails.

modified to work much better. The tires are the tires—either they spin or they don't. Same with the rear end. As long as everything is working okay inside and the ratio is correct, how can it be improved significantly? There can be some small gains in the transmission but usually they are very expensive (aluminum drums and needle bearing kits for example) to

get.

A race converter has a strange job. It needs to slip enough to get the engine in its powerband immediately, but at the same time be tight enough to transfer maximum power to the transmission.

Street Use—If the car is set up for street use, an 11" converter is the best overall plan. This is a good step up

If you are running a light car (under 2800 lbs) it will usually be faster with a two-speed Powerglide transmission. To install one, this special adapter plate and flywheel are required.

from the factory style HP or "hemi" converters. A good 11" converter is fine as a daily driver or for casual strip action. They also work especially well for restoration cars that want some more zip off the line, since most Mopar big-block engines are usually in fairly heavy cars.

Street/Strip Use—If more serious street action is desired, then a 10" converter is the next step up in the performance ladder. This type of converter will give the best compromise between street use and strip performance. They are about as wild as possible while still retaining some driveability.

Race Only—If the car is a race-only machine, an 8" inch converter is the only way to go. These race-only units will deliver maximum performance all the way down the track. While an 8" converter is great for drag racing at the strip, they are generally too loose for much street driving. For absolute maximum street performance, they can be used, but their loose nature tends to generate a lot of heat, so make sure to use a large transmission fluid cooler.

Stall Speed—To gain stall speed, a stock converter could have every other fin removed inside. It would stall at 5000 rpm but would be so inefficient that it probably wouldn't even move the car. This balance is what makes a good (true race) converter work better than a bad one.

A converter's stall speed is a function of the input torque. A good 11" street converter may stall to 2800 rpm behind a hot 440 cid engine, but the same converter behind a 572 cid nitrous engine may stall at 4500 rpm because of the increased torque input. Choose your converter based on its diameter, not some arbitrary advertised stall speed.

Flash Speed—What's actually more important than the stall speed is a converter's flash speed. This is the rpm that the converter will allow the engine to instantly rev to. It is usually higher than the stall speed. Ideally the flash speed should be up to the point of maximum torque output of the engine. For most track-only big blocks, this is usually about 4700–5300 rpm. The trick is to pick a converter that has a flash point of about 1800 rpm less than your shift point. This applies to a race-only vehicle, not to street cars.

Custom Converters—If you have a dyno sheet for your engine, most converter companies can make a custom converter to match the power curve of the engine. If the engine produces a lot of power (over 800 hp) consider using a converter with a steel stator in place of the stock style cast aluminum stator. Not only will this make the converter stronger, the manufacturer can change the pitch of the stator fins to increase performance. A custom converter can cost near $1000 and is worth every penny. Not only will a good converter pay for itself in increased performance, but also in increased durability. Face it, you can't win with broken equipment. I know of several 7-second drag cars that have used their converters for two or more seasons without any failures.

Transmission & Related Components

With the advent of electronics in racing, the manual transmission has almost disappeared from bracket racing. Because of the difficulty of cutting a narrow range of good reaction times, and the inconsistency of most drivers, the automatic transmission now rules the strip.

However, there are still racers with manual transmissions, and these trannys only need a few tricks to give a long life and good performance. A strong clutch is a must, because it will get abused in racing. Flywheel weight can be an area of tuning that may be worthy of some experimentation. A heavier car usually likes a heavier flywheel to get it moving off the line quicker due to the additional stored energy that the flywheel will have. This extra weight will also make the engine rev slower, so a light car may benefit from a lighter flywheel since the whole system will be able to move quicker.

Shifting will be easier if automatic transmission fluid is used in the manual transmission instead of the usual 80-weight gear lube. Usually, most manual transmission cars will go about a tenth faster with the lighter fluid.

Always make sure that the crankshaft has a pilot bushing installed to allow the use of a manual. There is a myth that all steel cranks have the provision for a pilot bushing, but this is not true. Always check to be sure.

Rear End & Tires

The only thing left in the drivetrain are the rear end gears and tires. Always choose the tires first and the gears second. For maximum performance, use the largest tires that fit under your car. The only connection all of your power has to the pavement is that contact patch of rubber.

Tire Diameter—On the subject of contact patch, tire diameter is just as important as tire width for a large contact patch. A large diameter tire will put more rubber on the road than a smaller diameter tire of equal width. This is why drag cars have such large rear tires.

For the front tires use the smallest that you can. Don't go too small for a car run on the street for obvious safety reasons. But on the track, you can experiment with front tire diameter to change reaction times if your car is

A two-step controller works with a transbrake to launch the car consistently and much harder than a foot-brake. The two-step limits the engine rpm to a pre-set level when the transbrake is engaged.

not running a delay box. A larger diameter front tire will usually have a slower reaction time but a better elapsed time than a shorter tire. This is due to the fact that the taller tire will allow the car to roll more before starting the clocks.

Rims—Always use lightweight rims to reduce unsprung weight. It has been said that saving a pound of unsprung weight is equal to eight pounds of sprung weight. I can't confirm this, but let's just say that a Pro Stock car uses a lot of expensive, lightweight components in this area. Carbon fiber brake rotors and titanium lug nuts, wheel studs, and spools are common.

Gear Ratio—After the tire size is established, estimate your trap speed and how much rpm you want to turn through the lights. With this information, use the formula on page 156 to determine what gear to use. If your calculation comes up with a ratio that is between two available ratios, choose the lower numerical one. Remember to consider the fact that the tires are going to grow at high speed and that there will be some

slippage in the converter. Most of the time, a bracket car will use between a 4.10 and 4.88 gear for best performance. Mopar engines can produce a ton of power at conservative rpm levels, so don't overdo it in the gear department. Put all that torque to work for you.

Front End Alignment

Always make sure to have a good front end alignment for performance and stability at high speed. Try for as much positive caster as possible for stability and zero toe-in for performance. Make all of your adjustments with the car raised one inch or so from static height as this will be the ride height at speed under acceleration.

Make sure that the toe pattern doesn't change as the front end travels up or the car will wander. Also make sure that the rear end is square in the car so that it is not trying to drive the car in any other direction other than straight ahead. Having friends at a front end shop is the key here, especially if they have a good alignment rack to experiment on.

FORMULAS

PEAK HORSEPOWER RPM
(16,000/displacement) x Head Flow CFM @ 10"
Example: A 440 cid engine with Indy Heads that flow 209 cfm @ 10"
(16,000/440) x 209 = 7600 rpm

HEAD PORT SIZE AREA
$Bore^2$ x Stroke x RPM/190,000
Example: Minimum port area for 496 cid (4.375" bore x 4.15" stroke) engine to go 6800 rpm
4.375^2 x 4.15 x 6800/190,000 = 2.843 square inches

HORSEPOWER POTENTIAL VS. HEAD FLOW
.257 x no. of cylinders x flow @ 28"
Example: How much horsepower will a B-1 head with 410 cfm flow @ 28" support?
.257 x 8 x 410 = 843 horsepower

BLOCK DECK HEIGHT
Block Deck Height = (Stroke/2) + Rod Length + Piston Compression Height + Deck Height
Where raised block deck height = 10.725", B deck height = 9.98"

HEADER LENGTH & DIAMETER
Length = $(850$ x $(360 —$ exhaust valve opening point$))$/RPM — 3
Diameter = $\sqrt{}$ (cid x 16.38/ x 16.38/8)/(length + 3) x 25 x 2.1

Example: 572 engine, exhaust valve opens 85 before BDC, desired rpm is 7000
Length: (850 x (360 —85)/7000 — = $(233750/7000)$ — 3 = 30.4"
Diameter = $\sqrt{}$ 572/8 x 16.38/(30.4 + 3) x 25   x 2.1
Diameter = $\sqrt{}$1171/835   x 2.1
Diameter = $\sqrt{}$ 1.40   x 2.1 = 2.49"
Suggestion: Set headers for in the middle of your rpm range

ENGINE DISPLACEMENT
Bore x Bore x Stroke x number of cylinders x .785

EXACT DRIVESHAFT RPM
MPH x 17.6/Tire Diameter x 3.141 x 60 x Gear Ratio
Example: 132 mph, 4.10 gears, 32" tires
132 x 17.6 / 32 x 3.141 x 60 x 4.10 = 2323/100.5 x 60 x 4.10 = 5685 rpm
This is driveshaft speed. Engine rpm will be equal driveshaft speed times slippage in clutch or torque converter.

REAR WHEEL HORSEPOWER
Horsepower = Vehicle weight / $(ET/5.825)^3$
Example: 2350-lb Pro Stock car, ET = 7.05 seconds
HP = $2350/(7.05/5.825)^3$
HP = $2350/1.21^3$ = 2350/1.773 = 1325 horsepower

A

Aftermarket
    blocks, 26–31
        aluminum or iron, 27–28
        choosing, 27–31
        Indy Maxx Blocks, 29–30
        Keith Black aluminum blocks, 30–31
        Mopar Mega blocks, 28–29
    cranks, 37
    heads, 75–86
    rods
        aluminum or steel, 46–47
Aluminum blocks, Keith Black, 30–31
Aluminum main caps, 24
Assembly tips, 135–140
    camshafts, 136
    engine break-in, 136
    general, 135–140
    photo tips, 137–140
    rings, 136
    torquing fasteners, 136

B

B engine cylinder head casting numbers, 10
Babbitt bearings, 56
Ballast resistors, 126–127
BDC (bottom dead center), 9, 16, 48
Bearing crush defined, 20
Bearings, 55–59
    Babbitt, 56
    cam, 55–56
    connecting rod, 56–58
    grooved, 58–59
    main, 58–59
    oil clearance, 59
    prepping rod, 57–58
    tri-metal, 56
Belt drives, 98
Big block
    specs, 12–13
        deck height, 13
        interchangeability, 13
    stock, 1–10
        B engine cylinder head casting numbers, 10
        background, 1–2

crankshaft vibration dampers, 9
    crankshafts, 7–8
    cylinder heads, 8–10
    engine block identification, 4–7
    identification numbers, 2–4
Big bore engines, 144–145
Billet cranks, 37
Block casting numbers, 4
Block identification, engine, 4–7
    B series 383 and 400 cid, 6
    condensed history, 7
    RB series 413, 426 & 440 cid, 6–7
Block serial stamping numbers, 5
Block-ups
    planning, budget-saving ideas, 15–16
        lightweight components, 16
        solid lifter cam, 16
    planning, goals
        safety, 15
        short block priority, 15
Blocks
    aftermarket, 26–31
    big, 1–10
    cylinder, 17–31
        aftermarket blocks, 26–31
        production blocks, 18–26
    cylinder, design features, 17–18
        head bolt patterns, 17
        measurements, 17–18
    Indy Maxx, 29–30
    KB blocks, 30–31
    Keith Black aluminum, 30–31
    Mopar Mega, 28–29
    production
        440 CID w/440, 142
    See also Big blocks
Blocks, production, 18–26
    400 blocks, 19–20
    440 blocks, 19
    basic prep & inspection, 20–21
        clean threads, 20
        deburr casting flash, 20–21
        fasteners, 20

torque main caps, 21
    cylinder boring & honing, 21–22
    decking, 22–23
    final prep, 23
    increasing strength, 23–26
        aluminum main caps, 24
        bushing lifter bores, 24–26
        cement waterjackets, 23–24
        miscellaneous oil modifications, 26
    initial selection, 18–20
    line honing, 21
Bolts, rod, 44
Brewer Heads, 84–86
Brodix heads, 80–84
    B-1, 80–81
    B-1 BS, 83–84
    B-1 MC, 81
    B-1 PS, 81
    B-1 TS, 81–83

C

Cam bearings, 55–56
    installation, 55–56
    styles, 56
Cams
    basics, 88–93
    custom, 93–95
        checking clearances, 94–95
        choosing duration, 93–94
        determining lift, 93
        fitting cams, 94
        intake centerline, 94
        lobe separation, 94
    drives, 95–98
        belt drives, 98
        gear drives, 97–98
        timing chains, 95–97
    hydraulic, 89–91
    roller, 92–93
    solid, 91–92
    solid lifter, 16
Camshafts, 88–98, 136
    recommendations, 91
    See also Cams
Caps, aluminum main, 24
Carburetors, selecting, 115–122
    carb considerations, 115–116

carb size, 118
tips, 118–120
    fuel lines, 119
    fuel pumps, 119–120
    jetting, 120
    modified carbs, 120
    vacuum vs. mechanical, 116–118
Casting numbers, 4
    B engine cylinder head, 10
    block, 4
CD (capacitive discharge), 124
CDI (capacitive discharge ignition), 124
Cement waterjackets, 23–24
Chains, timing, 95–97
Cid (cubic inch displacement), 4
Coils, 126
Composition gaskets, 86–87
Compression ratios, 51–52
Connecting rods, 41–47
    aftermarket rods, 46–47
    bearings, 56–58
Converters, torque, 147–148
Copper gaskets, 87
Crank balancing, 38–40
    balancing procedure, 38–39
        dynamic balancing, 38–39
        frequency specific, 39
        Mallory metal, 39
        static balancing, 38
    vibration dampers, 39–40
Crank triggers, 129
Crankcase, ventilation of, 54

INDEX

Cranks, 37–38
   aftermarket, 37
   billet, 37
   forged stock, 34
   stock, 33–34
Crankshafts, 7–8, 32–40
   design features, 32–33
      bearing sizes, 32
      journal size, 33
   interchanges, 7–8
   selection of, 33–38
      aftermarket cranks, 37
      making stroker cranks fit, 37–38
      modifying stock cranks, 34–37
      stock cranks, 33–34
   vibration dampers, 9
Cylinder
   blocks, 17–31
      aftermarket blocks, 26–31
      design features, 17–18
      production blocks, 18–26
   compression ratio (CR), 10
   displacement, 10
   heads, 8–10, 70–87
      casting numbers, 10
      design fundamentals, 9–10
      valve & port size, 10

D

Dampers
   fluid, 40
   vibration, 39–40
Deck plate, 22
Decking, 22–23
   parallel, 22
Design features, 11–13
   big block specs, 12–13
Distributors, 124–125, 128–129
Drives
   belt, 98
   gear, 97–98
Dry sump systems, 67–68
Dual-plane manifolds, 111
Dykes rings, 53–54

E

Engines
   400 CID stroker, 142–144
   440 CID w/440 block, 142
   451 cid, 143
   474 cid, 143
   496 cid, 143–144
   big bore, 144–145
      bore size, 144
      general parts, 145
      heads are key, 144–145
   block identification, 4–7
   block stamping numbers, 4
   break-in, 136
   combinations, 141–145
   general tips for all racing, 141–142
   street, 142
   track, 142
Exhaust systems, 132–134
   header design, 132–133
   header recommendations, 133–134
      collector length, 134

F

Fasteners, torquing, 136
Flow numbers, 71
Fluid dampers, 40
440 crank/400 block combo, 35–37
Friction, reducing, 54
Front end alignment, 149
Fuel
   lines, 119
   pumps, 119–120

G

Gapless rings, 54
Gaskets
   composition, 86–87
   copper, 87
   head, 86–87
Gear drives, 97–98
Grooved bearings, 58–59

H

Head gaskets, 86–87
Header design, 132–133
Heads, cylinder, 8–10, 70–87
   aftermarket heads, 75–86
      Brewer Heads, 84–86
      Brodix heads, 80–84
      Indy Cylinder Heads, 77–84
      Mopar Performance heads, 75–77
   head gaskets, 86–87
      composition gaskets, 86–87
      copper gaskets, 87
      recommendations, 86
   stock heads, 72–75
      layout & features, 73
      modifications, 74–75
      for racing only, 73–74
      recommendations, 73
   theory, 70–72
      flow numbers, 71
      port area vs. volume, 71
      port flow, 70–71
      porting heads, 71–72
Hydraulic cams, 89–91
Hypereutectic pistons, 49–50

I

Identification
   engine block, 4–7
   numbers, 2–4
      casting numbers, 4
      engine block stamping number, 4
Ignition
   basics, 123–125
      capacitive discharge (CD), 124
      distributor drives, 124–125
      distributors, 124–125
      triggers, 124
   system, 123–131
      Mopar conversion kits, 125–127
      racing tips, 128–131

Ignitions, multi-spark, 127–128
Indexing, throw, 35
Induction, 109–122
   intake manifolds, 109–115
   selecting carburetors, 115–122
Indy
   Cylinder Heads, 77–84
      440-1 heads, 78–79
      572-13 heads, 79–80
      S/R heads, 79
   Maxx Blocks, 29–30
Intake manifolds, 109–115

K

KB (Keith Black) aluminum blocks, 30–31

L

Lifter bores, bushing, 24–26
Lifter cam, solid, 16
Lines, fuel, 119
Locks & retainers, 104

M

Making stroker cranks fit, 37–38
Mallory metal, 39
Manifolds
   dual-plane, 111
   intake, 109–115
      operation, 109–110
   Mopar M-1, 112–113
   multiple carb, 114–115
   recommended, 110–113
   single-plane, 111–112
   stock, 111
   tuning & modifications, 113–114
   tunnel ram, 114–115
Mopar
   conversion kits, 125–127
      ballast resistors, 126–127
      chrome boxes, 125–126
      coils, 126
      orange boxes, 125
      super gold boxes, 126
   M-1 manifolds, 112–113
   Mega blocks, 28–29

Performance heads, 75–77
  stage 5 head, 75–76
  stage 6 head, 76–77
Multi-spark ignitions, 127–128

N

Nitrous oxide & pistons, 52
Numbers
  B engine cylinder head casting, 10
  block casting, 4
  block serial stamping, 5
  casting, 4
  engine block stamping, 4
  identification, 2–4

O

Oil pans
  tips, 63–64
  types of, 64–65
Oil pumps
  drives, 68–69
  upgrade, 61–62
Oil system, 60–69
Oil systems, 61–69
  design, 60–61
    pressure, 60–61
    suction, 61
  external, 65–67
  modifications
    dry sump systems, 67–68
    external oil system, 65–67
    general tips, 62–63
    high pressure vs. high volume, 62
    oil pan tips, 63–64
    oil pump drive, 68–69
    upgrade oil pumps, 61–62
Oils, 69
  maintenance of, 69
  synthetic, 69

P

Parallel decking, 22
Pin bosses, 50
Pins, wrist, 44–45
Pistons, 48–54

cast vs. forged, 49–51
Crankcase ventilation, 54
designing custom, 52–53
functions, 48–49
hypereutectic, 49–50
pin bosses, 50
and rings, 53–54
tips, 51–54
  compression ratios, 51–52
  nitrous oxide & pistons, 52
top & ringlands, 51
weights of, 48–49
Plate, deck, 22
Plugs, spark, 130–131
Port
  area vs. volume, 71
  flow, 70–71
Porting heads, 71–72
Production blocks, 18–26
Pumps, fuel, 119–120
Pushrods, 104–106
  lengths, 105
  stronger, 105–106

R

Racing engines, general tips for, 141–142
Racing tips, 146–149
  chassis, 146–149
  front end alignment, 149
  rear ends & tires, 149
  reducing weight, 146–147
  strategy for winning, 147
  torque converters, 147–148
  transmissions & related components, 148–149
RB (raised block) versions, 11
Rear ends & tires, 149
Resistors, ballast, 126–127
Retainers & locks, 104
Rings, 53–54, 136
  choosing, 54
  Dykes, 53–54
  gapping, 54
  reducing friction, 54
Rockers, roller, 107
Rod bearings, prepping, 57–58

Rod bolts, 44
Rod stress, reducing, 42–43
  beam polishing, 43
  limit Rpm, 42–43
  reducing weight, 42
  shot-peening, 43
Rods
  aftermarket, 46–47
  connecting, 41–47
  prepping stock, 43–45
    inspection, 43–44
    resizing, 44
    rod bolts, 44
    wrist pins, 44–45
  See also Pushrods
Rods, connecting
  prepping stock rods, 43–45
  stock rod types, 41–45
    dimensions, 42
    load capability, 42
    reducing rod stress, 42–43
    six-pack rods, 42
Roller cams, 92–93
Roller rockets, 107

S

Serial stamping numbers, block, 5
Single-plane manifolds, 111–112
Six-pack rods, 42
Spark plugs, 130–131
  gaps, 131
  heat ranges, 130
  with nitrous oxide, 130–131
Specifications, general, 13
Stock big block, 1–10
Stock cranks, 33–34
  forged, 34
  modifying, 34–37
  440 crank/400 block combo, 35–37
Stock heads, 72–75
Stock manifolds, 111
Stock rods
  prepping, 43–45
  types, 41–45
Stroker cranks, 37–38

SV (swept volume), 10
Synthetic oils, 69

T

TDC (top dead center), 9, 16, 48, 98
Throw indexing, 35
Timing chains, 95–97
Tires & rear ends, 149
Titanium valves, 100–101
Torque converters, 147–148
Transmissions & related components, 148–149
Tri-metal bearings, 56
Triggers, crank, 129
Tunnel ram manifolds, 114–115

V

Valve springs, 102–104
  pressure, 102
  retainers & locks, 104
  selecting proper spring pressure, 103–104
  setup, 102–103
Valves, 100–101
  lashes, 108
  one-piece, 101
  titanium, 100–101
Valvetrains, 99–108
  pushrods, 104–106
  roller rockets, 107
  tips, 106–108
  weights of, 99–100
V.E. (volumetric efficiency), 121
Vibration dampers, 39–40
VIP (Vehicle Identification Plate), 2

W

Waterjackets, cement, 23–24
Wires, 131
Wrist pins, 44–45

HANDBOOKS
Auto Electrical Handbook: 0-89586-238-7
Auto Upholstery & Interiors: 1-55788-265-7
Brake Handbook: 0-89586-232-8
Car Builder's Handbook: 1-55788-278-9
Street Rodder's Handbook: 0-89586-369-3
Turbo Hydra-matic 350 Handbook: 0-89586-051-1
Welder's Handbook: 1-55788-264-9

BODYWORK & PAINTING
Automotive Detailing: 1-55788-288-6
Automotive Paint Handbook: 1-55788-291-6
Fiberglass & Composite Materials: 1-55788-239-8
Metal Fabricator's Handbook: 0-89586-870-9
Paint & Body Handbook: 1-55788-082-4
Sheet Metal Handbook: 0-89586-757-5

INDUCTION
Holley 4150: 0-89586-047-3
Holley Carburetors, Manifolds & Fuel Injection: 1-55788-052-2
Rochester Carburetors: 0-89586-301-4
Turbochargers: 0-89586-135-6
Weber Carburetors: 0-89586-377-4

PERFORMANCE
Aerodynamics For Racing & Performance Cars: 1-55788-267-3
Baja Bugs & Buggies: 0-89586-186-0
Big-Block Chevy Performance: 1-55788-216-9
Big Block Mopar Performance: 1-55788-302-5
Bracket Racing: 1-55788-266-5
Brake Systems: 1-55788-281-9
Camaro Performance: 1-55788-057-3
Chassis Engineering: 1-55788-055-7
Chevrolet Power: 1-55788-087-5
Ford Windsor Small-Block Performance: 1-55788-323-8
Honda/Acura Performance: 1-55788-324-6
High Performance Hardware: 1-55788-304-1
How to Build Tri-Five Chevy Trucks ('55-'57): 1-55788-285-1
How to Hot Rod Big-Block Chevys:0-912656-04-2
How to Hot Rod Small-Block Chevys:0-912656-06-9
How to Hot Rod Small-Block Mopar Engines: 0-89586-479-7
How to Hot Rod VW Engines:0-912656-03-4
How to Make Your Car Handle:0-912656-46-8
John Lingenfelter: Modifying Small-Block Chevy: 1-55788-238-X
Mustang 5.0 Projects: 1-55788-275-4
Mustang Performance ('79-'93): 1-55788-193-6

Mustang Performance 2 ('79-'93): 1-55788-202-9
1001 High Performance Tech Tips: 1-55788-199-5
Performance Ignition Systems: 1-55788-306-8
Performance Wheels & Tires: 1-55788-286-X
Race Car Engineering & Mechanics: 1-55788-064-6
Small-Block Chevy Performance: 1-55788-253-3

ENGINE REBUILDING
Engine Builder's Handbook: 1-55788-245-2
Rebuild Air-Cooled VW Engines: 0-89586-225-5
Rebuild Big-Block Chevy Engines: 0-89586-175-5
Rebuild Big-Block Ford Engines: 0-89586-070-8
Rebuild Big-Block Mopar Engines: 1-55788-190-1
Rebuild Ford V-8 Engines: 0-89586-036-8
Rebuild Small-Block Chevy Engines: 1-55788-029-8
Rebuild Small-Block Ford Engines:0-912656-89-1
Rebuild Small-Block Mopar Engines: 0-89586-128-3

RESTORATION, MAINTENANCE, REPAIR
Camaro Owner's Handbook ('67-'81): 1-55788-301-7
Camaro Restoration Handbook ('67-'81): 0-89586-375-8
Classic Car Restorer's Handbook: 1-55788-194-4
Corvette Weekend Projects ('68-'82): 1-55788-218-5
Mustang Restoration Handbook('64 1/2-'70): 0-89586-402-9
Mustang Weekend Projects 2 ('68-'70): 1-55788-256-8
Tri-Five Chevy Owner's ('55-'57): 1-55788-285-1

GENERAL REFERENCE
Auto Math:1-55788-020-4
Fabulous Funny Cars: 1-55788-069-7
Guide to GM Muscle Cars: 1-55788-003-4
Stock Cars!: 1-55788-308-4

MARINE
Big-Block Chevy Marine Performance: 1-55788-297-5

TO ORDER CALL: 1-800-788-6262, ext. 1

HPBooks
A division of Penguin Putnam Inc.
375 Hudson Street
New York, NY 10014